Pure Chocolate

Rich, decadent, chocolate and—vegan? It can be difficult to find truly indulgent vegan desserts, especially chocolate. But for the first time, luscious chocolate cakes, brownies, truffles, puddings, ice creams, and more are within reach. This breakthrough book will delight and unite everyone who madly, deeply, truly loves chocolate desserts, whether vegan or otherwise.

While the health benefits of the cocoa bean are welcome, what we love most about chocolate is the taste. Today's chocoholics are interested in fine flavor, high-percentage, organic, and fair chocolate. All her desserts are vegan, some are gluten-free, and some are raw, but every one is absolutely chocolate and made with quality, easily sourced ingredients: minus the dairy, eggs, and white sugar.

Author, baking instructor, and vegan dynamo Fran Costigan has dedicated years to satisfying her sweet tooth while keeping it vegan through experimentation and long hours in the kitchen. Better-for-you interpretations of 120 favorite chocolate desserts pass the taste test: chocolate truffles, Brooklyn Blackout Layer Cake, Éclairs, White and Dark Chocolate Cheesecake, Black Bottom Cupcakes, Chocolate Pecan Pie, Mocha Crème Brûlée, Brownie Crumble Ice Cream, and even Moon Pies made with homemade vegan grahams! Her detailed instructions from setup to cooking to storing and keeping make for perfect outcomes every time: it's like a personal vegan baking class, right in your kitchen. You'll never have to pass up chocolate again.

Vegan
Chocolate

Vegan Chocolate

UNAPOLOGETICALLY LUSCIOUS
AND DECADENT DAIRY-FREE DESSERTS

by Fran Costigan

Photographs by Kate Lewis

RUNNING PRESS
PHILADELPHIA · LONDON

This book is dedicated to all
my chocolate-talking and chocolate-
eating, chocolate-obsessed family
and friends, colleagues, and students
who've said, "Chocolate makes everything better! Write the book."

ISBN 978-0-7624-4591-2

Library of Congress Control Number: 2013943523

E-book ISBN 978-0-7624-5067-1

9 8 7 6 5 4 3 2 1
Digit on the right indicates the number of this printing

Cover and interior design by Corinda Cook
Edited by Kristen Green Wiewora
Food photographer, food styling and prop styling: Kate Lewis /
    www.kk-lewis.com
Pastry assisants: Clare Gray and Christina Martin
Prop assistant: Maryellen Echle
Typography: Whitney, Sabon, and Tamarillo

Running Press Book Publishers
2300 Chestnut Street
Philadelphia, PA 19103-4371

Visit us on the web!
www.offthemenublog.com

CONTENTS

ACKNOWLEDGMENTS
6

INTRODUCTION
8

CHAPTER ONE
Ingredients, Sweeteners, Chocolates, and Equipment
12

CHAPTER TWO
Truffles
34

CHAPTER THREE
Cakes
62

CHAPTER FOUR
Showstoppers
90

CHAPTER FIVE
Cookies, Bars, and Little Bites
122

CHAPTER SIX
Pies and Tarts
148

CHAPTER SEVEN
Creams, Puddings, and Gels
172

CHAPTER EIGHT
Frozen Desserts
194

CHAPTER NINE
Confections
214

CHAPTER TEN
Beverages
236

CHAPTER ELEVEN
Master Recipes
260

RESOURCES
290

BIBLIOGRAPHY READING LIST
296

ORGANIZATIONS AND PUBLICATIONS
297

INDEX
298

Acknowlegments

I am blessed to a have a large and delightful community of family, friends, and colleagues to thank for the joy, inspiration, and encouragement they each bring to my life. My first thank you goes to my super agent, Sally Ekus, who supported me every step of the way, from idea to proposal and printed book, over and above what is reasonable. And, when I heard Lisa Ekus say, "I can't wait to read this proposal," I was extra-sure I had an idea whose time had come. Thank you to everyone at the awesome Lisa Ekus Group.

At Running Press Book Publishers, a publishing house I have long admired, I was lucky to have worked with a dream team. My editor, Kristen Green Wiewora's commitment to the project from the first phone conversation to the actual book never wavered. Art director and designer, Corinda Cook, took the manuscript and photos and created a truly beautiful book. My publicist, Gigi Lamm, worked with me enthusiastically to promote the book. Thanks also to Peggy Paul, Virginia Villalon, and Elizabeth Parson.

My first thoughts about doing an all-chocolate vegan book were: make it comprehensive, accessible, and stunning. I wanted lots of irresistible photographs to illustrate the fact that chocolate vegan desserts are on par with or better than the traditional counterparts. Photographer and stylist Kate Lewis's gorgeous photos are proof positive. Assisting Kate on the shoot were Clare Gray and Christina Martin, both specialists in vegan desserts who have assisted me for several years, and I appreciate their dedication and long hours in the kitchen.

I honor my family for patience during the year of Fran's one track mind, and making available to me their kitchens and space to write in the "country." Thank you to my sister-in-love, Professor Linda ("oh yes you can") Costigan Lederman; my daughter Tracy, a statistician who scaled recipes and ingredients, and her husband Rob, the "liquids guy"; and my son Michael and his lovely wife Linda, who know a thing or two about editing and producing. Special thanks to my precious grandchildren who helped select recipes. Georgia and Cecile the "Costigals," learned to taste test, and said enthusiastically of the ones they liked, "Put it in the book GFran!" The little boys, Seth and Eli, while not as verbal at two and a half and one and a half, just smiled and said "Nummy!" And thanks to Sheila Bender and Leah Breier, other writers in the family, who helped when I asked, and fast.

Colleagues and cookbook authors who graciously shared information and friends who offered support include: Nava Atlas, Robin Asbell, Max and Paul Binder, Daniel Biron, Kris Carr, Betsy Carson, Mary Doyle, Suzanne Fass, Jerry Lyn Field, Alessandra Felice, Natalie Freed, Bryanna Clark Grogan, Caryn Hartglass, Julie

Hasson, Liz Hoffman, Dr. Michael Klapper, Linda Long, John Joseph McGowen, Victoria Moran, Sharon Nazarian, Charlene Nolan, Jill Nussinow, Joy Pierson and Bart Potenza, Tal Ronnen, Suzy Rowley, Chad Sarno, Karen Basset Stevenson, Benay Vynerib, and Diane Weinz.

Thanks to the staff and assistants at the Natural Gourmet Institute and the Institute for Culinary Education for hosting my dessert classes, and to all the wonderful people who come to my classes, demonstrations, and conferences. I learn from you all every day.

Thank you to the ever-enthusiastic Jim Eber, who read my rough drafts, and with his unique ability to preserve what I wrote, made them better.

I could write another book about the making of the book, before and after, my assistant Megan Eaton came on board. Megan and I met at the Vida Vegan Blogger Conference held in Portland, Oregon in 2011. When back in New York, I worried aloud to our mutual friend, vegan consultant JL Fields, that keeping track of a dozen versions of a recipe, tester evaluations, and the intricacies of the computer in general had me anxious (okay hysterical). JL suggested I give Megan a call, which I did that Saturday night. On Sunday morning, Megan dug right in, setting up systems (hello Dropbox, Excel, notebooks, and daily lists) and formatting documents. In no time, Megan, a vegan who believes it is never too early to taste dessert, was thinking like a food writer and testing recipes, too.

My recipes were tested by real people in their real-life kitchens around the world, from newbies to pros, in New York City, Canada, and Australia. Thank you to my elite team for excellent work and comments that had us laughing along the way. Your comments and photos made clear which of the recipes were ready for prime time.

Nicole Axworthy

Jane Belt

Kelly Cavalier ("can I have all 8?!")

Monica Giannakopolous (and her entire family!)

Clare Gray

James Hultgren (testing while writing his thesis!)

Kimberly Marcus

Sharon Nazarian, "The Big City Vegan"

Lisa Pitman

Sabrina Ravello

Roberta Roberti

Kim and Ron Sansone

Debra Walter

Eric West

Introduction

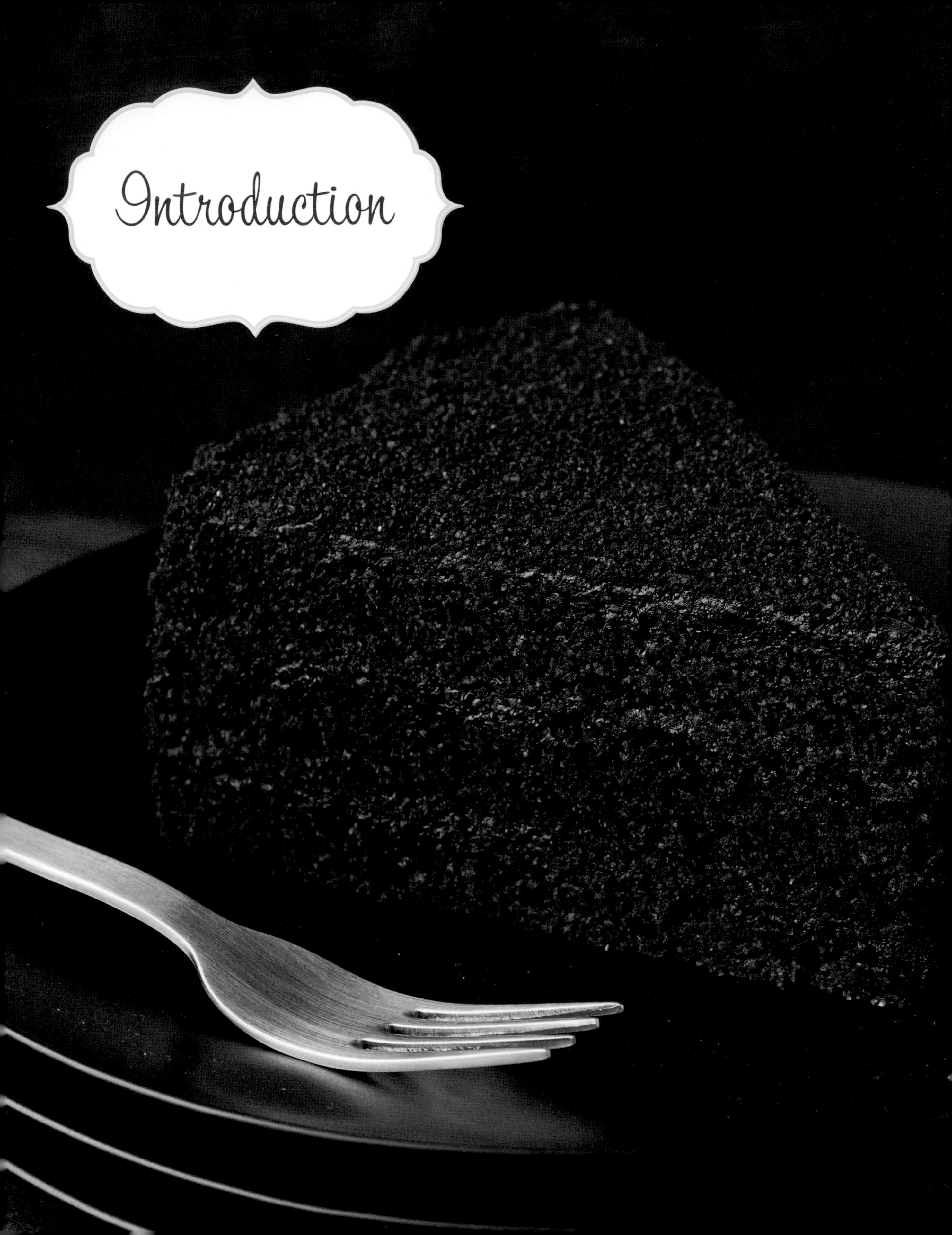

It doesn't matter where I am— a cocktail party, the dentist, the hairdresser—as soon as people learn about my work the conversation immediately turns into a discussion about diet, health, and chocolate. "Does dietary restriction mean chocolate deprivation?" (No, it doesn't!) "Can I eat safely and healthfully and still eat chocolate, too?" (Yes, you can!) "Can vegan chocolate desserts possibly taste as good as my old favorites?" (Absolutely! As good as, if not better!)

The same thing happens in my cooking classes. My chocolate-themed classes sell out the fastest, and in any class, faces brighten and hands shoot up whenever chocolate is mentioned. Opinions and memories of favorite chocolate desserts are always readily shared. But very quickly the usual concerns take over: "Is chocolate vegan?" "Are premium high-percentage vegan chocolates available?" "Is it organic? Fair? Single origin?" "Where can I buy it?" "How can I be sure it's safe?" I understand all their questions and concerns, and this book will answer those questions, address those concerns, and more.

My lifelong love of sweets—chocolate in particular—started very early: My mother, Shirley Bernstein, fed me chocolate ice cream for breakfast when I was a toddler. Truthfully, I have no memory of ice cream for breakfast. I do know I've always found milk impossible to swallow, so it is possible Mom resorted to this irresistible treat as a solution to the doctor's order, "Get milk into that child!" It also would have laid the earliest foundation for my chocoholic tendencies.

Not that my taste differed then from most children. Most of my childhood chocolate memories revolve around the standard fare of most of my neighborhood friends: Hostess Cupcakes, Devil Dogs, Oreo cookies, and the iconic Blackout Cake from Ebinger's Bakery in Brooklyn—perhaps the greatest chocolate cake of all time. For those who have never experienced that New York classic, it was a spectacular three-layer chocolate cake filled and frosted with thick chocolate pudding and then showered all over with chocolate cake crumbs.

That Blackout Cake and the home-style, frosting-swirled chocolate layer cake from Custom Bakers in Island Park, New York, were the two special-occasion treats I loved most growing up, and they remain among my favorite dessert memories. (My recipe for a vegan version of the Brooklyn Blackout Cake is in the "Showstoppers" chapter, page 94.)

Flash forward to my first job out of the New York Restaurant School: pastry chef at a gourmet takeout shop on Manhattan's Upper East Side. It was a dream come true. To everyone's delight, especially my own, I baked muffins, scones, popovers, cookies, pies, and cakes all day, using loads of butter, cream, eggs, and white sugar. Of course I tasted everything I made, but within a short time I began to experience digestive upsets and fatigue that made it increasingly difficult for me to work. After just nine months, I had to leave the job I loved in order to find out what was wrong.

In researching my symptoms, by chance I picked up the landmark book _Food and Healing_ by Annemarie Colbin, Ph.D. Her theory that food and health are linked made sense to me. I decided to eliminate all dairy and eggs—in fact, all animal foods—as well as refined sugar from my diet. I resolved to eat only seasonal, organic, whole foods. In other words, I began following a healthy, plant-based vegan diet. Almost immediately, I felt better—great, even. (It was not until sometime later that I learned, unsurprisingly, I was among the 75% of people worldwide who are lactose intolerant.)

For a while, keeping with my new way of eating, I shunned all sweets. But when my fourteen-year-old son said, "Mom, you can't put a candle in a baked sweet potato and call it my birthday cake," I realized I had gone too far! I came to my senses. I remembered that sweet treats are celebratory and an important part of a balanced life. Vegans—and all people with dietary considerations and restrictions—still celebrate birthdays, weddings, and anniversaries. We sit at the holiday table with family and friends. We love desserts as much as anyone else. My dietary considerations and restrictions were not going to deprive my family and me any longer.

Easier said than done, as they say. This was the late 1990s. I soon understood why my professional colleagues were skeptical, believing that "vegan pastry chef" was an oxymoron and that an "excellent vegan dessert" was a contradiction in terms. Vegan desserts were largely uncharted territory with no Facebook and only a few websites and cookbooks available to help. Unless you liked gummy and heavy health-food-style creations, you were out of luck. The biggest insult to me, as a chocoholic, were carob cakes being passed off as chocolate cakes.

Undeterred, I learned all I could about the properties of high-quality vegan ingredients. I tasted, tested, and tweaked, feeling certain that if I could link these ingredients with traditional pastry techniques, I'd get what I was after: *no-apologies-needed delicious desserts that just happen to be vegan*. I refused to accept the verdict, "Well, this is pretty good for what it is," or to use poor quality or analogue ingredients (e.g. margarine instead of butter). I dedicated myself to revamping the mediocre-to-awful vegan desserts and the inaccurate recipes I had found in first-generation vegan cookbooks. I had a lot of work to do.

My first real sense that I was on to something came after I enrolled in the Natural Gourmet Institute Chef Training Program and worked as a pastry chef at a busy organic dairy-free restaurant in Hell's Kitchen in New York City. The chef instructed me to follow the recipes exactly, since the desserts always sold out. I was puzzled by their popularity. I could taste the margarine in the frosting and understood that the tofu in the batter made the cake heavy. I knew I could do better. It took time and testing, but with the first successful version of my margarine-and-tofu-free Chocolate Cake to Live For, I knew I was right. The chocolate cake has since become my signature cake and is my most requested and discussed recipe. Love letters from fans and attention from the media continue to this day.

(The latest version of the cake, The Bittersweet Ganache–Glazed Chocolate Torte to Live For, is on page 68.)

After that breakthrough, I had ample opportunity to hone my craft as a pastry chef at New York City's renowned vegan restaurant, Angelica Kitchen, and develop new recipes for my proprietary vegan pastry classes at the Natural Gourmet Institute. I learned that pesticide- and herbicide-free ingredients are safer for consumers, growers, and the environment, and I committed to using organic ingredients. I realized new techniques were needed to make tender baked goods and started using whole grain flours, healthy plant-based liquid fats (like extra-virgin olive oil and other plant oils), and natural sweeteners. After researching the links between slavery and the production of sugar and chocolate, I opted to buy from companies with ethical policies in place. I was overjoyed to confirm that unsweetened cocoa powder and many fine chocolates—two of the most important ingredients in the pastry chef's pantry—can be vegan, organic, and fair trade.

My vegan recipes evolved from desserts I missed eating, as well as the desserts I see in restaurants and pastry shops, on cooking shows, in cookbooks, and in magazines. I'm inspired by requests I receive from home bakers and professionals who seek vegan versions of their favorite recipes. When I develop recipes, I work within vegan guidelines, use high-quality ingredients, adhere to foundational pastry techniques, and maintain the integrity of the original dessert. These factors result in desserts that are vegan by design only—they don't "taste vegan." I enjoy watching the joyous, if somewhat amazed, reactions when I reveal to doubters that the dessert they just devoured is vegan and I welcome the ensuing challenge: "You have to prove to me that this dessert is vegan!" (This is much more fun and satisfying than the days when defending meant proving that vegan desserts could be good at all.)

But I also know that none of this would mean anything to anyone using this book if my recipes did not

work, were impossible to make, and most importantly, did not taste great. Well, the proof is in the pudding—and the cookies, the cakes, the ice creams. . . . My recipes, from simply made Very Fudgy Chocolate Chip Brownies and Almost-Instant Chocolate Pudding to luxurious Bittersweet Chocolate Truffles and the elegant Opera Cake, will have even the most ardent choco-holics—including any "vegan dessert doubters"—too busy licking their plates to remember that every dessert is completely free of dairy, eggs, white sugar, choles-terol, and saturated fat.

For the dessert novice, this book is a practical guide to demystifying the art of vegan desserts, and for the professionals and everyone in between, it is a compre-hensive resource. That none of the recipes include chemically processed, fake, or hard-to-find ingredients is simply "icing on the cake" for the millions of us who, for one reason or another, have chosen a vegan diet.

What these recipe all do include is chocolate. In the past decade, chocolate has come a long way from Hershey's and Baker's chocolates favored by the doyenne of baking, Maida Heatter. Today's chocolate aficionados are interested in high-percentage, fair-trade, organic, gluten-free, and raw chocolates. They are pleased about the reported health benefits of their favorite bean. Now considered an affordable luxury, premium specialty chocolate bars crowd grocery store and supermarket shelves, no longer the exclusive provenance of a few upscale shops or online vendors. This is why, with the exception of a few recipes using chocolate chips, I use high-percentage dark chocolates in my recipes. I urge you to read the informative first chapter, which is structured so you can find what you need and start cooking immediately. As long as you stay within the range of percentages listed in each recipe, I leave the choice of brand to you—the chocolate that tastes good to you is the right one to use! Because what everyone loves most about chocolate is eating it. So, let's get into the kitchen and start playing with dark chocolate!

CHAPTER ONE

Ingredients, Sweeteners, Chocolates, and Equipment

Making desserts at home is a sure way to have fun and maybe even learn something new. You get tangible results that are guaranteed to bring happiness into your home. "Wow, you made this for me?" Make the desserts chocolate and the "Wow!" will be even louder and the thanks more effusive. Because who doesn't love chocolate?

This chapter gets you ready to deliver on that wow factor. The first part of the chapter includes a glossary of ingredients, as well as a how-to guide for using both vegan-specific items such as agar (the sea vegetable that gels), tofu, and nondairy milks, and standard ingredients found in any pastry kitchen (flours, leavening agents, starches, spices, fats, sweeteners, and chocolates). Many of these ingredients will be familiar but some might not be or might need more explanation.

The Equipment section provides guidance on how to select and use tools for the vegan pastry kitchen. I have indicated tools that are "essential" as well as those that are "nice to have," but the decision is ultimately yours. If you don't aspire to bake a lot of pies, you don't need multiple pie and tart pans. But in my opinion, no kitchen can ever have enough sturdy heatproof stainless steel bowls in a variety of sizes, extra sets of measuring cups for dry and wet ingredients, measuring spoons, whisks, and spatulas used to make all kinds of desserts.

The Ingredients

EXTRACTS AND ESSENCES (OILS)

Extracts and essences are distilled, concentrated flavorings from ingredients like plants, nuts, coffee, and spirits. Seek out real versions only—artificial flavorings, like vanillin, for example, taste "fake" and use coal tar and petroleum. Read the label and find pure flavorings. Essences are more potent than extracts, so less is needed. Store the bottles in a dark, cool place. I revere vanilla beans but they are expensive. I use beans only when I want to see the teeny seeds, and I save the bean pod for other uses (see Sidebar page 49).

Almond extract/oil is extracted from sweet almonds.

Chocolate extract made by infusing cacao beans in alcohol sometimes adding agave. The extract adds a subtle but definite chocolate note, and is worth seeking out.

Vanilla extract is made by infusing vanilla beans in alcohol. Organic and fair-trade pure vanilla and alcohol-free options are available.

FATS

Cocoa Butter is the fat extracted from the bean. Food grade cocoa butter is used as an ingredient in chocolate and baked goods. It is not a dairy product. Deodorized cocoa butter is processed through steam (not with chemicals), and the organic, fairly traded variety is easy to find (see Resources page 290). Cocoa butter is solid at room temperature: Shave or finely chop it, and melt it in a water bath until liquid before using.

Coconut Oil is the oil of the coconut. Choose a brand that is organic and non-GMO. Melt the amount of oil you need over low heat in a small saucepan. Store at room temperature. Do not worry if the oil that was solid when you bought it at the store has become liquid in your pantry. It is perfectly fine. (The oil melts at 76°F / 24°C.)

Coconut Butter (also called Creamed Coconut Concentrate) is a solid fat, which is made by puréeing coconut flesh. If you need to use melted coconut butter, follow the directions for melting coconut oil. Store at room temperature.

Extra-Virgin Olive Oil (mild tasting, fruity) is the pressed fruit juice of olives made without additives. The factors influencing its quality and taste include the varieties of olives used, the terroir, and how the oil is produced. For baking, I use the delicate, mild, and versatile Everyday Extra-Virgin Olive Oil from California Olive Ranch. I use one of the more assertive and floral varieties when I want the taste of the oil to be more pronounced. You can substitute neutral vegetable oils like sunflower or organic canola. Note that if canola is not organic is it a GMO. Store extra-virgin olive oil at room temperature in a dark bottle, capped tightly, away from heat.

WHEAT FLOURS

Organic all-purpose flour and **organic whole wheat pastry flour** are the two wheat flours I use most often. With only a few exceptions, I mix the flours in varying percentages, as I find this provides the best flavor and texture in baked goods. Organic all-purpose flour is a blend of hard red winter and spring wheat and has a protein content of 9.5 to 11%. Organic whole wheat pastry flour is milled from low-protein soft wheat and has a mellow 9% protein content and slightly nutty taste. (Note: Standard whole wheat flour has a protein content of about 14% and is not appropriate for cakes and pastries—do not substitute.) Organic flours are free of the chemicals used in the processing of conventional flours and are not bleached and bromated. Organic flours and grains are widely available in packages and in the bulk bins of natural food stores and larger markets. Store all flours in airtight bags or containers in the refrigerator for up to three months or in the freezer for up to six months. Whisk to fluff before measuring.

NON-WHEAT FLOURS

All-Purpose Gluten-Free Baking Mixes are combinations of starches and/or bean flours. Be sure to check the label of gluten-free baking mixes before you mix the batter. If guar or xanthan gum is not an ingredient in the pre-made mix, add the amount listed in the recipe. (My go-to gluten-free mix is Bob's Red Mill Gluten-Free Baking Mix—see Resources page 290—which does contain xanthan gum.)

Coconut Flour is gluten-free flour made from the fiber of coconut meat after most of the oil has been extracted. Low in digestible carbohydrates and a good source of protein, it adds a subtle sweetness to baked goods. It is thirsty flour that needs more liquid than most others. Use in combination with other flours.

Oat Flour is finely ground or pulverized oats (see Sidebar page 81 to make your own). The oats do not contain gluten, but cross contamination with wheat often keeps oats off limits to those who must avoid gluten. However, certified gluten-free oats are now available.

Essential Note About Proper Measuring of Dry Ingredients

Some cookbooks specify sifting before measuring, or spooning the flour into the measuring cup. Do not sift or spoon the flours or other dry ingredients into a measuring cup. The recipes in *Vegan Chocolate* use the *"whisk, dip, and sweep"* method of measuring. Using any other method will result in an unpredictable, and likely disappointing, result. Refer to the Introduction to Cakes (page 63) to learn how to use this method. Then use it, please!

FRUIT, DRIED

Choose sulfite-free dried fruits. Store in airtight containers in a cool pantry for up to six months.

GUMS

Agar/agar-agar/kanten is known as the "vegetable gelatin" but is actually not a protein; it is a vegetable gum derived from several species of red seaweed. Agar comes in flakes and as a powder, which are not interchangeable in recipes. (The powder is four to five times as strong as the flakes, and the flakes need to be softened before using.) Agar gels are firmer than those made with gelatin and set at room temperature, although refrigerating speeds the process. Agar gels also continue to set after they are made. For this reason, I usually combine agar and a root starch, for a creamier, softer result that doesn't grow rubbery. Agar is a natural product and varies in strength from batch to batch and among manufacturers. (I find Eden agar flakes to be the strongest and the most consistent. See Resources page 290.) You will have to test and adjust the gels as needed, following the directions for testing in the recipes. Store agar in a tightly covered container in a cool, dry place for up to two years.

Note: When converting recipes from gelatin to agar, use very slightly less agar.

Guar Gum is my new best friend: it's a thickener made from a bean that grows in India and Pakistan and has seven to eight times the thickening potency of arrowroot, cornstarch, and tapioca. As a result, the quantity of guar gum in the recipes is very small (from $1/16$ to 1 teaspoon), but it is essential for adding the "creamy" to ice cream (by slowing ice crystal formation) and for perfect nut milks and creams (by hindering separation). Do not use more than the amount listed to avoid an unpleasant taste or texture. I use guar gum from Bob's Red Mill and a bag will likely last for as long as you can store it in a tightly closed container or jar in the refrigerator, up to two years. (Guar gum is interchangeable with xanthan gum; both are used in gluten-free baked goods.)

Chia seeds (black and white) are gluten-free seeds that come from the desert plant *Salvia hispanica*. The seeds are even richer in Omega-3 fatty acids than flax seeds, and since chia is so rich in antioxidants, the seeds can be stored for long periods without becoming rancid. When mixed with water, ground chia forms a gel that thickens and binds. It's used as an egg white replacement in Chocolate-Dipped Coconut Macaroons (page 134) and to make the no-cook Chocolate, Date, and Coconut Chia Pudding (page 189). Refrigerate the chia seeds in a covered container for up to six months and the ground seeds for three months.

LEAVENING AGENTS

Traditional batter-based cakes rise because they are made with chemical leavening agents, such as eggs, baking powder, and baking soda. Vegan bakers can only use the latter two. Baking soda is an ingredient in baking powder, but they have crucial differences and I use them both in most of my baked desserts, unless natural cocoa powder is an ingredient (refer to page 29). When a recipe contains baking powder and baking soda, the baking powder does most of the leavening. The baking soda adds to the leavening, neutralizes the acids in the recipe, and adds tenderness. Instead of eggs, apple cider vinegar is the third in my holy trinity of making tender, risen cakes.

Apple Cider Vinegar (also called cider vinegar) has a pale to medium amber color. It acts in collaboration with the baking powder and/or soda to leaven cakes, and contributes a tender crumb. It is also used to sour or clabber nondairy milks and helps to tenderize pastry dough by hindering the formation of gluten. White vinegar can be substituted, but it is a highly processed product that I use only for cleaning. Refrigerate opened bottles of vinegar for up to six months, and store unopened bottles in a dark, cool place for a year.

Baking Powder (double-acting, aluminum-free) is a leavening agent for baked goods comprised of baking soda, cream of tartar or another acid, and starch (added to prevent moisture). It reacts twice, once when dissolved and again in the presence of heat. Whether or not you choose to believe the health claim that aluminum contributes to Alzheimer's, it does impart a tinny, off taste to baked desserts. So choose the widely available aluminum-free baking powder. Stored in an airtight container (marked with the date of purchase or the expiration date), baking powder should stay fresh for six months. Do not refrigerate. To see if your baking powder is still good: Add a teaspoon to a cup of hot water. If it bubbles vigorously, use it. When in doubt, toss it out.

Why I Use Ethical Ingredients

The historic link between chocolate, sugar, and slavery shamefully continues today. Reports of workers—especially children—enslaved or working long hours for pennies in places like Côte d'Ivoire have sparked widespread criticism of and within the chocolate industry, and show the stark contrast between the delicious treat we enjoy and the difficult working conditions of the people who produce it. The same can be said for sugarcane farming. That's why I seek out chocolates and sugars from companies with fair-trade policies in place. Some of the brands that I use are certified fair trade, some chose not to certify but are more than fairly traded, often paying above and beyond the prices set by the certifying agencies. A complete list of sources for organic and fair-trade ingredients is found in Resources, page 290.

Baking Soda is pure sodium bicarbonate. When baking soda is combined with moisture and an acidic ingredient (for example, yogurt, chocolate, or soured milk) the resulting chemical reaction produces bubbles of carbon dioxide that expand under oven temperatures, causing baked goods to rise. Stored in a covered container at room temperature, baking soda is said to last eighteen months. I replace mine every five months.

OTHER INGREDIENTS

Matcha is a premium green tea powder unique to Japan that is used for drinking as tea and as an ingredient in recipes. The complex flavor is slightly bitter, vegetal, and astringent, but when used as an ingredient, sparingly, the flavor becomes subtler. Matcha adds a lovely light green hue and unique flavor to a dish.

Miso, a staple Asian food, is a thick and salty paste with health supportive properties. Made by fermenting rice, barley, and soybeans, a small amount of white or sweet miso adds a subtle cheese note to desserts made with tofu. Store miso in the refrigerator for up to a year.

Do I Need to Use Organic Ingredients?

I choose to use ingredients that are produced without chemicals, pesticides, or other synthetic inputs. In addition, organic ingredients are never irradiated or genetically modified. But a recipe will work with non-organic ingredients. No matter what you choose, be an informed consumer. Big business is keenly aware of the exponential growth (read money to be made) of organics. There is even a term "industrial organic" for some of the biggest companies, while some smaller highly respected organic companies are now subsidiaries of big manufacturers, and some local farms may be "everything but organic," meaning they use organic practices but just do not have certification. The choice to use organic or conventional ingredients is, of course, yours.

NONDAIRY MILKS (COMMERCIAL)

Interest, choices, and availability have grown so much for these milks in the last few years that they are found in 7-Eleven! Use any of the following in recipes that specify "any nondairy milk:" **Almond Milk, Coconut Milk Beverage, Rice Milk,** or **Soymilk.** Use plain or vanilla versions in the recipes and look for brands with the fewest additives. Organic is recommended.

> ### Is Coconut Milk Vegetable-Based Heavy Cream?
> Refrigerate a can of full-fat coconut milk overnight in the coldest part of your refrigerator. Open the can and skim off the opaque layer on top. This is referred to as the coconut cream (and if the cream is sufficiently hardened, it can be whipped like heavy cream). Do not discard the watery milk under the cream. It can be used as a liquid in many desserts. Note: Coconut milk does not always separate; some manufacturers have added guar gum to canned coconut milk to prevent or retard separation.

Coconut milk that is canned, unsweetened, and full fat has the highest fat content (at 18 to 22%) of any of the commercial nondairy milks. Do not buy light coconut milk. Make your own by adding water, but do not substitute the "light" for undiluted coconut milk in recipes.

> ### Are Coconut Cream, Cream of Coconut, and Creamed Coconut the Same Product?
> No, and they are not interchangeable! Coconut Cream is the coconut oil–rich layer often found at the top of a can of cold full-fat unsweetened coconut milk. Cream of coconut is primarily defined as a mix of coconut milk and sugar (and other additives) used primarily in pina coladas and other drinks. Creamed coconut and coconut butter are one and the same: a slightly fibrous purée of whole coconut flesh.

NUTS AND SEEDS

All nuts pair exquisitely with chocolate! The high fat—it is good fat—content of nuts and seeds also makes them prone to becoming rancid. So while I always buy raw nuts, I also only buy them from stores with a fast turnover and store them in the refrigerator or freezer. For convenience, buy shelled nuts and for best tasting nuts, buy whole or halved nuts, not pieces. Always cover nuts when not using so they stay fresh and dry. Nuts and seeds develop flavor and crisp (and slightly stale nuts are improved) when they are roasted.

Almonds (sweet, whole unpeeled, raw) are delicately flavored and versatile. Actually, almonds are not tree nuts, but rather a seed of the fruit of the almond tree. Roast, blanch, or soak almonds following recipe directions.

Cashews (whole raw, roasted lightly, or soaked) are kidney-shaped nuts with mild to neutral flavor. When soaked in water, drained, and blended with fresh water or another liquid, they make an excellent substitute for dairy cream (see page 284).

Chestnuts are lower in fat than other nuts, which is one of the main reasons they are not interchangeable with other nuts in recipes. They are also not raw nuts; chestnuts are cooked and often puréed before using.

Coconut (dry, shredded) is the tropical nut and the source of desiccated (dry, shredded, unsweetened) coconut, coconut oil, coconut butter (a.k.a. creamed coconut concentrate), and coconut milk and milk beverage.

Hazelnuts (also called filberts) are a round nut also known as cobnut or filbert nut. They are used raw or roasted, or ground into a paste. The thin, dark brown skin is best removed before cooking. The best United States hazelnuts are grown in Oregon. Purchase whole nuts with skin on and roast and remove the skins before using (see Sidebar below).

Peanuts are legumes (groundnuts), not tree nuts. A species in the "bean" family, peanuts are much higher in protein than tree nuts. As peanuts are considered a major allergen, substitute another nut, if necessary.

Pecans are native to North America and high in vitamin E. The best are said to come from Georgia.

Pine nuts (also called pignoli and piñons) are mild and sweet, and very expensive. They come from Asia, Europe, and North America.

Pistachios have a unique green color and flavor. Do not buy the ones dyed red.

Sesame Seeds (light and black, hulled and unhulled) are one of the oldest foods in the world and are grown primarily in Africa and India. They are a staple of Middle Eastern and Asian cuisines (tahini is roasted sesame paste). But be careful. Although not listed as a major allergen in the United States, they are in Canada.

Walnuts are a hard-shelled nut, largely an American pedigree, and a hefty "meat." About two-thirds of the world's walnuts come from California. All nuts have health benefits, but walnuts are at the top of the list with the highest Omega-3 fatty acid content. (Omega-3 is said to be heart healthy.) For those (not me) who find their slightly bitter flavor unappealing, reduce the bitterness by removing some of the papery skins in a fine mesh sieve. If nut allergies are present, cacao nibs make a good replacement.

Roasting Nuts

Position a rack in the middle of the oven and preheat to 350°F / 180°C. Spread nuts in an even layer on a parchment-lined sheet pan. Roast for 6 to 10 minutes, stirring once, until the first nutty aroma wafts out of your oven. Watch carefully so the nuts do not burn—set a timer and don't walk away! Remove the pan from the oven and place on a wire rack. Let cool completely. The differences in oil content and freshness make an exact roasting time for any nut impossible, but properly toasted, all nuts will smell good and be warm to the touch with a uniformly golden or lightly browned color. Store roasted nuts in an airtight container.

STARCHES

Arrowroot, tapioca, and organic cornstarch are powdery, white starches used to thicken and add body and silken texture to sauces, puddings, and creams. Small amounts can also be used to replace some of the flour in baked goods to produce a more tender result. About 3% cornstarch or tapioca is added to confectioners' sugar to prevent caking. Unless the recipe specifies otherwise, the starches are dissolved in cool water (called "slurries") before being used. All starches can be stored in a cool dry place for up to two years.

Arrowroot or arrowroot flour is an easily digested combination of starches from several different tropical roots. Arrowroot thickens at a lower temperature than the other starches and will thin out or become stringy if cooked after the boil or stirred too vigorously. Don't buy the ridiculously expensive little spice-size jars of arrowroot. Buy in bulk or larger bags.

Organic Cornstarch (corn flour grown in UK/Australia) is ground starch isolated from the whole corn kernel. It must be cooked sufficiently or it will leave a chalky taste. Cook for 1 minute after the boil is reached. Note that unless cornstarch is organic it will certainly be genetically modified (a GMO).

Tapioca Flour or Starch is produced from dried manioc, which is the starch from the root of manioc or cassava. Unmodified tapioca starch can become stringy if overcooked. I prefer to use it in baked goods rather than puddings. Organic is available.

SEASONINGS AND SPICES

If you can't remember when you bought that jar of spice powder, or you can't tell what it is by sniffing, toss it out. Buy spices in small quantities, or from the bulk bin in stores with high turnover. They are less expensive that way and the spices will be fresher. Store spices in airtight jars or tins, labeled with the date of purchase, away from heat.

Salt is a crystalline mineral that is composed primarily of sodium chloride. If you are worried about cutting down on the amount of salt in your diet or have been warned by your doctor to do so, eliminate the processed food from your diet. That's where the salt lurks. Do not eliminate quality sea salt from desserts. They will not taste satisfactory. I use the following salts in my recipes: Fine sea salt is used in most recipes, as it dissolves easily. Flaked finishing salts are coarser and, depending on the variety, add moderate to strong flavor.

Ancho Chili Powder (made from dried Mexican poblano chiles) is distinguished by a characteristic rich red hue, mild heat, and complex fruity sweetness. The spice pairs beautifully with cinnamon in dark chocolate desserts.

Anise (also called aniseed and sweet cumin) is commonly used throughout the world, but less so in the United States. It is considered a digestive aid in some cultures. Perhaps this is why after dinner biscotti are often flavored with this spice. Buy anise as seeds, not ground. Toast the seeds lightly without oil in small skillet. Cool and grind in a spice grinder. Store in an airtight jar until needed.

Cardamom is an ancient spice native to India. The cardamom seeds are flavorful. If using whole pods, crush before using.

Cinnamon (or Ceylon in Sri Lanka) can come ground or in sticks. Perhaps the most beloved and certainly the most common of all the sweet spices, cinnamon is enjoying a surge due to its purported health benefits. Cinnamon is widely believed to improve blood glucose control. Most of the cinnamon sold in North America is cassia. Cassia, with its more robust, less sweet taste, can substituted.

Cumin is a flowering plant in the family Apiaceae, native from the east Mediterranean to India. Its seeds (each one contained within a fruit, which is dried) are used in the cuisines of many different cultures, in both whole and ground form. Buy the seeds instead of the ground spice. Follow the directions for toasting and grinding anise.

Ginger is a root and belongs to the same family as turmeric, cardamom, and galangal. Pungent, warming ginger is used in many cultures as a culinary spice as well as a medicine. My travel bag always holds ginger tea to soothe any digestive upset or ward off queasiness. Ginger is also considered one of the more potent anti-inflammatory spices. When it comes to food and flavor, the combination of ginger and chocolate is a personal favorite of mine, especially in Chocolate Ginger Ice Cream (page 208). Since the flavor of fresh ginger is variable, I save the fresh root for making miso soup, salad dressing, and savory dishes, in which a few more coins of fresh ginger can be added along the way. Of course, ground spices are variable too, so you may need more or less than is called for in a recipe.

SOY

Tofu (also called bean curd or soybean curd) was first used in China around 200 B.C.E. Tofu, which is made by curdling hot soymilk with a coagulant, has a flavor that ranges from nutty and somewhat "beany" to quite neutral, depending upon the type and manufacturer. When I changed my diet in the 1980s the tofu available tasted more like the soybean than it does today, and I didn't agree with macrobiotic friends who deemed the "Chocolate Pudding" made from blending tofu, cocoa, rice syrup or barley malt to be delicious. Two different types of tofu are used to make the recipes and they are not interchangeable. Whichever type is used, look for tofu that is organic or GMO-free. Use the right kind and quantity of tofu, sweeteners, flavorings, and chocolate or cocoa powder, and you can make wonderfully flavored desserts with no taste of bean whatsoever. Tofu is found in grocery stores, supermarkets, and Asian markets.

Firm (Chinese-style) tofu is found packed in water in sealed containers in the refrigerator section of markets. Drain and rinse firm tofu before using.

Firm or Extra-Firm Silken tofu has a higher water content and more neutral taste than firm Chinese-style tofu. Simply drain the silken tofu before using.

ZESTS

When finely grated zest is listed as an ingredient, use a Microplane rasp or zester. This simple tool takes off more of the zest while leaving behind the bitter white pith underneath. Scoop the zest into the measuring spoon without packing it down.

SUGARS AND SWEETENERS

Craving sweetness is in our DNA, making our desire for desserts undeniable. And yes, sweeteners are essential to most prepared desserts; you simply cannot bake a cake—well, not a good cake—without using real sugars. And no artificial sweeteners or conventional white sugar either, please! Organic sugar is vegan (see Sidebar, page 22) and free of pesticides and other poisons that are used to grow and process the conventional kind. That does not make organic sugar a health food, but it is better for the growers, the earth, and us. I also choose to use organic sweeteners from companies with fair-trade policies in place (see Sidebar page 16 and Resources page 290).

Today, consumers have a dizzying array of quality sugars and other sweeteners to choose from. Sugars alone range in flavor (mild to strong), color (pale blonde to dark brown), and size of the crystals (fine to coarse). This section helps you determine what they are, if they are interchangeable, and whether they are vegan.

I use two types of dry, or granulated, organic cane sugars: Organic Granulated Sugar and Organic Whole Cane Sugar. They are both made from sugar cane juice, but the end products are different and, for the most part, not interchangeable.

Organic Granulated Sugar is the all-purpose sweetener. Most of the molasses has been removed during processing so the color ranges from pale blonde to light beige. For tender baked goods, I recommend grinding organic sugar in a blender until it is superfine before using: in essence, making your own superfine, bakers, or castor sugar. (These sugars are one and the same.) Store in an airtight container until needed, and sift before using.

Organic Whole Cane Sugar (or whole cane juice, evaporated cane juice, or dehydrated cane juice) is a dark brown coarse sugar containing all the molasses in the cane and must be ground to a powder before using to ensure the sugar dissolves properly in baked goods and other desserts. Depending on the size of your blender, grind 1 to 2 cups at a time. (Do not be alarmed at the dust that rises when you open the blender lid.) You can grind the sugar ahead and store in an airtight container. Sift before using. Use in recipes calling for brown sugar, which is most often conventional white sugar with molasses added (see Resources page 290).

Note: Jaggery from India, piloncillo from Mexico and Latin America, and rapadura from South America are forms of non-granulated whole cane sugar. I don't recommend grating and using them in the recipes since their moisture content is variable.

Organic Confectioners' Sugar (also called icing sugar) is powdered white sugar with about 3% cornstarch or tapioca added to prevent clumping. Because of this added starch, it can't be substituted in baked goods for granulated sugars. Confectioners' sugar is used in icings, sweets, and whipped cream. Glazing sugar is confectioners' sugar made without the added starch; it can be directly substituted for confectioners' sugar. Make your own from organic granulated cane sugar in a high-speed blender or clean spice or nut grinder.

Coconut Sugar (or coconut palm sugar) is a sustainable sugar made from the sap of the coconut palm tree flower. Its flavor reminds me of a mild brown sugar with caramel overtones that I have come to appreciate, particularly in coconut-based desserts. Make sure to buy palm sugar from a reputable supplier, as much of what is sold in Asian markets contains a blend of fillers like white cane sugar. Grind to a powder before using and store in an airtight container.

Maple Sugar is evaporated maple syrup and was for many years the only sugar I used. But as my desserts have become more refined, I reserve this sugar to use in maple-forward desserts or as a garnish. Grind if very coarse and store in an airtight container.

Pure liquid sweeteners (syrups) retain the flavor from and color of their source plant. Formulas can be found for substituting liquid and dry sweeteners, but I do not find any to be consistently reliable, so mine change from recipe to recipe.

Is That Sugar Vegan?

The majority of white cane sugar is processed with bone char (charcoal) used as a decolorizing agent and is, therefore, not vegan. Organic sugars are never processed with bone char (or genetically modified) and are always vegan. Organic sugars have larger crystals than conventional white sugar and grinding them before using will result in baked goods with the best crumb and grit-free sauces and creams. For grinding instructions, see Organic Whole Cane Sugar. Bone char is never used in the processing of sugar beets either, so beet sugar is always vegan. But sugar beets are a genetically modified crop, and health-conscious and eco-vegans have turned instead to organic sugars.

Do Vegans Eat Honey?

Vegans do not eat dairy (milk, butter, cream, cheese, or yogurt—not even from goat's or sheep's milk), eggs (not even organic or free range), gelatin, white sugar processed with bone char (charcoal), or honey. The rules have been absolute, but recently, honey has become controversial among vegans because of the importance of bees to our environment. Honey is an animal product, which is verboten to vegans. Large commercial beekeeping companies engage in cruel factory farming practices. There are, however, dedicated beekeepers that employ humane practices and support and encourage bee populations. This is crucial in a world that is facing a frightening depopulation of bees called Colony Collapse Disorder. Without enough bees to pollinate crops, we have a shortage of food that impacts vegans and non-vegans alike. I do not use honey in my recipes, but this does not translate to my saying that all honey is off-limits. My own research into the bee problem and controversy included seeing two of the excellent documentaries made on the subject: *Queen of the Sun* and *Vanishing of the Bees*. My advice is to educate yourself on the situation and decide what feels right to you.

Agave Syrup (or nectar) is a very sweet, free-flowing sweetener produced from several species of agave. Most agave syrup comes from Mexico and South Africa and is found in both raw and cooked versions; the raw is darker in color and has a more pronounced flavor. Agave is primarily fructose. Do not use agave in baked goods; it bakes sticky cakes. Maple syrup can be substituted for agave. Store in a cool dry pantry or keep refrigerated.

Brown Rice Syrup (or nectar) is amber-colored and is a very thick and sticky sweetener made by culturing cooked rice with enzymes to break down the starches. It is half as sweet as sugar, with a lovely mild caramel taste. It is not suitable for cakes, making them damp and heavy, and cookies made with it are often too hard unless the rice syrup is used in combination with another sweetener. Because it is so thick, rice syrup should be heated slightly to make measuring easier. To heat, open the jar of syrup and place it in a saucepan of very hot water. Stir a few times until it is liquefied. Measure as directed. Cool and wipe the jar. Cover tightly and return it to the pantry. It has a shelf life of about a year, and, once opened, it should be stored in a cool, dry place. Do not refrigerate.

Maple Syrup is made from the sap of the sugar maple. A gallon of syrup, depending on the quality, requires thirty-five to fifty gallons of sap. I prefer dark syrup, Grade B, with its more assertive flavor, for baking, but Dark Amber, Grade A, can be used. The maple flavor is actually not apparent in desserts that are not designated as maple. Store in the refrigerator or freezer to prevent foaming or mold; it will become more viscous but will not freeze solid (see Resources page 290).

Molasses is a by-product of sugarcane processing and retains all the chemicals used in any processing, so buy organic molasses! It has a strong flavor and is used sparingly in combination with other sweeteners. Store in a cool dry pantry.

Sorghum is a Southern/Midwestern American sweetener extracted from a cereal grass that is enjoying a much-deserved revival. It tastes like a light, more complex molasses, and may be substituted for molasses. Store in the refrigerator.

About Chocolate

Chocolate: Good and good for you!

The botanical name of the tree where the magical cocoa bean comes from is *Theobroma cacao*, which is commonly translated to mean "food of the gods" or "God food." Either way, the divine nature of chocolate is indisputable. Harder to sort out is the research linking myriad health benefits to chocolate consumption, and answering one question I am continually asked: "Is chocolate really healthy?" Yes, tests have proven that natural dark chocolate contains beneficial antioxidants called flavanols and resveratrol. Enjoying a daily dose of quality, high-percentage, perfectly gorgeous chocolate makes *me* feel happy. Unless an allergy, sensitivity, or other medical condition requires you to avoid eating chocolate, then you should enjoy it, too! Happy has *definitively* been proven to be healthy. That is as far as I go in promoting chocolate as a health food.

Personally, I don't need more reasons to eat chocolate. I don't remember a time when I was not wild for chocolate. I do remember a time when my chocolate dreams included waxy foil-wrapped Kisses and colorful candies that "melt in your mouth, not your hand." That changed during my first trip abroad, to Switzerland in the late 1970s, where I had my chocolate epiphany. Creamy, dark, and not too sweet, I couldn't get enough. This was long before people talked about quality dark chocolate, percentages, or single estate. This was not the chocolate I found in the bodegas or drug stores around New York City, but I knew I couldn't go back to the "candy" chocolate I'd been eating at home. Since that awakening, my love for chocolate has been obsessive and has even bordered on irrational. When my wallet was stolen on a crowded bus I rushed home to cancel the credit cards and notify the bank, and as I did I thought, "Well, okay, at least they didn't get my chocolate bar."

While savoring a piece of quality dark chocolate in a moment of crisis or calm is divine, what thrills me most is using chocolate to make glorious desserts. That's why writing a cookbook filled with the best chocolate desserts everyone can enjoy, whether or not dietary considerations are an issue, became my passion. This section offers specific information and answers to questions about the kinds of chocolates used in the recipes and how to work with them so you can better understand and share my passion. More detailed information is found in the chapters.

DARK AND PREMIUM CHOCOLATE: JUST THE FACTS

There is no official standard for what defines "premium" or "dark" chocolate. The finest "dark" chocolate usually has no milk solids, but many other brands do. Dark chocolate can be labeled as unsweetened, bittersweet, or semisweet, but except for 100% unsweetened chocolate all of them could have milk. Dark chocolate for my purposes should only contain a percentage of something from the cocoa bean (meaning cocoa powder, nibs, liquor, butter, etc.) and vegan sugar. Optional ingredients may include lecithin and vanilla.

ABOUT PERCENTAGES

High-percentage chocolates contain more cocoa mass and less sugar, but what those percentages mean is rarely clear and not all bars of the same percentage taste the same. Let's look at chocolate labeled 70%. This type of chocolate contains about 70% cocoa liquor and 30% sugar. Different combinations of cocoa solids and cocoa butter can total the same percentage, and manufacturers rarely give you the breakdown. So, one bar can have 45% cocoa mass and 25% cocoa butter and another can have 60% cocoa mass and 10% cocoa butter but both would be listed as 70%

Is Chocolate Vegan?

Chocolate is vegan when it contains no milk solids of any kind, and the sugar used in processing is vegan. Vegan sugar has not been processed with bone char. All organic sugar is vegan. As for the milk, you would certainly not be alone if you were surprised to learn that up to 12% milk or milk solids is legally allowed to be present in the dark chocolate you may have added to your shopping cart, or in the bar you planned to give to your son's vegan girlfriend. I was very surprised (and confused) the first time I noticed milk listed on a non-milk chocolate bar, and I am sorry to report that this trend is becoming more common. Depending upon your reason for avoiding dairy, this news might be annoying, disappointing, or dangerous. For people with severe allergies to dairy, the presence of milk products in non-milk chocolate can be deadly. It is, therefore, of the utmost importance that you carefully read labels *every time*, even when you are purchasing a favorite vegan brand. Only certified vegan chocolates and kosher chocolates, which are made in dedicated milk-free facilities, are reliably free of dairy. (Note that this is a different story from the "made on shared equipment" chocolates.) If in doubt, contact the manufacturer and ask about the machinery and the process. Sources for vegan sugars and chocolates are found in Resources (page 290).

cocoa or cacao. Even if the percentages of cocoa mass and cocoa butter were identical, other factors, including quality of the cocoa beans, roasting processes, and other ingredients contribute to the taste. As a result, some lower-percentage chocolates taste "darker" than higher-percentage bars, and vice versa. Some are brilliant and some are awful. You will have to do some tasting and take notes! (This is hardly homework to complain about.)

While your palate should determine the percentage you prefer to eat out of hand, it is necessary to adhere to the percentages in the recipes. My understanding of high-percentage chocolates changed radically when I was doing the research for this book. I had been listing the high-percentage chocolates in my recipes as bittersweet, followed by the range of percentages to be used. My friend Jim Eber had just finished co-writing *Raising the Bar: The Future of Fine Chocolate* with Pam Williams. I showed him some of my recipes and he informed me that dark chocolate (then specifying the percent) was more correct, espe-

cially if I explained that there are no standards. I was quite stubborn about this for a while, but I understand the validity of their argument and the confusion that surrounds percentages and chocolate even at the high end. As long as you stay within the percentages of chocolates listed in the recipes, use chocolate you like eating out of hand, and follow my directions, good results are assured.

A Note about Substitutions

I do not recommend using cocoa powder and fat in place of chocolate, although many such conversions exist. The recipes contained in this book are developed to make the finest version of a dessert without dairy or eggs, solid shortening, or refined sugars, but with the best chocolate.

TYPES OF CHOCOLATES

Unsweetened Chocolate usually has a cocoa mass of 99 to 100%. It is used mainly for cooking..

Bittersweet Chocolate is required by the FDA to contain at least 35% cocoa liquor—after that, there is no restriction on ingredients. What a surprise this was to me. Clearly there is a huge difference between a 35% bittersweet chocolate and one that is 84%! Most dark chocolate that contains no milk is 60% or above, but this is not a rule.

Semisweet Chocolate or Sweet Chocolate is still considered dark chocolate even though the percentage of chocolate required by the FDA is just 15%. This chocolate is used in the book only in the form of chocolate chips and chocolate chunks. Standard chocolate chips/morsels are known as "baking resistant chocolate" since they stay whole in baked goods. Do not be tempted to substitute any chips or chunks for the higher-percentage chocolates—your truffles, glazes, and other recipes will fail.

White Chocolate usually contains little cocoa mass (except for cocoa butter) and almost always contains milk or cream powder, which makes it unsuitable for vegans. Vegan white chocolate chips, which are admittedly low quality, can be found in kosher marts and at online retailers. A few recipes list white chocolate as an ingredient. An excellent raw "golden" white chocolate is made in the United States by Organic Nectars, and I have sampled some very good ones in Europe.

Find listings of chocolates and ordering information in Resources (page 290).

HOW TO STORE CHOCOLATE

Chocolate will keep for a year at room temperature if kept below 70°F / 21°C. Keep the chocolate well wrapped in a dark pantry away from strong smelling foods. If your chocolate has a white film on it (called bloom), it may have been stored in too warm a place or condensation has occurred. Do not discard bloomed chocolate. While it does mar the appearance and texture, it can be melted and used in baking.

HOW TO CHOP CHOCOLATE

Chop chocolate very fine on a completely dry cutting board with a heavy serrated knife or a chef's knife, or chop it finely (or even grind to a powder) in a food processor. I batch-prep chocolates when I've got a little down time, wiping the board and knife (or food processor) with a dry kitchen cloth when switching brands and percentages. I weigh and double bag the chopped chocolate airtight in 4, 8, and 16-ounce / 113, 227, and 454-gram portions. I then label the bags to indicate the amounts, brands, percentages, tasting notes, and dates of chopping. This is slightly messy but extremely delicious work that means a faster start to making chocolate desserts.

HOW TO MELT CHOCOLATE IN A WATER BATH

I do not melt chocolate in a microwave. I melt chocolate in a water bath, which is a homemade double boiler, as follows. Pour a few inches of water into a saucepan. Set a heatproof bowl on the pan, making sure the bottom of the bowl sits above the water. Now remove the bowl and heat the water to a simmer. Put the chopped chocolate into the bowl and place the bowl on the saucepan. Keep the water at the lowest simmer. Wait until the chocolate has melted halfway to the center and start stirring with a silicone spatula. Remove the bowl from the heat when the chocolate is nearly, not completely, melted. Stir off heat until it is melted. If the chocolate is melted in advance as part of your *mise en place*, keep the bowl of chocolate over the warm water so it remains liquid.

TEMPERING CHOCOLATE

Tempering is simply melting chocolate in a controlled way so the fat crystals are stable. The chocolate bars that you purchase are already tempered. However, when chocolate is melted that changes, and the chocolate must be tempered again. The traditional manner of tempering chocolate is labor intensive. Professionals use tempering machines. I make small batches of tempered chocolate as needed using the easy-to-master seed method. And when I do not wish to temper chocolate for truffles, I dip truffle centers in melted untempered chocolate, and dust with cocoa or another dry coating. I call this the hybrid method of coating (see page 37). I store chocolate-coated cookies, cakes, and transfer sheet chocolate shapes in the freezer, where the sheen stays pristine.

TO SEED TEMPER CHOCOLATE

10 ounces / 283 grams dark chocolate (70 to 75%), divided

1. Chop 2 ounces / 57 grams of the chocolate into medium chunks and set aside until needed.

2. Finely chop the remaining 8 ounces / 227 grams of chocolate. Place in a heatproof bowl set over a saucepan of barely simmering water. Stir once or twice with a silicone spatula until the chocolate is almost, but not completely, melted. The chocolate should be about 100 to 110°F / 38 to 43°C now. If not, keep stirring.

3. Remove the bowl from the saucepan to the counter, and add the reserved pieces of unmelted chocolate (the "seeds"). Whisk the seeds vigorously until they are melted. Check the temperature. When the temperature drops into the low 80s, you want to slowly bring it back up to between 88°F and 90°F / 31°C and 32°C over the warm water. This is the working range you need for dipping.

4. Spread a small amount of melted chocolate on a plate; the chocolate should harden in a few minutes and remain shiny. If it doesn't, repeat the tempering process.

REUSE EXTRA TEMPERED CHOCOLATE

Let your leftover tempered chocolate harden, then cover and store it at room temperature. You can re-temper it up to two more times.

DECORATING WITH CHOCOLATE

Chocolate Curls require only one 4-ounce / 113-gram block of chocolate at room temperature and a bowl or piece of parchment paper to hold the curls. Hold the block of chocolate in one hand and, using a swivel type vegetable peeler, peel the length of one side of the piece of chocolate. Continue to peel the chocolate until you have made enough curls. Use immediately or freeze in an airtight container.

For **Chocolate Shavings**, take 4 ounces / 113 grams of chocolate, chilled and cut into chunks that fit comfortably in your hand. Grate the chocolate directly onto the cake or dessert you are finishing, using a Microplane zester or the smallest holes of a box grater.

Chocolate Transfer Sheets are rectangular acetate sheets embossed with cocoa butter and food coloring and are available in hundreds of designs that give chocolate desserts a professional, finished appearance and a distinctive touch. Logos and personalized designs can be special ordered. Depending on your needs, you may not need to use the whole sheet, so cut the transfer sheet to your desired size. Place the textured side face up on a baking sheet.

To use transfer sheets, spoon tempered chocolate onto the textured side in a thin layer, using an offset spatula to spread the chocolate over the entire sheet, so that all of the edges are covered. (Apply it sparingly. You can always add more if you need to.) It's okay if the chocolate goes past the edges. Allow the chocolate to sit for six to eight minutes until it is no longer shiny. Refrigerate until the chocolate is set but not brittle before cutting into shapes with a sharp knife or decorative cutters. If the chocolate starts to shatter, it is too cold. Allow time for it to warm before proceeding. Do not discard the acetate sheet after the transfer has occurred. Use it as a landing place for enrobed truffles.

I frequently use melted chocolate that has not been tempered to make transfer sheet designs, allowing them to harden in the refrigerator. After cutting, I store the shaped chocolates in an airtight container in the freezer where they stay shiny until needed. This may be heresy, but it works for me.

Note: 4 to 5 ounces / 113 to 141 grams of melted or tempered chocolate covers one average transfer sheet.

Are Natural and Dutch-Process Cocoa Powders Interchangeable?

A recipe should specify which kind of cocoa powder to use, but if it does not, here is a clue: When baking soda is the leavening agent, use natural cocoa. If baking powder is used alone or in combination with soda, use Dutch process. If you cannot find Dutch process, use both baking powder and baking soda. Some recipes like the Brooklyn Blackout Cake (page 94), for example, use a natural cocoa and baking soda recipe. I added a variation using Dutch-process cocoa and baking powder and soda for testers outside the United States who told me they couldn't find natural cocoa. Don't substitute one for the other in batter recipes.

Note: It is easier to swap the types of cocoa powders in sauces and ice creams, but taste will be affected. And, if you vary ingredients or make substitutions from what is written, results will not be the same. That said, personal preference in the choice of cocoa is often based on what people ate as children.

Finally, never substitute sweetened or drinking cocoa for unsweetened cocoa powder.

Which Is It: Cacao or Cocoa?

Both can be correct. Most commonly, "cacao" refers to the pod and the fresh seeds or beans and sometimes is used to describe the pure chocolate paste or "liquor" of the bean. "Cocoa" is the more common name for the processed (fermented, dried, and roasted) beans. "Cocoa butter" is the fat extracted from those beans, and "nibs" are the broken pieces of the fermented, roasted bean. When the fat is extracted from the liquor, the result is cocoa / cacao powder. Today, with the increased interest in raw foods, cacao has come to signify raw chocolate products; the raw community very rarely uses the word "cocoa." To keep it simple in this book, cocoa will be used in all but the raw recipes.

Are all Cocoa Powders Alike?

All cocoa powder is unsweetened and is relatively low in fat (10 to 22%). Some premium cocoa is as high as 24% and I have seen low-fat versions under 10%, which is unacceptable for dessert. Cocoa powder is packed with more flavor per ounce than any other form of chocolate and is the best choice for batter-based desserts. There are two main types of unsweetened cocoa powder: natural (non-alkalized) and Dutch-process (alkalized) and two subtypes: raw (natural) and black (alkalized). A well-stocked chocolate dessert pantry includes all kinds. Store in a cool, dark place (not in the refrigerator) for up to two years.

Note: The weights for Dutch-process and natural (non-alkalized) cocoa powders differ slightly, and may vary from brand to brand. This is due to the variable amount of fat in the cocoa powders. The differences are very small; do not be concerned.

Dutch-process cocoa powder is made from beans that have been washed with a potassium solution to neutralize their acidity and make the cocoa more soluble. It gets its name from a Dutch chemist and chocolate maker, Coenraad van Houten, who is credited with inventing the process for "Dutching" cocoa. Dutch-process cocoa contributes a mellow but complex flavor and can stand alone in uncooked desserts. Some recipes call for cocoa powder to be "bloomed" in hot water or another hot liquid in order to intensify the flavor.

Black cocoa powder is highly alkalized. (Think Oreo cookies for an idea of the color this cocoa imparts.) Substitute it for only a small percentage of the Dutch cocoa in the recipe. It will not add to the flavor and, when used to excess, can ruin a dessert.

Natural cocoa powder is made from beans that are simply roasted and then pulverized into a fine powder. Natural cocoa powder is often described as fruitier, but I find it sour. In my opinion, natural cocoa is best in recipes containing large amounts of sweetener that are baked or cooked or otherwise transformed. Raw cacao powder, made from unroasted beans, is available.

Try a few of these cocoa powders to see which you like best. Sniff the powder; it should smell roughly of chocolate with a hit of acid (see Resources page 290).

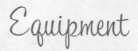

Equipment

My kitchen space in New York City is limited. Much of the equipment I use and recommend has served me over many years. But no matter how much space you have, the key is to invest in quality heavy pans that won't warp, and easy-to-use, accurate measuring utensils. The "essential" (marked with a *) and nice to have equipment that follows can easily be found on- and off-line in department stores, kitchenware shops, restaurant supply stores, and catalogs. Think before you buy: If you like to bake cakes, buy more cake pans; if you don't think you'll be baking pies, hold off on the pie pan.

Acetate Sheets create a nice clean finish for enrobed truffles.

* Blender (Standard or High Speed) is helpful for grinding and powdering organic sugar, making nut milks and creams, smoothies, ice cream bases, and more. A standard blender is fine, but fair warning: I've burned out a few. You don't need more than high-low, on, off—but get one with a decent motor. A high-speed blender is not essential but can be life-changing. Until this book, I never specified using a high-speed blender because of its cost. But my Vitamix really is a game changer. It powders sugars and makes velvet-smooth nut creams in a minute. You can even cook pudding to a boil (see page 282).

* Baking sheets (also seen as baking sheet pans and jellyroll pans) in 18 x 13 x 1-inch / 46 x 33 x 2.5-cm half-sheet pans and 13 x 9 x 1-inch / 33 x 23 x 2.5-cm quarter-sheet pans: You'll need two of each. Buy only heavy commercial-weight aluminum (it won't buckle in a hot oven) with a light-colored finish to promote heat absorption and prevent burning. They should last a lifetime.

Blowtorch: A butane torch found in hardware stores is much less expensive than the smaller ones in specialty shops and works great, but either will do. Using a blowtorch to make crème brûlée is fun and easy.

* Bowls (heatproof, stainless steel) in all sizes from very small to very large, for everything from mixing batters to melting chocolate over a water bath, to making giant salads before you indulge in chocolate. Have a few that are deeper than they are wide. Start with one, two, and three-quart bowls that nest. Note: As I do not use a microwave, I don't need glass bowls. I have a restaurant's supply of stainless steel mixing bowls that never break.

Cake Decorating Turntable is best made of heavy metal, but a plastic turntable will do. Mine is an Ateco that I have owned for twenty-five years.

* Cake Pans in the following sizes and quantities: 8 x 3 and 9 x 3-inch / 20 x 7.5 and 23 x 7.5-cm round cake pans (two of each size for cakes); 8 to 8½- x 3-inch / 20 to 21 x 7.5-cm springform pan for assembling desserts (one), and 8 x 3 and 9 x 3-inch / 20 x 7.5 and 23 x 7.5-cm square pans (one or two of each).

* Cardboard Cake Circles in 8 and 9-inch (20 and 23-cm) sizes are extremely helpful for supporting and moving cake layers.

Chocolate Dipping Forks: A three-prong stainless steel dipping fork is the tool I use for dipping truffle centers in and out of the melted chocolate coating. I sometimes use a large dinner fork, but dipping forks are easier to use.

Citrus Reamer is a terrific little wooden tool for getting juice out of a lemon or lime, but a fork will work fine.

* **Cutting Boards,** one reserved for chocolate and another for nuts and fruits and everything else. I like flexible boards for ease of moving the chopped ingredients.

* **Food Processor** for grinding nuts, making nut butters, powdering chocolate, creaming creams, and much more. Buy a processor with a good motor. I have not found the mini processors to be useful.

* **Knives** of the following sizes/types: 3 to 3½-inch / 7.5 to 8.9-cm paring knife (to peel fruit, cut decorations, loosen stuck cakes), 8 to 10-inch / 20 to 25-cm heavy chef's knife (to chunk large pieces of chocolate), and a stiff 10-inch / 25-cm serrated bread knife (to chop the chocolate fine and for torte cakes).

* **Ice cream maker** for making ice creams. I use a self-freezing electric unit. Models with removable canisters are less expensive, but you need to freeze the canister for 24 hours before each use. Both will work to make the ice creams in this book.

* **Measuring Cups:** For dry ingredients, I suggest keeping three sets of nesting metal cups in your kitchen. For measuring liquid ingredients, 1, 2, 4, and 8-cup liquid measures with pouring spouts are ideal; I find the 4-tablespoon (60-ml) mini measuring cups invaluable for small amounts.

* **Mixers** (electric) are essential for the few recipes that require the use of an electric mixer, but don't go buying a new one for me! My Kitchen Aid is a dented relic but otherwise fine. An electric hand mixer is fine, too.

* **Muffin tins and liners** are essential for making cupcakes in standard size (12-cup) and mini (12 or 24-cup) versions.

Nut Grinder for the fluffiest nut powders. I do grind nuts in the food processor, but at less than $20.00, my nut grinder was a worthwhile purchase. You can also grind small quantities of sugar in a nut grinder.

Oil Sprayer (Pump) for oiling baking pans without aerosol. I prefer the Misto Olive Oil Sprayer.

* **Parchment paper** for cakes which are always lined with parchment paper cut to fit. Sheets that measure 18 x 13 inches / 46 x 33 cm are easier to handle and more economical than the rolls, and can be cut to line baking sheets and every other kind of pan. You can also buy precut circles to fit 8 and 9-inch / 20 and 23-cm cake pans for convenience.

Pastry bags and tips for piping icing and decorating. I don't do much piping, but when I do, I use disposable bags in 10 to 12-inch or 16 to 18-inch sizes. The tips I use most often are the round and star tips. (You can write in chocolate with a small bag and a little round tip.)

* **Pastry brushes** (silicone) for oiling pans. Standard size is approximately 7.5 inches / 19 cm.

* **Pie pan, glass** (one or two 9 to 9½-inch / 23 to 24-cm) not only for baking pies but also to hold cocoa coatings and a full recipe of ganache as it sets. You can check the bottom of the pie crust for color when you bake in glass (I like Pyrex).

* **Ramekins** (3-ounce / 88-ml) for serving puddings, mousse, and crème brûlées, and small ones to hold ingredients for *mise en place*, and tests of creams, gels, and ganache.

* **Rolling Pin** to make pies. I use a tapered wooden pin. I have used wine bottles. The pin is better.

Scale (digital) for accurate measuring of ingredients and because many fine chocolates do not come in pre-measured packages. Good scales can be had for about $30.00. You can use a non-digital scale or even a postal scale.

Scissors to open packages, cut parchment, and more.

* **Skewers and Toothpicks** (wooden) are better for testing cakes than metal cake testers because crumbs adhere, making it possible to gauge whether or not the interior of the cake is gummy and needs further baking.

* **Spatulas** (metal, offset) in medium and small for leveling dry ingredient measures, spreading batter into pans, and frosting cakes; use wide ones for moving layers. My hands are small and I use the small size most often, feeling that I have best control.

* **Spatulas** (silicone, heatproof) in medium, small, and very small sizes, and multiples of each for mixing batters, stirring hot liquids, and moving mixtures from one vessel to another.

* **Strainers** (stainless steel) for sifting dry ingredients (a large-size medium mesh strainer) and to strain lemon juice and dust cocoa or confectioners' sugar over a dessert (a smaller mesh strainer).

* **Tart pan** (removable bottom, 9 to 9½-inch / 23 to 24-cm non-stick) for baking tarts. This is the only nonstick item I own.

* **Thermometer** (instant read) for tempering chocolate. But I find my wrist and fingers are pretty accurate at telling temperature.

* **Thermometer** (oven) to keep in your oven and check before you bake every single time. I keep two in my oven.

* **Timers** because you just need to burn something once to understand why.

* **Vegetable Peeler** for removing citrus peel and making chocolate curls.

* **Wire Racks** to speed the cooling of cakes and other baked goods. Several rounds and one or two sized for your baking sheets.

* **Wire Whisks** for aerating dry ingredients, sifting, mixing batter, and stirring cooked mixtures. I recommend small, medium, and large whisks with flexible but not soft wires. I have no use for silicone heatproof whisks, finding them too soft to be useful. A flat whisk is handy for stirring chocolate sauces.

* **Zester** for making fine zest, grating nutmeg, and shaving chocolate. I prefer a Microplane.

Measuring the Batter Allows Different Size Baking Pans

The recipes in the book can be scaled up or down. For example, a double recipe of a cake that makes two 9-inch rounds also makes an 18 x 13-inch sheet cake, or 24 regular sized cupcakes, or many more mini cupcakes. When you measure and record the batter yield for your favorite recipes, switching between rounds, sheets, and cupcakes is easy.

CHAPTER TWO

Truffles

A chocolate truffle has nothing in common with the highly coveted, wildly expensive fungus that grows underground, except its roundish shape and potent flavor. The latter makes it a chocolate lover's dream, especially when dusted with cocoa powder or enrobed in chocolate. Typically, chocolate truffles—even the dark chocolate ones—are made with cream or butter and sometimes corn syrup. Not here. In my recipes, all but the Raw Superfood Truffle are made using high-percentage dark chocolate, meaning more chocolate flavor and less sugar. Nondairy milk, yogurt, cashew cream, and even orange juice replace the dairy cream. There are some flavorings for the liquids and small amounts of extra-virgin olive oil here and there but that's all there is to it. Truffle ganache and shaped truffles can even be made ahead and refrigerated or frozen for whenever you need them. The hard part then isn't making these truffles but choosing which ones! So, are you in the mood for a bittersweet bite, or perhaps one flavored with ginger or espresso? How about something Aztec-spiced? The nondairy yogurt-based Crème Fraîche Truffles (page 60) and the juice-based Chocolate Orange Sesame Truffles (page 58) are standouts, too. Just remember, whatever you choose, use a chocolate you enjoy eating on its own, since the flavor of the chocolate is apparent in the finished truffle.

Fran's Rulebook for Successful Chocolate Truffles

1. Review the "About Chocolate" section of Chapter One (page 24).

2. Read the recipe all the way through and plan your time.

3. Prepare your *mise en place*: finely chop or temper the chocolate, grind sugar, gather the equipment.

4. Allow the chocolate to melt slowly into the hot liquid. This is an essential technique for velvety smooth truffles!

5. Don't over-whisk; over-mixing can turn a bowl of gorgeous ganache gritty.

6. Test a spoonful in the refrigerator to judge the final consistency.

7. Keep the ganache at room temperature for 30 minutes before moving it into the refrigerator (it is sensitive to changes in temperature).

8. Shape the truffles when the ganache is set but not so hard it crumbles.

If you follow all these rules correctly, your ganache will be glossy and gorgeous. If not, refer to the troubleshooting guide on page 37.

USING A WATER BATH

A water bath, also known as a *bain-marie*, is a double boiler you make using a saucepan filled with a few inches of water and a heatproof bowl. Remember to set up one to use if the ganache does not melt completely, and to keep chocolate liquefied when melted in advance. See page 28 for setting up and using a water bath.

SERVING

Truffles taste best at room temperature. Remove them from the refrigerator 1 hour before serving.

KEEPING

Place truffles in single layers in an airtight container, separating the layers with parchment paper, and refrigerate for up to five days. Or freeze truffles for up to one month in a tightly covered container. Allow the truffles to thaw in the refrigerator, then keep them at room temperature for two hours before serving.

OPTIONS FOR FINISHING YOUR TRUFFLES

Cocoa Coating: Truffles that are rolled in cocoa powder, nuts, or other dry coatings are quick, easy to make, and very attractive. These truffles often have a more solid center than truffles enrobed in a chocolate shell (see next section) made from tempered chocolate. To make cocoa-dusted truffles, simply roll the truffle centers in sifted Dutch-process cocoa powder to which salt or spices may have been added. The cocoa powder adds flavor and texture. Allow ½ cup Dutch-process cocoa powder (sifted) per recipe, and add any spice or salt that may be listed in the recipe to the cocoa.

Enrobing in Tempered Chocolate: Coating truffles with melted, tempered chocolate adds a chocolate coating that stays streak-free. Tempering is simply melting chocolate in a controlled way so the fat crystals are stable. Chocolate bars are already tempered, but when chocolate is melted that changes and the chocolate must be tempered again. The traditional manner of tempering chocolate is a labor intensive process that involves checking the temperature many times. (Professionals use tempering machines.) I make small batches of tempered chocolate as needed using the easy-to-master "seed method" (see page 28). That said, the only time I temper chocolate for enrobing truffles is when they will not have another coating, such as cocoa powder.

Remove the centers from the refrigerator about 5 minutes before enrobing. The centers should be chilled but not icy cold or the coating might crack. (If this happens, drop the truffle into cocoa powder and follow the hybrid method (see page 37). To dip, have the melted, or melted and tempered, chocolate in a deep bowl. Drop a chilled truffle center into the chocolate, and use a chocolate dipping fork to make sure it is submerged. Use the fork to remove the truffle. Hold it over the bowl to allow the excess chocolate to drip back into the bowl, and wipe the bottom of the truffle gently on the side of the bowl. Place on parchment and allow to set. Repeat with the rest of the centers. Refrigerate briefly to allow the coating to harden.

Melted Chocolate and Cocoa Coating: The Hybrid Method

When I do not wish to temper chocolate, I dip truffle centers in melted chocolate, and then roll in cocoa powder or another dry coating. The cocoa will hide any imperfections and the truffles will still look like their dusty fungus namesake.

FOR 24 TO 28 TRUFFLES:

¼ cup / 25 grams Dutch-process cocoa powder, more as needed

Pinch fine sea salt, or to taste

8 ounces / 227 grams dark chocolate (68 to 72%), finely chopped

1. Refrigerate the truffle centers until cold, about 1 hour, or up to overnight. If stored in the freezer, move to the refrigerator 4 hours before enrobing.

2. Sift the cocoa into a shallow dish such as a pie plate. Sprinkle with the sea salt.

3. Melt the chocolate in a heatproof bowl set over a pan of simmering water, stirring a few times until the chocolate is melted. Remove the saucepan from the heat but keep the bowl over the hot water.

4. Enrobe the truffle centers in the melted chocolate following the directions on page 36.

5. Drop the enrobed truffles into the cocoa powder, and roll each until coated.

6. Drop the cocoa-dusted truffles into a fine mesh strainer and shake gently to remove the excess cocoa. Refrigerate for 20 minutes to allow the chocolate to set. Remove from the refrigerator 1 hour before serving.

KEEPING

Refrigerate in an airtight container for up to one week.

Note: Allow leftover chocolate to harden. Melt again and use when you need liquid chocolate as an ingredient.

TROUBLESHOOTING	
Bits of chocolate still not melted	Set the bowl over the water bath and stir until melted.
Grainy ganache	Remove about one third of the ganache to another bowl. Whisk in 2 tablespoons of warmed nondairy milk. Add the ganache back into the main bowl and whisk until smooth. Your ganache should be shiny and smooth now.
Oily ganache	Remove about one fourth of the ganache to another bowl. Whisk in 2 tablespoons of cold nondairy milk. If this works, repeat until all the ganache is fixed. If not, discard the ganache and start over.

THE RECIPES

Bittersweet Chocolate Truffles

Bittersweet Cashew Cream Truffle Squares

Lemon Olive Oil Truffles

Spicy Ginger Truffles

Chai-Spiced Truffles

Curry in a Hurry Truffles

Aztec Truffles

Raw Cacao Superfood Truffles

Espresso Truffles

Chocolate Orange Sesame Truffles

Crème Fraîche Truffles

Bittersweet Chocolate Truffles

Classic chocolate truffles are sinfully indulgent, melt-in-your-mouth, bite-sized confections made from ganache (an emulsion of chocolate and heavy cream). Truffles sometimes include butter, as well as spices, coffee or tea, liqueurs, nuts, and even fruit purées for flavor. Vegan truffles, also based on ganache, are just as luxurious, velvety smooth, and indulgent—but not sinful. A variety of nondairy milks replace the heavy cream and no butter is added. And here is the best part: After making and tasting hundreds of truffles made with nondairy milks, I am convinced they taste more intensely chocolaty than their heavy cream–based cousins.

MAKES ABOUT 30 (1-INCH / 2.5-CM) TRUFFLES

8 ounces / 227 grams dark chocolate (70 to 72%), finely chopped

¾ cup plus 2 tablespoons / 210 ml unsweetened organic almond milk or soymilk

2 tablespoons / 26 grams organic granulated sugar

⅛ teaspoon fine sea salt

1 teaspoon / 5 ml pure vanilla extract

2 teaspoons / 10 ml mild tasting extra-virgin olive oil

A few pinches of flaked sea salt, for coating and serving (optional)

Dutch-process cocoa powder for coating (optional)

1. Add the chocolate to a heatproof bowl and set aside while you heat the milk.

2. Pour the milk into a small saucepan. Add the sugar and salt. Cook over medium heat, whisking a few times, to a low boil.

3. Immediately remove the saucepan from the heat. Pour the hot milk over the chocolate all at once. Rotate the bowl so the chocolate is completely submerged. Cover the bowl with a plate and let stand undisturbed for 4 minutes.

4. Add the vanilla and olive oil and whisk from the center out only until smooth and glossy. (If the chocolate is not completely melted, refer to page 36 for instructions on using a water bath to melt the chocolate.)

5. Keep the bowl of ganache at room temperature while you test the final consistency. A properly made truffle ganache is firm enough to scoop and shape but still tastes creamy. Dip a teaspoon into the ganache, set the coated spoon on a small plate, and refrigerate for 10 to 15 minutes. After chilling, the ganache on the spoon should be smooth and firm but still taste creamy. It is unlikely, but if the glaze is too firm, add a tablespoon of room temperature milk and repeat the test. Add a second tablespoon if needed.

6. Cool the ganache in a shallow dish at room temperature for 30 minutes. (The ganache sets up fastest and most evenly in a 9-inch / 23-cm glass pie pan or similar dish.) Refrigerate uncovered until the surface is no longer soft, then place a piece of parchment paper or plastic wrap directly onto the surface of the ganache, covering it completely, and refrigerate for at least 3 hours or until very firm. The ganache can be refrigerated at this point for up to 1 week in an airtight container.

MAKE THE TRUFFLE CENTERS

Line a shallow container with parchment. Remove the ganache from the refrigerator. Use a spoon to scoop out 1-inch / 2.5-cm pieces of ganache and another to push the ganache off the spoon into the container. (If you prefer more uniform truffles, use a ½-tablespoon scoop.) When a half dozen or so are made, roll and press the pieces into irregularly shaped rounds. Repeat until all the ganache has been used, washing and drying your hands as needed. (If at any time the ganache becomes too soft to shape, refrigerate until cold and proceed.) Cover and refrigerate the truffle centers in layers separated by parchment paper for 15 to 25 minutes before finishing with the cocoa coating.

FINISH THE TRUFFLES

Choose one of the following three methods from the chapter introduction (page 36) to suit your time or taste: roll in cocoa powder and flaked sea salt, coat in melted chocolate and cocoa powder (the hybrid method), or enrobe in tempered chocolate. Place the coated truffles in the refrigerator to set for 30 to 45 minutes. Sprinkle the truffles with a few grains of flaked sea salt, if you like, just before serving.

Bittersweet Cashew Cream Truffle Squares

This three-ingredient, one pot, luxuriously creamy chocolate truffle is incredibly quick and easy. However, unlike the truffles made with other nondairy milks, the Basic Thick Cashew Cream used in this recipe must first be warmed gently over low heat with very finely chopped chocolate or, better yet, chocolate that has been powdered in a food processor. Smaller particles ensure that the chocolate will melt quickly into the warm liquid, resulting in a smooth ganache with minimal stirring.

MAKES 30 TO 36 (3/4-INCH / 2-CM) SQUARE TRUFFLES

1 cup / 240 ml Basic Thick Cashew Cream (page 284)

7 ounces / 198 grams dark chocolate (72 to 75%)

1 teaspoon / 5 ml pure vanilla extract

Dutch-process cocoa powder or chopped nuts, for coating (optional)

1. Pour the Basic Thick Cashew Cream in a small saucepan and set aside.

2. Chop or break the chocolate into pieces, then process in a food processor until powdered. Add the chocolate to the cashew cream and cook over very low heat, stirring slowly and constantly with a silicone spatula until the chocolate is about two-thirds melted, about 1 minute.

3. Immediately remove the saucepan from the heat and continue to stir gently until the chocolate is completely melted and the ganache is smooth. Stir the vanilla into the ganache.

4. Line an 8 x 8-inch / 20 x 20-cm pan with parchment paper large enough to hang over the sides. Spoon the ganache into the pan and smooth the top. (You want to make a block of ganache that is ½ to 1 inch / 1.3 to 2.5 cm-thick.) Refrigerate for 2 to 3 hours until firm and then transfer to the freezer. Freeze for 4 hours or overnight until quite firm.

5. When the ganache is firm, lift the block onto a cutting board with the help of the parchment paper. Square the edges with a sharp knife and cut the block into squares. If the ganache gets soft, refrigerate until chilled. (If the ganache is too soft to cut, work with half or even a quarter of the block at a time, keeping the rest refrigerated.)

FINISH THE TRUFFLES

Pour the cocoa powder into a fine mesh strainer and lightly sift the cocoa powder over the truffle squares. (If the squares are very cold, the cocoa may not adhere. If that happens, allow them to soften slightly for a few minutes.) Sprinkle with chopped nuts or seeds of your choice if you like. You may also coat them in melted chocolate and cocoa powder (the hybrid method), or enrobe in tempered chocolate (see page 28). Place the finished truffles in the refrigerator to set for 30 to 45 minutes.

Lemon Olive Oil Truffles

The majority of people who rave about these truffles express surprise at the same time, saying they wouldn't have imagined liking chocolate and lemon together. I too was once surprised at how unusually well-suited lemon and chocolate are, and these truffles are singularly divine. It is best to use a chocolate that is not too bitter so that the lemon flavor comes through. While I do specify percentages in the recipes, I rarely recommend brands, believing that personal preferences rule. However, in this recipe, I especially like Whole Foods Market's 71% Costa Rican Dark Chocolate and Amano's Ocumare 70% from Venezuela. I also prefer using neutral rice milk, but almond milk is another option. Flaked lemon salt is worth seeking out: see page 293.

**MAKES ABOUT 40
(1-INCH / 2.5-CM) TRUFFLES**

8 ounces / 227 grams dark chocolate (70 to 72%), finely chopped

2/3 cup / 160 ml rice milk or almond milk

1 tablespoon / 13 grams organic granulated sugar

Zest from 1 medium organic lemon, removed in thin strips

1/8 teaspoon fine sea salt

1 tablespoon / 15 ml fruity extra-virgin olive oil, such as arbequina

1 tablespoon / 15 ml freshly squeezed lemon juice, strained

1 to 2 drops pure lemon oil (optional)

Dutch-process cocoa powder for coating (optional)

1/2 teaspoon flaked sea salt or lemon salt, for coating and serving (optional)

1. Set a fine mesh strainer over a heatproof liquid measuring cup for straining the heated milk. Add the chocolate to a bowl and set aside while you heat the milk.

2. Pour the milk into a small saucepan. Add the sugar, lemon zest, and salt. Cook over medium heat, whisking a few times, to a low boil.

3. Immediately remove the saucepan from the heat. Cover the saucepan and let the milk sit for 20 minutes to infuse with the flavor of the lemon, stirring a few times.

4. Pour the milk through the strainer into the measuring cup. Discard the solids. Wash and dry the saucepan. Return the milk to the saucepan and cook over medium heat until small bubbles are visible around the sides.

5. Pour the hot milk over the chocolate all at once. Rotate the bowl so the chocolate is completely submerged. Cover the bowl with a plate and let stand undisturbed for 4 minutes.

6. Add the olive oil and lemon juice and whisk from the center out only until smooth and glossy. (If the chocolate is not completely melted, refer to page 36 for instructions on using a water bath to melt the chocolate.) Taste and add the lemon oil if desired.

7. Keep the bowl of ganache at room temperature while you test the final consistency. A properly made truffle ganache is firm enough to scoop and shape but still tastes creamy. Dip a teaspoon into the ganache, set the coated spoon on a small plate, and refrigerate for 10 to 15 minutes. After chilling, the ganache on the spoon should be smooth and firm, but still taste creamy. It is unlikely, but if the glaze is too firm, add a tablespoon of room temperature milk and repeat the test. Add a second tablespoon if needed.

8. Cool the ganache in a shallow dish at room temperature for 30 minutes. (The ganache sets up fastest and most evenly in a 9-inch / 23-cm glass pie pan or similar dish.) Refrigerate uncovered until the surface is no longer soft, then place a piece of parchment paper or plastic wrap directly onto the surface of the ganache, covering it completely, and refrigerate for at least 3 hours, or until very firm. The ganache can be refrigerated at this point for up to 1 week in an airtight container.

MAKE THE TRUFFLES

Line a shallow container with parchment. Remove the ganache from the refrigerator. Use a spoon to scoop out 1-inch / 2.5-cm pieces of ganache and another to push the ganache off the spoon into the container. (Or, if you prefer more uniform truffles, use a ½-tablespoon scoop.) When a half dozen or so are made, roll and press the pieces into irregularly shaped rounds. Repeat until all the ganache has been used, washing and drying your hands as needed. (If at any time the ganache becomes too soft to shape, refrigerate until cold and proceed.) Refrigerate the truffles in layers separated by parchment paper for 15 to 25 minutes before finishing.

FINISH THE TRUFFLES

Choose one of the following three methods from the chapter introduction (page 36) to suit your time or taste: roll in cocoa powder and flaked lemon salt or sea salt; coat in melted chocolate and cocoa powder (the hybrid method); or enrobe in tempered chocolate. Place the coated truffles in the refrigerator to set for 30 to 45 minutes. Sprinkle the truffles with a pinch of flaked sea salt if desired before serving.

Spicy Ginger Truffles

The pungent ground ginger cooked into coconut milk to flavor these ultra creamy truffles elicited this comment from my friend Lisa Pitman, an accomplished cook from Toronto: "Not only are these exquisite, they are perfect for sharing when you want to spice things up with a certain someone." How you spice things up is up to you, but make sure you add enough ground ginger to ensure that at least these truffles are up to the task. Remember: bittersweet chocolate will temper the flavor of the ginger. Using coconut sugar adds a subtle caramel note to the spiciness, but mixing organic granulated sugar and whole cane sugar works just as well. Either way, just follow the recipe carefully and your reward will be luxurious truffles to serve after a meal of vegetable curry.

MAKES ABOUT 30
(1-INCH / 2.5-CM) TRUFFLES

8 ounces / 227 grams dark chocolate (68 to 71%), finely chopped

¾ cup / 180 ml unsweetened canned full-fat coconut milk, well-stirred (do not use light)

2 tablespoons / 18 grams coconut sugar or 1 tablespoon each organic whole cane sugar (9 grams) and granulated sugar (13 grams)

1 tablespoon / 6 grams ground ginger, divided, or more to taste

⅛ teaspoon fine sea salt

1 teaspoon / 5 ml pure vanilla extract

1 teaspoon / 5 ml mild tasting extra-virgin olive oil

Dutch-process cocoa powder, for coating (optional)

¼ teaspoon flaked sea salt, for coating, plus more for sprinkling on finished truffles (optional)

Candied ginger, slivered, for serving (optional)

1. Set a fine mesh strainer over a heatproof liquid measuring cup for straining the heated milk. Add the chocolate to a heatproof bowl and set aside while you heat the milk.

2. Pour the milk into a small saucepan. Add the sugar, 1½ teaspoons / 3 grams of the ground ginger, and the salt. Cook over medium heat, whisking a few times, to a low boil.

3. Immediately remove the saucepan from the heat. Cover the saucepan and let the milk sit for 10 minutes to infuse with the flavor of the ginger, stirring a few times. The heat of the ginger should be pronounced, so taste the milk now. If not, add a little more ginger to taste and let the milk infuse another few minutes.

4. Pour the milk through the strainer into the measuring cup. Discard any solids.

5. Wash and dry the saucepan. Return the spiced milk to the saucepan and cook over medium heat until small bubbles are visible around the sides.

6. Pour the hot milk over the chocolate all at once. Gently rotate the bowl so the chocolate is completely submerged. Cover the bowl with a plate and let stand undisturbed for about 4 minutes.

7. Add the vanilla and olive oil and whisk from the center out only until smooth and glossy. (If the chocolate is not completely melted, refer to on page 36 for instructions on using a water bath to melt the chocolate.)

8. Keep the bowl of ganache at room temperature while you test the final consistency. A properly made truffle ganache is firm enough to scoop and shape but still tastes creamy. Dip a teaspoon into the ganache, set

the coated spoon on a small plate, and refrigerate for 10 to 15 minutes. After chilling, the ganache on the spoon should be smooth and firm, but still taste creamy. It is unlikely, but if the glaze is too firm, add a tablespoon of room temperature milk and repeat the test. Add a second tablespoon if needed.

9. Cool the ganache in a shallow dish at room temperature for 30 minutes. (The ganache sets up fastest and most evenly in a 9-inch / 23-cm glass pie pan or similar dish.) Refrigerate uncovered until the surface is no longer soft, then place a piece of parchment paper or plastic wrap directly onto the surface of the ganache, covering it completely, and refrigerate for at least 3 hours, or until very firm. The ganache can be refrigerated at this point for up to 1 week in an airtight container.

MAKE THE TRUFFLE CENTERS

Line a shallow container with parchment. Remove the ganache from the refrigerator. Use a spoon to scoop out 1-inch pieces of ganache and another to push the ganache off the spoon into the container. (If you prefer more uniform truffles, use a ½-tablespoon scoop.) When a half dozen or so are made, roll and press the pieces into irregularly shaped rounds. Repeat until all the ganache has been used, washing and drying your hands as needed. (If at any time the ganache becomes too soft to shape, refrigerate until cold and proceed.) Cover and refrigerate the truffle centers in layers separated by parchment paper for 15 to 25 minutes before finishing with the cocoa coating.

FINISH THE TRUFFLES

Choose one of the following three methods from the chapter introduction (page 36) to suit your time or taste: roll in cocoa powder, the remaining ginger, and flaked sea salt; coat in melted chocolate and cocoa powder (the hybrid method); or enrobe in tempered chocolate. Place the coated truffles in refrigerator to set for 30 to 45 minutes. Sprinkle the truffles with a pinch of ginger powder and a few grains of flaked sea salt just before serving, or press a small sliver of candied ginger into each.

Chai-Spiced Truffles

For most Americans, chai (rhymes with "pie") is synonymous with tea bags, or a drink at Starbucks. In India, chai refers to a spiced milk tea that is generally made from rich black tea, heavy milk, a regional combination of spices, and sweetener. Indian chai produces a warming soothing effect, and is said to be a natural digestive aid; the spices used are anti-inflammatory. In this recipe, rich coconut milk stands in for the heavy milk. The strong black tea can be brewed from either bags or leaves.

MAKES ABOUT 26 TO 28 (1-INCH/2.5-CM) TRUFFLES

6 ounces / 170 grams dark chocolate (70 to 72%), finely chopped

3 black or chai tea bags

¾ cup / 180 ml boiling water

1½ teaspoons / 3 grams ground ginger, divided

1 teaspoon / 4 grams garam masala, plus more for coating

¾ teaspoon / 2 grams ground cinnamon

⅜ teaspoon grated nutmeg

6 cardamom pods, lightly smashed

1 vanilla bean, seeds scraped

⅜ teaspoon fine sea salt

5 twists black pepper

6 tablespoons / 54 grams coconut sugar (substitute 3 tablespoons each organic whole cane sugar and organic granulated sugar)

3 tablespoons / 45 ml almond milk

Scant ¼ teaspoon flaked salt, crushed, plus ¼ teaspoon for coating

Dutch-process cocoa powder, for coating (optional)

1. Put the chocolate to a heatproof bowl and set aside while you make the chai concentrate.

2. Place the 3 tea bags in a medium saucepan and pour the boiling water over them. Add half the ginger, the garam masala, cinnamon, nutmeg, cardamom, vanilla bean, sea salt, and pepper. Stir and simmer over the lowest heat for 5 minutes.

3. Remove the saucepan from the heat. Cover and set aside to infuse for 20 minutes.

4. Remove the tea bags from the chai concentrate, squeezing to release any tea. Strain the concentrate into a 1-cup/250-ml measure through a fine mesh strainer and press on the solids to release all the liquid. Discard the solids.

5. Rinse the saucepan and return 6 tablespoons/90 ml of the concentrate to the saucepan (refrigerate any extra for tea). Add the sugar and almond milk and bring to just under the boil over medium heat, stirring until the sugar is dissolved.

6. Pour the mixture over the chocolate all at once. Rotate the bowl so the chocolate is completely submerged. Cover the bowl with a plate and let stand undisturbed for 4 minutes.

7. After 4 minutes, whisk from the center out only until smooth and glossy. (If the chocolate is not completely melted, refer to page 36 for instructions on using a water bath to melt the chocolate.) Slowly stir the remaining ginger into the ganache.

8. Keep the bowl of ganache at room temperature while you test the final consistency. A properly made truffle ganache is firm enough to scoop and shape but still tastes creamy. Dip a teaspoon into the ganache, set the coated spoon on a small plate, and refrigerate for 10 to 15 minutes.

After chilling, the ganache on the spoon should be smooth and firm, but still taste creamy. It is unlikely, but if the glaze is too firm, add a tablespoon of room temperature milk and repeat the test. Add a second tablespoon if needed.

9. Cool the ganache in a shallow dish at room temperature for 30 minutes. (The ganache sets up fastest and most evenly in a 9-inch/23-cm glass pie pan or similar dish.) Refrigerate uncovered until the surface is no longer soft, then place a piece of parchment paper or plastic wrap directly onto the surface of the ganache, covering it completely, and refrigerate for at least 3 hours, or until very firm. The ganache can be refrigerated at this point for up to 1 week in an airtight container.

MAKE THE TRUFFLE CENTERS

Line a shallow container with parchment. Remove the ganache from the refrigerator. Use a spoon to scoop out 1-inch/2.5-cm pieces of ganache and another to push the ganache off the spoon into the container. (If you prefer more uniform truffles, use a ½-tablespoon scoop.) When a half dozen or so are made, roll and press the pieces into irregularly shaped rounds. Repeat until all the ganache has been used, washing and drying your hands as needed. (If at any time the ganache becomes too soft to shape, refrigerate until cold and proceed.) Cover and refrigerate the truffle centers in layers separated by parchment paper for 15 to 25 minutes before finishing with the cocoa coating.

FINISH THE TRUFFLES

Choose one of the following three methods from the chapter introduction (page 36) to suit your time or taste: roll in cocoa powder, garam masala, and flaked sea salt; coat in melted chocolate and cocoa powder (the hybrid method); or enrobe in tempered chocolate. Place the coated truffles in the refrigerator to set for 30 to 45 minutes.

Reusing Seeded Vanilla Beans

When you cook with seeded vanilla beans, the beans have lost too much of their flavor to be reused in cooking. But do not throw them away! Rinse and dry the beans and then add them to a jar of granulated sugar. The beans will infuse the sugar with vanilla flavor. Or add them to a jar of pure vanilla extract to reinforce its flavor.

Curry in a Hurry Truffles

Turmeric, a strongly flavored orange and yellow spice used in curry dishes and South Asian and Middle Eastern cuisine, contains curcumin, a compound that is widely believed to help to prevent infection. (The spice has also been used in India's traditional Ayurvedic remedies for 2,500 years.) Turmeric is also said to be anti-inflammatory. The flavor is very pungent and a little goes a long way, so many people choose to swallow turmeric capsules instead of eating a daily quotient. Here's a delicious answer. Use a teaspoon or more of mild, medium, or hot curry to flavor nondairy milk and healthy, sinfully easy curry truffles become a super way to help the "medicine" go down.

Note: Make sure to use a fresh, full-flavored curry powder. The recipe was developed using a medium-hot curry powder, but you may use mild or hot instead. You will find a great selection of flavorful, fresh spices in ethnic and specialty markets (see Resources page 290).

MAKES 26 TO 30
(1-INCH / 2.5-CM) TRUFFLES

8 ounces / 227 grams dark chocolate
   (68 to 71%), finely chopped
³/₄ cup / 180 ml almond milk,
   or soymilk
4 teaspoons / 12 grams coconut sugar
   or organic granulated sugar
2 teaspoons / 4.5 grams curry powder
¹/₈ teaspoon sea salt
1 teaspoon / 5 ml pure vanilla extract
Flaked salt, crushed, for coating
   (optional)
Dutch-process cocoa powder,
   for coating (optional)

1. Add the chocolate to a heatproof bowl and set aside while you heat the milk.

2. Pour the milk into a small saucepan. Add the sugar, curry, and salt. Cook over medium heat, whisking a few times, to a low boil.

3. Pour the hot milk over the chocolate all at once. Rotate the bowl so the chocolate is completely submerged. Cover the bowl with a plate and let stand undisturbed for 4 minutes.

4. Add the vanilla extract and whisk from the center out, only until combined. (If the chocolate is not completely melted, refer to page 36 for instructions on using a water bath to melt the chocolate.)

5. Keep the bowl of ganache at room temperature while you test the final consistency. A properly made truffle ganache is firm enough to scoop and shape but still tastes creamy. Dip a teaspoon into the ganache, set the coated spoon on a small plate, and refrigerate for 10 to 15 minutes. After chilling, the ganache on the spoon should be smooth and firm, but still taste creamy. It is unlikely, but if the glaze is too firm, add another tablespoon of room temperature milk, and repeat the test. Add a second tablespoon if needed.

6. Cool the ganache in a shallow dish at room temperature for 30 minutes. (The ganache sets up fastest and most evenly in a 9-inch / 23-cm glass pie pan or similar dish.) Refrigerate uncovered until the surface is no longer soft, then place a piece of parchment paper or plastic wrap directly onto the surface of the ganache, covering it completely, and refrigerate at least 3 hours, or until very firm. The ganache can be refrigerated at this point for up to 1 week in an airtight container.

MAKE THE TRUFFLE CENTERS

Line a shallow container with parchment. Remove the ganache from the refrigerator. Use a spoon to scoop out 1-inch pieces of ganache and another to push the ganache off the spoon into the container. (If you prefer more uniform truffles, use a ½-tablespoon scoop.) When a half dozen or so are made, roll and press the pieces into irregularly shaped rounds. Repeat until all the ganache has been used, washing and drying your hands as needed. (If at any time the ganache becomes too soft to shape, refrigerate until cold and proceed.) Cover and refrigerate the truffle centers in layers separated by parchment paper for 15 to 25 minutes before finishing with the cocoa coating.

FINISH THE TRUFFLES

Choose one of the following three methods from the chapter introduction (page 36) to suit your time or taste: roll in cocoa powder and flaked sea salt, coat in melted chocolate and cocoa powder (the hybrid method), or enrobe in tempered chocolate. Place the coated truffles in the refrigerator to set for 30 to 45 minutes.

Aztec Truffles

Savory spices incorporated into desserts yield fabulous results, but restraint is necessary, particularly when the spices are potent. Remember: adding spice is easy; removing it, especially in this recipe, is often impossible. While the dark chocolate in this recipe will temper the potency of the spice, use the minimum amount of ancho chili to start, tasting as you go. Then, add cautiously until the flavor reaches your preferred level of heat.

MAKES 28 TO 30
(1-INCH / 2.5-CM) TRUFFLES

8 ounces / 227 grams dark chocolate (70% to 72%), finely chopped

3/4 cup / 180 ml almond milk or soymilk

2 tablespoons / 26 grams organic granulated sugar

1 1/4 to 1 1/2 teaspoons / 2 to 3.5 grams ancho chili powder, plus 1/4 teaspoon for cocoa coating, if using

3/8 teaspoon ground cinnamon

1/8 teaspoon fine sea salt, plus 1/8 teaspoon for coating

2 teaspoons / 10 ml mild tasting or fruity extra-virgin olive oil

1/2 teaspoon pure vanilla extract

Dutch-process cocoa powder, for coating (optional)

MAKE THE GANACHE

1. Put the chocolate to a heatproof bowl and set aside while you heat the milk. (Have a fine mesh strainer nearby for straining the milk over the chocolate.)

2. Pour the milk into a small saucepan. Add the sugar, 1 1/4 teaspoons of the chili powder, cinnamon, and salt. Cook over medium heat, whisking a few times, to a low boil.

3. Remove the saucepan from the heat. Let the milk sit for 30 minutes to infuse with the flavor of the spices, stirring a few times. The heat of the chili powder should be pronounced, so taste the milk now. If not, add some or all of the remaining 1/4 teaspoon chili powder and let the milk infuse for another few minutes.

4. Warm the milk over medium heat until small bubbles are visible around the sides. Immediately remove the saucepan from the heat.

5. Pour the milk quickly through the strainer over the chocolate all at once. Rotate the bowl so the chocolate is completely submerged. Cover the bowl with a plate and let stand undisturbed for 4 minutes.

6. Add the olive oil and the vanilla and whisk from the center out only until smooth and glossy. (If the chocolate is not completely melted, refer to page 36 for instructions on using a water bath to melt the chocolate.)

7. Keep the bowl of ganache at room temperature while you test the final consistency. A properly made truffle ganache is firm enough to scoop and shape but still tastes creamy. Dip a teaspoon into the ganache, set the coated spoon on a small plate, and refrigerate for 10 to 15 minutes. After chilling, the ganache on the spoon should be smooth and firm, but still taste creamy. It is unlikely, but if the glaze is too firm, add a tablespoon of room temperature milk, and repeat the test. Add a second tablespoon if needed.

(recipe continues)

8. Cool the ganache in a shallow dish at room temperature for 30 minutes. (The ganache sets up fastest and most evenly in a 9-inch / 23-cm glass pie pan, but a wide bowl is fine too.) Refrigerate uncovered until the surface is no longer soft, then place a piece of parchment paper or plastic wrap directly onto the surface of the ganache, covering it completely, and refrigerate for at least 3 hours, or until very firm. The ganache can be refrigerated at this point for up to one week in an airtight container.

MAKE THE TRUFFLE CENTERS

Line a shallow container with parchment. Remove the ganache from the refrigerator. Use a spoon to scoop out 1-inch / 2.5-cm pieces of ganache and another to push the ganache off the spoon into the container. (If you prefer more uniform truffles, use a ½-tablespoon scoop.) When a half dozen or so are made, roll and press the pieces into irregularly shaped rounds. Repeat until all the ganache has been used, washing and drying your hands as needed. (If at any time the ganache becomes too soft to shape, refrigerate until cold and proceed.) Cover and refrigerate the truffle centers in layers separated by parchment paper for 15 to 25 minutes before finishing with the cocoa coating.

FINISH THE TRUFFLES

Choose one of the following three methods from the chapter introduction (page 36) to suit your time or taste: roll in cocoa powder, cinnamon, ancho chili powder, and flaked sea salt; coat in melted chocolate and cocoa powder (the hybrid method); or enrobe in tempered chocolate. Place the coated truffles in the refrigerator to set for 30 to 45 minutes.

Raw Cacao Superfood Truffles

Most raw date chocolate truffle recipes, while delicious, taste very similar. That is, they taste more like date confections to me than chocolate. In my recipe, the chocolate taste is pronounced, and the combination of the superfoods lucuma and maca, plus a small amount of coconut sugar, results in a more complex flavor. For a "raw friendly" not "raw really" truffle, use lightly toasted pecans (page 19).

**MAKES 30 TO 36
(1-INCH / 2.5-CM) TRUFFLES**

½ cup / 55 grams raw pecan halves

4.5 ounces / 126 grams pitted Medjool dates (about 8 large or ½ cup packed)

3 tablespoons / 15 grams raw cacao powder, plus more for coating (optional)

3 tablespoons / 27 grams lucuma

1 tablespoon plus 2 teaspoons / 33 grams maca

3 tablespoons / 27 grams coconut sugar, plus more for rolling (optional)

½ teaspoon alcohol-free vanilla extract

1. Chop the pecans in a food processor by pulsing the machine a few times, then process to a fine meal. Do not process so long that the nuts become butter.

2. Add the dates, cacao powder, lucuma, maca, coconut sugar, and vanilla extract and process until the mixture looks like fine crumbs. The mixture will not be a paste, but it will hold together when pressed between your fingers.

3. Spoon the dough into a small bowl. Scoop out 1-tablespoon portions and press between your fingers until the dough holds together. Roll into rounds in the palms of your hands.

4. Roll the truffles in the extra coconut sugar or keep them plain.

5. Refrigerate for 1 hour to allow the flavors to develop before serving. Enjoy these truffles at room temperature or chilled. The truffles will stay fresh for a few weeks, but I like the flavor best when eaten within one week. Freeze in an airtight container for up to one month.

Espresso Truffles

Coffee lovers like me will want to try one of these instead of their usual afternoon espresso. To make a truffle that tastes even more strongly of the coffee bean, use any of the premium espresso or coffee-flavored chocolates that are available in larger markets, but be sure to stay within the percentages listed in the recipe. Taste a few of the chocolates first, since flavor profiles vary. I do not recommend using chocolates that contain ground coffee beans. The truffles will taste gritty. With or without the addition of Kahlua or another coffee-flavored liqueur, this is a wonderful truffle to serve after a meal or as a midday coffee break.

**MAKES ABOUT 30
(1-INCH / 2.5-CM) TRUFFLES**

**8 ounces / 227 grams dark chocolate
(70 to 72%), finely chopped**

**¾ cup plus 2 tablespoons / 210 ml
unsweetened organic almond milk
or soymilk**

**3 tablespoons / 14 grams instant
espresso powder**

**2 tablespoons / 26 grams organic
granulated sugar**

⅛ teaspoon fine sea salt

1 teaspoon / 5 ml pure vanilla extract

**2 teaspoons / 10 ml mild tasting
extra-virgin olive oil (optional,
but recommended for sheen)**

**1 tablespoon / 15 ml Kahlua or other
coffee-flavored liqueur (optional)**

**Dutch-process cocoa powder,
for coating (optional)**

1. Set a fine mesh strainer over a heatproof liquid measuring cup for straining the heated milk. Add the chocolate to a heatproof bowl and set aside while you heat the milk.

2. Pour the milk into a small saucepan. Add the espresso, sugar, and salt. Cook over medium heat, whisking a few times, to a low boil.

3. Immediately remove the saucepan from the heat. Cover the saucepan and let the milk sit for 20 minutes to infuse with the flavor of the espresso, stirring a few times.

4. Pour the milk through the strainer into the measuring cup. Discard any solids.

5. Wash the saucepan. Reheat the infused milk to just under a boil.

6. Pour the very hot milk over the chocolate all at once. Rotate the bowl so the chocolate is completely submerged. Cover the bowl with a plate and let stand undisturbed for 4 minutes.

7. Add the vanilla, olive oil, and Kahlua (if using) and whisk from the center out only until smooth and glossy. (If the chocolate is not completely melted, refer to page 36 for instructions on using a water bath to melt the chocolate.)

8. Keep the bowl of ganache at room temperature while you test the final consistency. A properly made truffle ganache is firm enough to scoop and shape but still tastes creamy. Dip a teaspoon into the ganache, set the coated spoon on a small plate, and refrigerate for 10 to 15 minutes. After chilling, the ganache on the spoon should be smooth and firm, but still taste creamy. It is unlikely, but if the ganache is too firm, add a tablespoon of room temperature milk and repeat the test. Add a second tablespoon if needed.

9. Cool the ganache in a shallow dish at room temperature for 30 minutes. (The ganache sets up fastest and most evenly in a 9-inch / 23-cm glass pie pan or similar dish.) Refrigerate uncovered until the surface is no longer soft, then place a piece of parchment paper or plastic wrap directly onto the surface of the ganache, covering it completely, and refrigerate for at least 3 hours, or until very firm. The ganache can be refrigerated at this point for up to 1 week in an airtight container.

MAKE THE TRUFFLE CENTERS

Line a shallow container with parchment. Remove the ganache from the refrigerator. Use a spoon to scoop out 1-inch / 2.5-cm pieces of ganache and another to push the ganache off the spoon into the container. (If you prefer more uniform truffles, use a ½-tablespoon scoop.) When a half dozen or so are made, roll and press the pieces into irregularly shaped rounds. Repeat until all the ganache has been used, washing and drying your hands as needed. (If at any time the ganache becomes too soft to shape, refrigerate until cold and proceed.) Cover and refrigerate the truffle centers in layers separated by parchment paper for 15 to 25 minutes before finishing with the cocoa coating.

FINISH THE TRUFFLES

Choose one of the following three methods from the chapter introduction (page 36) to suit your time or taste: roll in cocoa powder, coat in melted chocolate and cocoa powder (the hybrid method), or enrobe in tempered chocolate. Place the coated truffles in refrigerator to set for 30 to 45 minutes.

Pairing Chocolate and Wine

Pair dark chocolate with an eco and vegan-friendly red wine. I recommend Carmaratina (Sangiovese 50%; Cabernet Sauvignon 45%; Merlot and Syrah 5%) from Italy's Querciabella winery with the Bittersweet and Espresso Chocolate Truffles in particular. The winery's owner, Sebastiano Castiglioni, a.k.a. The Eco Warrior, uses cruelty-free biodynamics to produce award-winning organic, non-GMO wines in prime Chianto Classico vineyards. Two other vegan reds that pair well with chocolate desserts are made by the Vegan Vine winery in California: their Cabernet and red blend. Refer to Resources (page 290) for more information about vegan wines.

Chocolate Orange Sesame Truffles

Fresh orange juice and finely minced orange zest are cooked with thick tahini (sesame seed paste) and a small amount of agave syrup to make the liquid for this unusual chocolate truffle with a slightly chewy texture. While this truffle ganache is not perfectly smooth, the truffles taste very creamy, and the coating of lightly toasted black and natural-colored sesame seeds provides color and crunch. Note that raw tahini is sweeter than the roasted kind, but either can be used. Serve this chocolate confection after a Middle Eastern or Moroccan meal.

MAKES 20 TO 24 (1-INCH / 2.5 CM) TRUFFLES

4 ounces / 113 grams dark chocolate (70 to 72%), finely chopped

Finely minced zest of half a medium organic orange

3 tablespoons / 45 ml freshly squeezed orange juice

¼ cup / 60 ml agave syrup

1 tablespoon / 15 ml raw or roasted tahini, stirred

1 ½ tablespoons / 13 grams natural sesame seeds, lightly toasted

1 ½ tablespoons / 13 grams black or white sesame seeds, lightly toasted

1. Put the chocolate into a small heatproof bowl.

2. Mix the orange zest and juice and agave in a small saucepan. Cook over medium heat just to a boil.

3. Reduce the heat to low and add the tahini, whisking vigorously. The mixture will thicken immediately. Do not be concerned if it looks broken or curdled. It will smooth out as you whisk. Simmer the mixture for 30 seconds until it is shiny and smooth. Remove from the heat.

4. Wait about 30 seconds until the mixture is no longer steaming and pour it over the chocolate. Cover the bowl with a plate. Wait 1 minute and then stir until the chocolate is completely melted. Remember: the ganache will not be perfectly smooth.

5. Cool to room temperature, stirring a few times with a silicone spatula.

6. Spoon into a small shallow container and refrigerate uncovered for about 2 hours until the ganache is firm. The ganache can be covered and refrigerated at this point for up to 1 week.

MAKE THE TRUFFLE CENTERS

Remove the ganache from the refrigerator. Use a spoon to scoop out 1-inch pieces of ganache and another to push the ganache off the spoon into the container. When half the ganache has been used, roll the pieces into logs about 1 inch long, washing and drying your hands as needed. (If at any time the ganache becomes too soft to shape, refrigerate until cold and proceed.) Cover and refrigerate the truffle centers for 15 to 25 minutes to set for before shaping and finishing with the sesame seed coating.

COAT THE TRUFFLES

Mix the sesame seeds in a small bowl. Sprinkle about 2 tablespoons / 18 grams on the bottom of a shallow container. Put a few logs at a time into the bowl of sesame seeds and roll until lightly coated. Pinch the ends to form the oval quenelle shapes. Place the finished truffles in the refrigerator to set for 35 to 45 minutes.

Crème Fraîche Truffles

Crème fraîche (literally "fresh cream" in French) is a rich cream that is soured naturally. It is smooth and velvety and has a wonderful tangy flavor. To get that same tangy taste in these vegan truffles, I use unflavored coconut milk or soy yogurt. I am not suggesting that vegan yogurts are the same as *crème fraîche*, but their tangy flavor works well to mimic the soured cream. For a more subtle taste, use a vanilla-flavored yogurt. As no sweetener is used in this recipe, the chocolate flavor in the truffles is very pronounced. Use a dark chocolate that you love to eat in the percentage range below. It is important to chop or process the chocolate until it is almost powdered so that it will melt quickly into the warmed yogurt.

    Note: The liquid ingredient in this recipe is nondairy yogurt. The yogurt, like the cashew cream in the Bittersweet Cashew Cream Truffle Squares (page 43), is warmed gently, rather than being cooked until hot. The saucepan is removed from the heat before the powdered chocolate is added. The chocolate in both this recipe and the cashew cream based–truffle should be ground in a food processor or chopped as small as possible. Smaller particles of chocolate ensure that the chocolate will melt quickly into the warm liquid, resulting in a smooth ganache with minimal stirring. Overheating will result in the separation of the cocoa butter. If this does happen, however (and you'll know it by the white streaks in the chilled truffle mixture), do not despair. Do not heat the ganache. In this particular recipe, even streaky ganache will taste smooth in the finished truffle.

MAKES 24 (1-INCH / 2.5-CM) TRUFFLES

½ cup plus 2 tablespoons / 150 ml nondairy yogurt: coconut, almond or soy, vanilla-flavored or plain

¼ cup / 60 ml mild tasting extra-virgin olive oil

Pinch fine sea salt

8 ounces / 227 grams dark chocolate (70 to 72%), chopped until nearly powdered or ground in a food processor (see Note above)

½ teaspoon pure vanilla extract

Dutch-process cocoa powder, for coating (optional)

1. Mix the yogurt, olive oil, and salt in a small saucepan. Warm the mixture over low heat, just until a bubble or two (but not more) appear at the edge.

2. Immediately remove the saucepan from the heat. Wait about 30 seconds and add the ground chocolate all at once. Stir with a silicone spatula only until the chocolate is melted and the ganache is smooth. Spoon into a bowl and add the vanilla.

3. Keep the bowl of ganache at room temperature while you test the final consistency. A properly made truffle ganache is firm enough to scoop and shape but still tastes creamy. Keep the bowl of ganache at room temperature while you test the final consistency. Dip a teaspoon into the ganache, set the coated spoon on a small plate, and refrigerate for 10 to 15 minutes. After chilling, the ganache on the spoon should be smooth and firm, but still taste creamy. It is unlikely, but if the glaze is too firm, add another tablespoon of room temperature yogurt, and repeat the test. Add a second tablespoon if needed and so on.

4. Cool the ganache in a shallow dish at room temperature for 30 minutes. (The ganache sets up fastest and most evenly in a 9-inch / 23-cm glass pie pan or similar dish.) Refrigerate uncovered until the surface is no

longer soft, then place a piece of parchment paper or plastic wrap directly onto the surface of the ganache, covering it completely, and refrigerate for at least 3 hours, or until very firm. The ganache can be refrigerated at this point for up to 1 week in an airtight container.

MAKE THE TRUFFLE CENTERS

Line a shallow container with parchment. Remove the ganache from the refrigerator. Use a spoon to scoop out 1-inch / 2.5-cm pieces of ganache and another to push the ganache off the spoon into the container. (If you prefer more uniform truffles, use a ½-tablespoon scoop.) When a half dozen or so are made, roll and press the pieces into irregularly shaped rounds. Repeat until all the ganache has been used, washing and drying your hands as needed. (If at any time the ganache becomes too soft to shape, refrigerate until cold and proceed.) Cover and refrigerate the truffle centers in layers separated by parchment paper for 15 to 25 minutes before finishing with the cocoa coating.

FINISH THE TRUFFLES

Choose one of the following three methods from the chapter introduction (page 36) to suit your time or taste: roll in cocoa powder, coat in melted chocolate and cocoa powder (the hybrid method), or enrobe in tempered chocolate. Place the coated truffles in the refrigerator to set for 30 to 45 minutes.

CHAPTER THREE

Cakes

"Anyone who spends any time in the kitchen eventually comes to realize that what he or she is looking for is the perfect chocolate cake," writes Laurie Colwin in *Home Cooking*. I couldn't agree more. I have spent the better part of my life in search of that cake, and recipes in the next two chapters are the most recent results of my search and the most popular among my family, friends, clients, and students. Moist and absolutely chocolate, yet cholesterol-, dairy-, egg-, and refined sugar–free, these are chocolate cakes made better—and easier! And, it's a fact that making vegan cakes is easier than many traditional from-scratch cakes. There is no waiting for eggs or butter to come to room temperature (and egg-free cake means you can safely lick the bowl without the risk of salmonella). You need only two bowls, a strainer for sifting, a couple of whisks and silicone spatulas, and the standard measuring and baking equipment. Parchment paper is a must, and cake cardboards are good to have. They support the layers and make transferring them easy. In addition, nearly every one of these cakes can be baked ahead, wrapped, and frozen. As a rule, the fillings and frostings benefit from advance preparation and most need time to set up properly, and cold cakes are easier to split, fill, and frost.

Measuring Dry Ingredients Using *"Whisk, Dip, and Sweep"*

Do not spoon the flour into the cup or sift it before measuring. Doing so will change the weight and will adversely affect the result.

- Whisk the dry ingredients in their container or bag before measuring. (To measure small amounts of starches, fluff with a fork before measuring.)
- Dip a dry measure into the flour, over-fill the cup, and level the top with the flat side of an offset spatula or dinner knife. Do not shake, estimate, or pack the ingredient in the cup.
- Put the measured dry ingredients in a medium-fine strainer set over a mixing bowl.
- Sift the dry ingredients by whisking them through the strainer. Set aside until needed. This can be done hours in advance. Whisk before proceeding.

Let The Leavening Agents Do Their Job!

Keep the dry and liquid ingredients separate until the oven is ready and the pans are prepared. The dry and liquid ingredients can be prepared in advance and whisked just before combining; just hold out the vinegar until it is time to make batter.

Fran's Rulebook for Successful Cakes

The same techniques apply for all of the cakes, from the simplest mix-bake-eat cakes served directly from the pan to the multi-layer showstoppers in the next chapter. Note: Rarely does the amount of vegan batter fill a pan more than a scant half full unless the pan has a center tube.

1. Review the "About Chocolate" section of Chapter One (page 27).

2. Read the recipe all the way through and plan your time.

3. Prepare your *mise en place* (from gathering the equipment and preparing the pans to grinding sugar, chopping or melting the chocolate, and roasting or cooling nuts, seeds, and flakes).

4. Position the oven racks as directed; cakes bake on the middle rack, cupcakes on the rung just above.

5. Preheat the oven and allow enough time for the oven to reach the correct temperature. An oven thermometer is essential.

6. Pan size matters! Use the correct size pan, and prepare it according to the recipe.

7. Measure ingredients carefully, using the correct measuring utensil and method. The recipes in this book use the *"whisk, dip, and sweep"* method of measuring dry ingredients, unless otherwise noted (see page 63). Measure liquid ingredients using liquid measuring cups—measure the oil first and the liquid sweeteners will slip right out!

8. Get the cakes right into the oven and allow some space between multiple pans.

9. Check the cake for doneness but wait until 5 minutes before the minimum baking time or you risk having the center of the cake collapse. Open the door as little as possible so the oven temperature doesn't drop. The top should look dry with no shine at the center and the edges will have started to pull away from the sides of the pan. Do not poke the cakes in the center—even gently; they are soft when warm.

10. Cool the cakes in the pan on an elevated wire rack, then get these moist cakes out of the pan and onto the wire rack quickly (about 10 minutes). It is okay to cool the cakes bottom side up, and don't worry if it sticks to the rack. Frosting will cover up any marks.

TROUBLESHOOTING	
Cake broke, or the center didn't bake well	Sorry. If the frosting can't cover it, make a trifle from the good pieces or make cake crumbs (see page 65).
Frosting too soft	Refrigerate it longer.
Frosting too firm to spread, even at room temperature	Mix in some nondairy milk or water until the desired consistency is reached.

The Frosting on the Cake

How-to details are found in the recipes, but there is one basic rule you must always follow: Allow time for the frosting or glaze to come to room temperature. Frostings should be creamy and glazes thick but pourable — test the consistency by spreading some on a piece of bread so you don't mess up the cake.

I use an offset spatula to spread the frosting over the cake (any size that feels comfortable in your hand will do), starting with the bottom layer.

When decorating frosted cakes, I keep it simple. I have never mastered the pastry bag, but I honestly like the elegant look of a simply glazed or frosted cake. Instead, I apply fresh edible flowers, use a garnish that has some link to the flavors of the cake, or make a simple bottom edge by patting cake crumbs, finely chopped nuts, or coconut on the sides, all of which can be used on top as well to camouflage my imperfect technique.

MEASURING FILLINGS AND FROSTINGS

You'll need the following amounts (approximately) for each kind of cake. Measure the amount of frosting to be used between each layer to ensure you have enough for the whole cake.

POURABLE GLAZES, INCLUDING GANACHE	
12 standard size (½ cup capacity) cupcakes	1 cup / 240 ml
Top and sides 8-inch round layer cake	1½ cups / 360 ml
Top and sides 9-inch round layer cake	2 cups / 480 ml
Top 9 x 12-inch sheet cake	2 cups / 480 ml
THICK FROSTINGS	
Top and sides 8-inch round 2-layer cake	1¾ cup / 420 ml
Top, sides and middle 8-inch round layer cake	2¾ to 3 cups / 660 to 720 ml
Top and sides 9-inch round 2-layer cake	2 to 2¼ cups / 480 to 540 ml
Top, sides and middle 9-inch round 2-layer cake	3¼ to 3½ cups / 780 to 840 ml
12 standard size (½ cup capacity) cupcakes	2 to 2¼ cups/ 480 to 540 ml
Per layer 8-inch round	½ to ¾ cup / 120 to 180 ml
Per layer 9-inch round	¾ to 1 cup / 180 ml to 240 ml

Making Cake Crumbs for Decorating or Crumb Crusts

Break a couple of cupcakes or any leftover cake (even stale cake will do) into small pieces. Dry the cake in a 350°F / 180°C oven for ten to fifteen minutes. (The exact time depends on the relative dryness or moistness of the cake.) When the pieces of cake are almost completely dry, cool, then crumble them into more uniform pieces with your hands or grind them into fine crumbs in a food processor. Use immediately or store in an airtight container in the freezer for up to two months. An 8-inch layer makes 3 cups / 390 grams fine dry crumb.

THE RECIPES

Bittersweet Ganache-Glazed Chocolate Torte to Live For

The No-Oil-Added Chocolate Torte to Live For

Chocolate, Orange, and Almond Olive Oil Cake

Chocolate Pecan Cranberry Coffee Cake

Mix-in-the-Pan Chocolate Cake

Brownie Pudding Cakelettes

Banana Cacao Nib Snack Cake

Vanilla Chocolate Chip Cupcakes

Chocolate Fudge Cupcakes

Black Bottom Cupcakes

Chocolate Date Muffins

Bittersweet Ganache– Glazed Chocolate Torte to Live For

The name for this cake dates back over twenty years to the day I was sure I had cracked the code for the perfect chocolate cake that was also vegan. I invited three friends over (non-vegan, as it happened) to taste the cake with me. After a big forkful each, we stopped, looked at each other, and said almost in unison, "Now this is a cake worth living for!" At least that is how I remember it. Since then, this has become my signature cake and remains the one most discussed, requested, Google-searched, praised, and served of all my cakes. Versions of what my assistants, interns, catering clients, friends, family, and I refer to as "TCC2L4" have appeared in both of my previous books, but I couldn't leave it out of my first all-chocolate book. This version is a single cake layer twice glazed with the glossy dark Bittersweet Chocolate Ganache Glaze. (You can of course simply double the recipe and bake a layer cake if that's what you prefer.) A "tinkerer" by nature, I have changed little bits of the recipe over the years, using a little less nondairy milk and substituting mild extra-virgin olive oil for the organic canola oil. Note that you will have more glaze than is needed for the recipe, but you can reuse the glaze that drips onto the parchment under the icing rack. After the excess has hardened, scoop it up, spoon it into a container, and cover and refrigerate or freeze for another use.

MAKES ONE (9-INCH / 23-CM) TORTE, 8 TO 10 SERVINGS

½ cup / 70 grams organic whole wheat pastry flour

½ cup / 64 grams organic all-purpose flour

¼ cup plus 1 tablespoon / 31 grams Dutch-process cocoa powder

¼ cup / 50 grams organic granulated sugar, finely ground in a blender

1 teaspoon / 5 grams aluminum-free baking powder

1 teaspoon / 5 grams baking soda

½ teaspoon / 2.5 grams fine sea salt

¼ cup / 60 ml mild tasting extra-virgin olive oil or organic neutral vegetable oil

½ cup / 120 ml pure maple syrup, Grade B or dark amber

¾ cup plus 2 tablespoons / 210 ml any nondairy milk

1 ½ teaspoons / 7.5 ml pure vanilla extract

½ teaspoon chocolate extract (optional)

1 teaspoon / 5 ml apple cider vinegar

1 recipe Bittersweet Chocolate Ganache Glaze (page 264)

1. Position a rack in the middle of the oven and preheat to 350˚F / 180˚C. Oil the sides and bottom of the cake pan and line the bottom with a parchment circle or paper cut to fit. Do not oil the paper.

2. Place a wire mesh strainer over a medium bowl. Add the pastry flour, all-purpose flour, cocoa, sugar, baking powder, baking soda, and salt to the strainer and stir with a whisk to sift the ingredients into the bowl. (If any small bits remain in the strainer, add them to the mixture in the bowl.) Whisk to aerate the mixture.

3. Whisk the oil, maple syrup, nondairy milk, vanilla, chocolate extract (if using), and vinegar in a separate medium bowl until completely combined. Immediately pour into the dry mixture and whisk until the batter is smooth. Pour the batter into pan. Rotate the pan to level the batter and tap it lightly on the counter to get rid of some of the air bubbles.

4. Bake the cake on the center rack for 28 to 32 minutes, or until the top of the cake is set, the sides have started to pull away from the pan, and a wooden toothpick or skewer inserted into the center comes out clean or with just a few moist crumbs.

5. Place the pan on a wire rack and cool for 5 minutes. Run a thin spatula around the sides of the cake to release the sides of the cake from the pan. Invert the layer onto the rack, remove the pan, and carefully peel off the parchment paper. Invert again, top side up on the rack, to cool completely. When the cake is completely cool, slide a cardboard circle or a flat plate underneath. Cover the cake tightly in plastic wrap and refrigerate until cold before glazing.

GLAZE THE CAKE

1. Place the cake on an icing rack set over a parchment-lined baking pan.

2. Pour slightly less than 1 cup / 240 ml of the Bittersweet Chocolate Ganache Glaze into a measuring cup with a spout. Center the cup over the cake and pour the glaze onto center of the cake. Coax the glaze to the edges and down the sides by tilting the baking sheet or using an icing spatula. Use the spatula to spread the glaze onto the sides.

3. Allow the glaze to set undisturbed for 15 minutes, then refrigerate the cake for 10 minutes.

4. Refill the measuring cup with another scant cup of the glaze, and add another coating. This time, don't try to move the glaze around with the spatula after it has been applied. Doing so will mar the finish. But extra glaze drizzled freeform on the cake looks great and hides any problems. Refrigerate to set the glaze.

SERVING

For the neatest slices, cut the cake while it is cold but serve at room temperature.

KEEPING

The glazed cake can be refrigerated for up to two days, unwrapped or in a cake box. (Keep the cake away from strong odors.) The cake can be frozen for up to one month: Wrap the cake tightly in a layer of plastic wrap and another layer of aluminum foil, or slip it into a zipper-lock bag and squeeze out the air.

VARIATIONS

Embellished Torte to Live For: The torte needs no fancying up—I like its elegant simplicity and often serve it without any further embellishment, other than possibly painting a line of extra glaze on each plate, off-center, and adding a pile of fresh berries or sliced fruit. But the following variations add wow: sprinkle the top of the cake with gold luster dust, add chocolate transfer sheet cut-outs (page 29), or place any of the truffles found in Chapter Two on the not-quite-set ganache.

Gluten-Free Chocolate Torte to Live For: Replace the pastry and all-purpose flours with 1 cup of all-purpose gluten-free baking mix. (I recommend Bob's Red Mill.) If your gluten-free mix does not contain xanthan or guar gum, add $3/8$ teaspoon xanthan gum to the dry ingredients. Bake for 25 to 27 minutes.

The No-Oil-Added
Chocolate Torte to Live For

Full disclosure: as a rule, I do not make or enjoy eating so-called fat-free cakes. I find the texture gummy when one hundred percent of the fat is replaced by fruit purée. And the fact that more sugar is necessary in oil-free, fruit purée-added baked goods is off-putting as well. So, when my daughter Tracy called to tell me she'd forgotten the oil in my Chocolate Torte to Live For recipe and liked the cake, I doubted her assessment, although she is one smart cookie and a baker. "No," she insisted, "It's denser and different, Mom, but really good." Still, I didn't intend to try "Tracy's recipe" until I was invited to present dessert demonstrations at the McDougall Celebrity Chef Weekend in Santa Rosa, California, where oils are prohibited in recipes. The cake was a resounding success and I have served it many times since. Sometime later, though, I decided to try using some canned coconut milk in the recipe. I'm not suggesting this change fits into a very lowfat eating plan, but I do prefer the taste and texture of this variation. The final word I leave to you. In keeping with the no-oil-added theme of this cake, I suggest frosting with Bittersweet Chocolate Ganache Glaze (page 264), which is naturally oil-free and low in sugar.

MAKES ONE (9-INCH / 23-CM) TORTE, 8 TO 10 SERVINGS

½ cup / 64 grams organic all-purpose flour

½ cup minus 1 tablespoon / 60 grams organic whole wheat pastry flour

1½ tablespoons / 9 grams arrowroot or organic cornstarch (10.5 grams)

¼ cup plus 1 tablespoon / 31 grams Dutch-process cocoa powder

¼ cup / 50 grams organic granulated sugar, finely ground in a blender

1 teaspoon / 5 grams aluminum-free baking powder

1 teaspoon / 5 grams baking soda

½ teaspoon fine sea salt

¼ teaspoon ground cinnamon

½ cup / 120 ml unsweetened canned full-fat coconut milk, well-stirred (do not use light)

½ cup / 120 ml almond milk or water

½ cup / 120 ml pure maple syrup, Grade B or dark amber

1 teaspoon / 5 ml pure vanilla extract

1 teaspoon / 5 ml chocolate extract (optional)

1 teaspoon / 5 ml apple cider vinegar

1. Position a rack in the middle of the oven and preheat to 350°F / 180°C. Oil the sides and bottom of the cake pan, and line the bottom with a parchment circle. Do not oil the parchment.

2. Place a wire mesh strainer over a medium bowl. Add the all-purpose flour, pastry flour, arrowroot, cocoa, sugar, baking powder, baking soda, salt, and cinnamon to the strainer. Stir with a wire whisk to sift the ingredients into the bowl. (If any small bits remain in the strainer, add them to the mixture in the bowl). Whisk to aerate.

3. In a separate medium bowl, whisk the coconut milk, almond milk, maple syrup, vanilla, chocolate extract (if using), and vinegar until completely blended. Pour into the dry mixture and whisk until the batter is smooth. Pour the batter into the pan.

4. Bake on the center rack for 25 to 30 minutes, or until the top is set, the sides have started to pull away from the pan, and a wooden toothpick or skewer inserted into the center comes out clean or with just a few moist crumbs.

5. Cool the pan on a wire rack for 10 minutes. Run a thin knife between the cake and inside of the pan, and invert onto a rack. Remove the pan and carefully peel off the parchment paper. Invert again, top side up on the rack to cool completely. Refrigerate the cake briefly before glazing.

SERVING

Serve the cake glazed with Bittersweet Chocolate Ganache Glaze (page 264).

KEEPING

The glazed or unglazed cake can be refrigerated for up to two days, unwrapped or in a cake box. (Keep the cake away from strong odors.) The cake can be frozen for up to one month: Wrap the cake tightly in a layer of plastic wrap and another layer of aluminum foil, or slip it into a zipper-lock bag and squeeze out the air.

Chocolate, Orange, and Almond Olive Oil Cake

I was determined to create a vegan version of an orange-scented cake with an unusual creamy interior that I enjoyed on a trip to Italy a few years ago. I could distinctly taste each element in the original, so I thought it would be a reasonably easy cake to convert. But the right texture—creamy, not gummy—was elusive. When I finally perfected the recipe, I realized that as hard as it had been to get the cake right, it was now one of my easiest cake recipes. If you have ground almonds in your freezer, as I usually do, it takes almost no time to prep. But don't rush the baking and final steps: it is important to bake the cake until it is dark golden-brown for the best texture, and to sprinkle a layer of chopped almonds on the serving plate so that the bottom of the cake doesn't stick to the plate.

This recipe calls for two kinds of almonds, unpeeled sweet whole almonds and Marcona almonds from Spain, but you can use all sweet almonds if that's what you have on hand. In that case, sprinkle a little more flaked salt over the top of the cake since Marcona almonds are already salted and fried in oil when you buy them. To highlight the taste of the olive oil in the cake, use one of the more pungent varieties. Just make sure you select oil that you really like, since you will taste it even after the cake is baked.

MAKES ONE (8½-INCH / 21-CM) CAKE, 8 TO 10 SERVINGS

3/4 cup / 99 grams organic all-purpose flour

1/2 cup / 70 grams organic whole wheat pastry flour

3/4 cup / 159 grams organic granulated sugar

1 teaspoon / 5 grams baking soda

1/2 teaspoon fine sea salt

1/4 teaspoon aluminum-free baking powder

1/2 cup / 60 grams ground roasted unpeeled whole almonds (page 19), divided

1 cup / 240 ml freshly squeezed orange juice

1/3 cup / 80 ml fruity olive oil, such as arbequina

Finely grated zest of 2 large oranges, preferably organic

1 tablespoon / 15 ml apple cider vinegar

1/2 teaspoon pure vanilla extract

1/2 teaspoon pure almond extract

1 recipe Chocolate Orange Glaze (page 269)

1 ounce / 28 grams Marcona almonds, coarsely chopped (or use more whole almonds chopped and sprinkled with sea salt)

Flaked sea salt, for serving (optional)

1. Position a rack in the middle of the oven. Preheat to 350°F / 180°C. Oil the cake pan and line the bottom with a parchment circle. Do not oil the parchment.

2. Place a wire mesh strainer over a medium bowl. Add the all-purpose flour, pastry flour, sugar, baking soda, salt, and baking powder to the strainer and stir with a whisk to sift the ingredients into the bowl. (If any small bits remain in the strainer, add them to the mixture in the bowl.) Add ¼ cup plus 2 tablespoons of the ground almonds and stir with a wire whisk to combine and aerate the mixture.

3. In a separate bowl, whisk together the orange juice, oil, zest, vinegar, and vanilla and almond extracts until completely combined. Immediately pour into the dry mixture and whisk until the batter is smooth.

4. Pour the batter into the prepared pan. Rotate the pan to level the batter and tap it lightly on the counter. Bake for 43 to 45 minutes or until the cake is dark golden-brown, the sides have started to pull away from the pan, and a wooden

(recipe continues)

toothpick or skewer inserted into the center comes out clean or with just a few moist crumbs. The cake will have risen considerably, but will become more compact as it cools.

5. Place the pan on a wire rack. Carefully run a thin knife between the cake and the inside of the pan. Cool for 5 minutes. Invert the cake onto the rack. Remove the pan and the parchment paper. If the bottom of the cake feels very wet, sprinkle with 1 tablespoon of the reserved ground almonds, pressing lightly so they adhere. Cool the cake completely without inverting it. Make the glaze while the cake cools.

ASSEMBLE THE CAKE

Sprinkle a serving plate with the remaining ground whole almonds. The almonds will keep the moist cake from sticking to the plate. Slide a 9-inch / 23-cm cardboard cake board under the cake and gently slide the cake off the board onto the plate. It will be bottom side up.

Drizzle or spread the Chocolate Orange Glaze on top of the cake and sprinkle with the Marcona almonds. Refrigerate the cake until the glaze is set.

SERVING

Slice the cake cold but serve at room temperature with the optional sprinkling of flaked sea salt. Drizzle the plates with olive oil if using.

KEEPING

I like the texture and flavor of the cake best the day it is made, but the cake will hold overnight at room temperature loosely wrapped in parchment. The cake freezes well for up to one month with no loss of flavor, but do not add the chopped nuts until the cake is defrosted. Wrap the cake tightly in a double layer of plastic wrap and slip it into a large zipper-lock bag. Defrost the cake unwrapped. Refrigerate the glaze in a covered container for up to three days. Allow the glaze to return to room temperature before using.

Zesty Organic Citrus

The aromatic oils in citrus zest are prized for the flavor they add to many desserts and savory dishes, but the waxes and chemicals that are routinely applied to these fruits are not. For this reason, I only use the zest of organic, unsprayed citrus fruit. The zest is the thin colored outer skin of the rind. The white pith underneath this skin is very bitter and should never be used.

Zest is easily removed with a citrus zester, a vegetable peeler, or a small sharp knife. The best tool for finely grating zest is a Microplane. But no matter the tool, just wash and thoroughly dry all citrus fruits first. If you are using the zest only, wrap the naked fruit tightly in plastic wrap and refrigerate, so that it does not dry out. Actually, I zest organic citrus even if the recipe calls for the fruit or juice only. Peel the zest from the citrus and freeze in an airtight zipper-lock bag until needed. For a refreshing drink, add the frozen zest to tea or a glass of water. If you cannot find organic citrus, use a ¼ teaspoon of corresponding citrus oil for every tablespoon of zest in the recipe.

Chocolate Pecan Cranberry Coffee Cake

What is a coffee cake? Is it cake to be eaten with a cup of coffee at breakfast or as a snack on your coffee break? Food historians generally agree that the concept of coffee cake (eating sweet cakes with coffee) most likely originated in Northern/Central Europe sometime in the seventeenth century. Coffee cakes are typically single-layer cakes flavored with cinnamon and other spices, nuts, and fruits, with a streusel or crumb topping, often glazed lightly. In a previous cookbook, I called a recipe the "Uncoffeecake," but I think I was trying to conquer my coffee habit at the time. That cake won the blue ribbon at a county fair, proving that no matter what you call them, coffee cakes are delicious. I wouldn't be surprised if this recipe won a ribbon, too. Enjoy a slice with coffee, tea, or a glass of wine.

Cranberries, pecans, and oats are health-promoting foods, and I prefer them in this recipe. But feel free to use any combination of dried fruit and nuts you like. As a beach lover, my visual cue for the crumb, which needs to be moistened but not wet, is the consistency of damp sand. The cake is moist and flavorful without a glaze, but if you like your crumb cakes glazed, I suggest the Chocolate Confectioners' Sugar Glaze on page 267.

MAKES ONE (9-INCH / 23-CM) CAKE, 10 TO 12 SERVINGS

CRUMB

½ cup / 57 grams dried cranberries

Zest and juice of a medium organic orange

¾ cup / 79 grams pecans, roasted and cooled, coarsely chopped (see page 19)

¼ cup / 25 grams rolled oats, toasted and cooled (see page 81)

½ cup / 83 grams organic whole cane sugar, ground in a blender until powdered

2 tablespoons / 30 ml mild tasting extra-virgin olive oil

2 tablespoons / 21 grams vegan chocolate chips

CAKE

1 cup / 129 grams organic all-purpose flour

¾ cup / 103 grams organic whole wheat pastry flour

¼ cup / 25 grams Dutch-process cocoa powder

⅓ cup / 64 grams organic granulated sugar

1 teaspoon / 5 grams aluminum-free baking powder

1 teaspoon / 5 grams baking soda

½ teaspoon ground cinnamon

½ teaspoon fine sea salt

¼ cup plus 1 tablespoon / 75 ml mild tasting extra-virgin olive oil

¾ cup / 180 ml pure maple syrup, Grade B or dark amber

¾ cup / 180 ml any nondairy milk

1 tablespoon / 15 ml pure vanilla extract

1 tablespoon / 15 ml apple cider vinegar

⅛ teaspoon pure orange oil (optional)

⅓ cup / 57 grams vegan chocolate chips

½ cup / 120 ml Chocolate Confectioners' Sugar Glaze (page 267, optional)

MAKE THE CRUMB

1. Mix the cranberries and orange juice in a small bowl and soak for 10 minutes, or until softened. (The amount of time needed depends on the dryness of the fruit.)

2. Drain the cranberries, reserving 1 tablespoon / 15 ml of the juice. Return the cranberries to the bowl, and add the pecans, oats, whole cane sugar, zest, and oil. If the crumb is dry, add the reserved tablespoon of juice. Think damp sand. Stir the chips into the crumb and set aside while you make the cake.

(recipe continues)

MAKE THE CAKE

1. Position a rack in the center of the oven and preheat to 350°F / 180°C. Oil the sides and bottom of a 9-inch round cake pan and line the bottom with a parchment circle (or paper cut to fit). Do not oil the paper.

2. Place a wire mesh strainer over a medium bowl. Add the all-purpose flour, pastry flour, cocoa, sugar, baking powder, baking soda, cinnamon, and salt to the strainer and stir with a whisk to sift the ingredients into the bowl. (If any small bits remain in the strainer, add them to the mixture in the bowl.) Whisk to aerate the mixture.

3. Whisk the oil, maple syrup, nondairy milk, vanilla, vinegar, and orange oil (if using) in a separate medium bowl until completely combined. Immediately pour into the dry mixture and whisk until the batter is smooth. Stir the chocolate chips into the batter.

4. Pour about half the batter into the prepared cake pan. Sprinkle with half the crumb, going light on the center. Pour the remaining batter over the crumb, using a small spatula or thin knife to spread batter to the sides of the pan if necessary. Sprinkle the remaining crumb over the batter, again keeping the center relatively light on crumb.

5. Bake for 55 to 60 minutes, or until the cake has begun to pull away from the sides of the pan and a wooden toothpick or skewer inserted into the center comes out clean or with just a few moist crumbs.

6. Cool the pan on a wire rack for 10 minutes. Place a piece of parchment on top of the cake and invert. Remove the pan and carefully peel off the parchment paper. Invert the cake again, top side up on the rack and cool to room temperature before cutting and serving.

SERVING

Serve the cake at room temperature, or warm slices in the oven at 325°F / 160°C for 5 minutes. If you are glazing the cake, wait until after it is warmed and drizzle with Chocolate Confectioners' Sugar Glaze.

KEEPING

Store the cake in a covered container overnight at room temperature. Refrigerate wrapped tightly for up to three days.

Mix-in-the-Pan Chocolate Cake

When my children were young, they loved to make this cake with me. Over the years, I have seen the recipe called Crazy Cake and Dump Cake, but we called our version Holes-in-the-Moon Cake since three lunar-like depressions are made in the dry ingredients before mixing. These days, my grandchildren make this cake, but they just call it Mix-in-the-Pan Chocolate Cake, and that's what I have called it here in their honor—today's children are so succinct! Whatever you call it, the original recipe is one of those "accidentally vegan" cakes created during wartime when butter and eggs were in limited supply, but it remained a perennial favorite. My upgrades to the original are few—why mess with success? But these things do improve this moist, chocolaty cake immeasurably: sifting the dry ingredients into the pan and using high-quality cocoa powder and organic whole wheat pastry flour. Most importantly, do not make the cake if you don't have natural cocoa—it won't taste good. And since the pan cannot be lined (the paper will interfere when the batter is mixed), don't try to turn the cake out of the pan.

MAKES ONE (9-INCH / 23-CM) ROUND CAKE OR ONE (8-INCH / 20-CM) SQUARE

- 1 cup / 129 grams organic all-purpose flour
- ½ cup / 70 grams organic whole wheat pastry flour
- 1 cup / 207 grams organic granulated sugar
- ¼ cup / 20 grams natural cocoa powder (non-alkalized)
- ⅜ teaspoon ground cinnamon
- ½ teaspoon fine sea salt
- 1 teaspoon / 5 grams baking soda
- ⅓ cup / 80 ml mild-tasting olive oil or organic neutral vegetable oil
- 1 tablespoon / 15 ml apple cider vinegar
- 1 teaspoon / 5 ml pure vanilla extract
- 1 cup / 240 ml chilled water or nondairy milk

1. Position a rack in the center of the oven and preheat to 350°F / 180°C. Oil the sides and bottom of the cake pan. Do not line with parchment.

2. Place a wire mesh strainer over a medium bowl. Add the all-purpose flour, pastry flour, sugar, cocoa powder, cinnamon, salt, and baking soda to the strainer and stir with a whisk to sift the ingredients into the bowl. (If any small bits remain in the strainer, add them to the mixture in the bowl.) Whisk to aerate the mixture.

3. Spoon the dry ingredients into the baking pan. Use a spoon to make three depressions in the mixture.

4. Pour the oil into one hole, the vinegar into another, and the vanilla into the third. Pour the chilled water or milk all over everything in the pan. Use a fork or whisk to mix until the batter is smooth.

5. Bake for 33 to 35 minutes until a toothpick inserted in the center of the cake comes out clean or with only a few moist crumbs. Set on a wire rack until just slightly warm (about 15 minutes) before cutting slices or squares.

SERVING

The cake is excellent served straight out of the pan, but if it's more dessert you crave, jazz it up with a hefty drizzle of All-Purpose Chocolate Syrup (page 274), or take it further still by adding a scoop of one of the ice creams in Chapter Eight.

KEEPING

Store the cake covered at room temperature for one day or refrigerate for up to two.

Brownie Pudding Cakelettes

There is almost nothing I'd rather bake and eat than these curious cakes that separate into two layers—moist cake and chocolate sauce—as they bake. I've often wondered if old-time pudding cakes were the pioneers for today's refined molten chocolate cakes. Frankly, I like pudding cakes better and they are certainly easier to make. While topping each cake with a scoop of Chocolate Espresso Gelato (page 198) may seem required, these cakes are fabulous served au natural. Bake the cakes during dinner and serve warm for dessert. The oat flour (see Sidebar, page 81) is easy to make, but you can use an extra tablespoon of pastry flour instead of the oat flour.

MAKES 6 CAKELETTES

- ³/4 cup plus 2 tablespoons / 108 grams organic whole wheat pastry flour
- ³/4 cup / 127 grams organic whole cane sugar, ground in a blender until powdered
- ¹/2 cup / 58 grams Dutch-process cocoa powder, divided
- 1 tablespoon / 6 grams arrowroot or tapioca starch (7 grams)
- 1 tablespoon / 6 grams oat flour (substitute 1 tablespoon / 10 grams whole wheat pastry flour)
- 2 teaspoons / 10 grams aluminum-free baking powder
- ¹/2 teaspoon baking soda
- ¹/4 teaspoon fine sea salt
- 1 cup / 207 grams organic granulated sugar
- ¹/2 cup / 120 ml any nondairy milk, at room temperature
- ¹/4 cup / 60 ml coconut oil, melted, or mild tasting extra-virgin olive oil
- 1 teaspoon / 5 ml pure vanilla extract
- 1¹/2 cups / 360 ml boiling water

1. Position a rack in the middle of the oven and preheat to 350°F / 180°C. Place six ¹/2-cup / 120-ml ovenproof ramekins on a parchment-lined sheet pan. Oil the sides and bottoms of the cups.

2. Place a wire mesh strainer over a medium bowl. Add the pastry flour, whole cane sugar, ¹/4 cup / 25 grams of the cocoa, the arrowroot, oat flour, baking powder, baking soda, and salt to the strainer and stir with a wire whisk to sift the ingredients into the bowl. (If any small bits remain in the strainer, add them to the mixture in the bowl.) Whisk to aerate the mixture.

3. Sift the remaining ¹/4 cup of the cocoa and the granulated sugar through a sieve into a small bowl and set aside.

4. Whisk the nondairy milk, oil, and vanilla in a separate small bowl until completely combined. Pour into the dry mixture and stir with a silicone spatula until the batter is smooth. Expect the batter to be fairly thick.

5. Divide the batter among the prepared ramekins, using a scant ¹/3 cup / 80 ml of batter for each. Sprinkle the top of each cake with scant 3 tablespoons of the cocoa/sugar mixture. Pour ¹/4 cup / 60 ml of the boiling water over each; do not stir.

6. Set the baking pan on the center rack of the preheated oven. Bake for 30 minutes.

7. Open the oven door and carefully and quickly insert a dinner knife in the center of each cake. If the sauce center is oozy and has thickened, remove the cakelettes from the oven. If not, return the cakes to the oven for 3 to 5 minutes longer. Expect the cake and sauce to have oozed over the sides. Remove from the oven and set the baking pan on a wire rack. Wait about 10 minutes, or until the cakes are no longer steaming hot before serving.

(recipe continues)

SERVING

The cakelettes are best served warm, but they taste good at room temperature or even chilled, although the textures will be different. Add a small scoop of any of the frozen desserts in Chapter Eight.

KEEPING

The cakelettes can be baked up to two days ahead and refrigerated in an airtight container. Warm in a 350°F / 180°C oven for 5 to 8 minutes or eat the cakes chilled.

From Rolled Oats to Oat Flour

You can make your own oat flour using rolled oats you toast and grind in a blender. Preheat the oven to 325°F / 160°C. Spread the oats on a parchment-lined baking sheet. Toast the oats in the oven for 5 minutes, then remove and cool completely. Use the toasted oats in recipes like the Chocolate Pecan Cranberry Coffee Cake (page 75).

To make oat flour, grind the toasted oats in a blender or clean coffee or nut grinder until they are the fine consistency of flour (a food processor does not make fine enough flour). Depending on the type of blender, grind ½ to 1 cup of oats at a time (about 50 to 100 grams). Each cup of oat flour requires approximately 1¼ cups / 125 grams of rolled oats.

Banana Cacao Nib Snack Cake

My freezer always holds a bag of frozen ripe bananas for making smoothies and banana muffins and bread. As I noticed myself (not infrequently) slathering chocolate icing on those banana muffins and adding cacao nibs or cocoa powder to my banana-creamed smoothies, it became clear to me that I needed to give the banana bread the same treatment and add a light, moist chocolate banana cake to my repertoire. Just one frozen banana, half puréed into the batter and half diced, adds more than a hint of banana to this quickly mixed and baked cake. The crunchy texture and intense, slightly bitter flavor of cacao nibs, which are cracked and hulled cocoa beans, make them a perfect replacement for walnuts, a boon to the nut-allergic. I prefer chocolate-coated sweet nibs as opposed to the plain ones, but either way, nibs are a healthy and delicious addition to all kinds of treats.

MAKES ONE (8 X 8-INCH / 20 X 20-CM) PAN, 8 TO 10 SERVINGS

½ cup / 64 grams organic all-purpose flour

½ cup / 70 grams organic whole wheat pastry flour

3 tablespoons / 18 grams Dutch-process cocoa powder

¼ cup / 50 grams organic granulated sugar

½ teaspoon aluminum-free baking powder

½ teaspoon baking soda

¼ teaspoon fine sea salt

⅔ cup / 160 ml any nondairy milk

3 tablespoons / 45 ml maple syrup, Grade B or dark amber

¼ cup / 60 ml mild tasting extra-virgin olive oil or organic neutral vegetable oil

1 teaspoon / 5 ml pure vanilla extract

1 medium very ripe banana, frozen

2 tablespoons / 20 grams cacao nibs, plain or sweet

1. Position a rack in the middle of the oven and preheat to 350°F / 180°F. Oil the baking pan and line the bottom with parchment paper cut to fit. Do not oil the paper.

2. Place a wire mesh strainer over a medium bowl. Add the all-purpose flour, pastry flour, cocoa, sugar, baking powder, baking soda, and salt to the strainer. Stir with a whisk to sift ingredients into the bowl. (If any small bits remain in the strainer, add them to the mixture in the bowl.) Whisk to aerate the mixture.

3. Pour the nondairy milk, maple syrup, oil, and vanilla into a blender and blend on high until combined. Cut the banana in half and cut one half into 1-inch / 2.5-cm pieces. Put the pieces back into the freezer. Add the remaining banana half to the blender and blend only long enough to purée.

4. Pour the liquid ingredients into the dry and stir with a silicone spatula until the batter is smooth. Expect the batter to be thick. Mix the diced banana into the batter and spoon into the prepared pan. Level the top with a spatula and sprinkle with the cacao nibs.

5. Bake for 23 to 25 minutes until the cake is set, the sides have pulled away from the pan, and a wooden toothpick or skewer inserted into the center comes out clean or with just a few moist crumbs.

6. Place the cake on a wire rack. Cool for 15 minutes until just warm, or cool to room temperature and warm in a 300°F / 150°C oven for a few minutes before serving.

SERVING

Cut the cake in squares and serve directly from the pan. It's a great snack cake and doesn't need any frosting or glaze, but if you prefer a little extra something, drizzle with any of the chocolate syrups in Chapter Eleven.

KEEPING

Store the cake into a covered container at room temperature overnight. Refrigerate for up to two days.

VARIATION

Banana Walnut Snack Cake: Instead of cacao nibs, sprinkle with same amount of finely chopped walnuts.

Vanilla Chocolate Chip Cupcakes

Occasionally, I crave a vanilla cupcake instead of chocolate, but I still want it well studded with vegan chocolate chips and topped with swirls of rich frosting. Piping the frosting through a pastry bag and sprinkling the cupcakes with more chocolate chips is my idea of pretty and delicious.

MAKES 12 STANDARD SIZE CUPCAKES OR 24 MINIS

1½ teaspoons / 7.5 ml apple cider vinegar

¾ cup / 180 ml soymilk or almond milk

½ cup plus 1 tablespoon / 73 grams organic all-purpose flour

½ cup / 70 grams organic whole wheat pastry flour

½ cup plus 1 tablespoon / 124 grams organic granulated sugar

1 teaspoon / 5 grams baking powder

¼ teaspoon baking soda

½ teaspoon fine sea salt

¼ cup / 60 ml mild tasting extra-virgin olive oil or organic neutral vegetable oil

1 tablespoon / 15 ml pure vanilla extract

⅓ cup / 61 grams mini vegan chocolate chips, divided

Creamy Chocolate Cupcake Frosting (page 270)

1. Position a rack in the upper third of oven and preheat to 350°F / 180°C. Line a 12-cup standard cupcake tin with paper liners.

2. In a small bowl, mix the vinegar and milk. Set aside for 10 minutes to clabber.

3. Place a wire mesh strainer over a medium bowl. Add the all-purpose flour, pastry flour, sugar, baking powder, baking soda, and salt to the strainer. Stir with a whisk to sift the ingredients into the bowl. (If any small bits remain in the strainer, add them to the mixture in the bowl.) Whisk to aerate the mixture.

4. Stir the oil and vanilla into the clabbered milk. Add the wet ingredients to the dry and whisk until the batter is smooth. Stir about half the chocolate chips into the batter.

5. Divide the batter evenly between the cups, filling each about halfway full. Sprinkle the remaining chocolate chips on top of the batter, dividing evenly between the cups. Bake for 17 to 18 minutes or until a wooden toothpick or skewer inserted into the center comes out clean or with just a few moist crumbs.

6. Cool the tin on a wire rack for 5 minutes. Lift each cake onto the rack and cool completely. Refrigerate until cold before finishing with Creamy Chocolate Cupcake Frosting (page 270).

KEEPING

Refrigerate the cupcakes in a covered container for up to two days. The cupcakes can be frozen in an airtight container for up to one month. Defrost uncovered at room temperature.

Clabbered Milk

Adding vinegar or lemon juice to milk makes a soured or clabbered milk substitute, but I believe that vinegar is more reliable. Of the nondairy milks, only soy and almond have enough fat to sour. The soured milk will look slightly curdled.

Chocolate Fudge Cupcakes

These moist, dark chocolate cupcakes crowned with big swirls of Thick and Glossy Fudge Frosting (page 271) and an abundance of chocolate curls or sprinkles are guaranteed to sell out at any bake sale and to disappear from party platters. No one I've ever met can resist an all-chocolate cupcake that tastes great! That they are vegan is just a nice bonus. And while I prefer the Thick and Glossy Fudge Frosting, you may use any of the frostings or fillings in Chapter Eleven instead.

Tip: Use chocolate-flavored nondairy milk for an extra chocolaty flavor.

MAKES 12 STANDARD SIZE CUPCAKES

1 cup / 129 grams organic all-purpose flour

3/4 cup / 103 grams organic whole wheat pastry flour

1/2 cup / 111 grams organic granulated sugar

1/3 cup / 25 grams natural cocoa powder (non-alkalized)

1 teaspoon / 5 grams baking soda

1/2 teaspoon fine sea salt

1 1/4 cups / 300 ml any nondairy milk

1/3 cup / 80 ml mild tasting extra-virgin olive oil or organic neutral vegetable oil

1 tablespoon / 15 ml apple cider vinegar

1 1/2 teaspoons / 7.5 ml pure vanilla extract

1 teaspoon / 5 ml chocolate extract (optional)

Thick and Glossy Fudge Frosting (page 271)

1. Position an oven rack in the top third of the oven and preheat to 350°F / 180°C. Line a 12-cup standard size cupcake tin with paper liners.

2. Place a wire mesh strainer over a medium bowl. Add the all-purpose flour, pastry flour, sugar, cocoa, baking soda, and salt to the strainer. Stir with a whisk to sift the ingredients into the bowl. (If any small bits remain in the strainer, add them to the mixture in the bowl.) Whisk to aerate the mixture.

3. In another medium bowl, whisk the milk, oil, vinegar, vanilla, and chocolate extract (if using) until thoroughly combined. Immediately pour into the dry ingredients and whisk until the batter is smooth. You will notice bubbles in this active batter.

4. Divide the batter evenly between the cups, filling each about two-thirds full. Bake for 20 to 25 minutes, or until a wooden toothpick or skewer inserted into the center comes out clean or with just a few moist crumbs.

5. Set the tin on a wire rack. After 5 minutes, remove the cupcakes from the tin. Allow the cupcakes to cool to room temperature on the rack. Refrigerate until cold before frosting.

KEEPING

Refrigerate the cupcakes in a covered container for up to two days. The cupcakes can be frozen in an airtight container for up to one month. Defrost uncovered.

Black Bottom Cupcakes

Was this long-time favorite, slightly odd-looking icing-free cupcake the result of a mistake? "Oops! I dropped cheesecake batter in the Devil's food cupcake batter!" The chocolate-flecked vegan cream cheese bakes into chocolate cupcakes for a treat as yummy, if not yummier, than the dairy version. Since the cake was already dairy- and egg-free in many of the original recipes (a.k.a. accidently vegan), and nondairy cream cheese spread is easily found in natural food stores and larger supermarkets, creating an actual recipe to follow was literally and figuratively "a piece of cake." Chocolate chips add to the flavor of the filling, and chia gel replaces the egg. The resulting bites of heaven fairly beg for a glass of ice-cold nondairy milk or a freshly made espresso (the latter is my choice). If you want to add some finesse, dip the cold cupcakes in Bittersweet Chocolate Ganache Glaze (page 264). The filling will still peek through.

Note: Keep the "cream cheese" in the refrigerator until ready to use, but do not freeze it. When making the regular-sized cupcakes, the tins will be almost completely full. If you are making minis, go for a maximum of two-thirds full and no more than 1½ teaspoons of filling.

MAKES 12 STANDARD-SIZE CUPCAKES OR 24 MINIS

FILLING

1½ teaspoons / 3 grams ground chia seeds

1½ tablespoons / 22.5 ml warm water

8 ounces / 227 grams nondairy cream cheese spread, very cold

9 tablespoons / 56 grams organic confectioners' sugar, sifted

2 teaspoons / 10 ml pure vanilla extract

2 ounces / 85 grams vegan chocolate chips

CAKE

1 cup / 129 grams organic all-purpose flour

½ cup / 70 grams organic whole wheat pastry flour

¾ cup / 159 grams organic granulated sugar

¼ cup / 50 grams organic whole cane sugar, ground in a blender until powdered

¼ cup plus 1 tablespoon / 25 grams natural cocoa powder (non-alkalized)

1 teaspoon / 5 grams baking soda

¼ teaspoon fine sea salt

1 cup / 240 ml any nondairy milk

¼ cup plus 2 tablespoons / 90 ml mild tasting extra-virgin olive oil or organic neutral vegetable oil

1 tablespoon / 15 ml apple cider vinegar

1 teaspoon / 5 ml pure vanilla extract

1 teaspoon / 5 ml chocolate extract (optional)

MAKE THE FILLING

1. Mix the chia and water and set aside for a couple of minutes. Mix with a fork until thoroughly combined. Repeat twice, 5 minutes apart. The chia gel can be made a day ahead and refrigerated in a covered container. Mix before using.

2. Beat together the cream cheese, sugar, and vanilla with an electric mixer. Add the chia gel and mix on medium for another 30 seconds until incorporated. Stir the chocolate chips into the filling. Refrigerate in a covered container while you make the cupcakes.

(recipe continues)

MAKE THE CUPCAKES

1. Position a rack on the rung just above the center of the oven and preheat to 350°F / 180°C. Lightly oil the top only of a 12-cup cupcake tin to make any bake-overs easier to clean, and line with paper liners that are slightly higher than the cups.

2. Put a wire mesh strainer over a medium bowl. Add the all-purpose flour, pastry flour, granulated sugar, whole cane sugar, cocoa, baking soda, and salt to the strainer. Stir with whisk to sift the ingredients into the bowl and whisk to aerate. (If any very small bits remain in the strainer, add them to the mixture in the bowl.) Whisk to aerate the mixture.

3. In a separate small bowl, mix the nondairy milk, oil, vinegar, vanilla, and chocolate extract (if using) until thoroughly mixed. Immediately pour into the dry ingredients. Whisk hard until the batter is smooth.

4. Fill the cups close to three-quarters full with batter.

Spoon or scoop 3 tablespoons of the filling—but not more—into the center of each cake. The cups will be filled almost to the top. That's okay.

5. Bake for 25 to 27 minutes, or until the edges of the cakes are firm when lightly tapped and the filling is set. Set the tins on a wire rack for 10 minutes. The filling will collapse into the cakes while they cool. Remove the cupcakes from the tin, and cool completely on a wire rack before serving.

SERVING

I like to serve the cupcakes slightly chilled for the best flavor, but some of my testers liked the cakes best at room temperature. You'll just have to make two batches and try them each way to decide!

KEEPING

Refrigerate in an airtight container for up to three days.

Chocolate Date Muffins

This is a satisfying muffin filled with chunks of sweet dates and chocolate chips, and made with oat flour, which adds a bit of sweetness and boosts nutrition. It also has a secret identity: spread your muffin with any of the frostings in Chapter Eleven, and your muffin becomes a cupcake.

Note: It's easiest to cut sticky dates when you freeze the dates briefly (about 5 minutes) before cutting. Sprinkle them with 2 tablespoons / 26 grams of the sugar in the recipe, and they will clump less. If using coconut oil as the fat, make sure the other ingredients are at room temperature or the oil will harden into clumps during mixing.

MAKES 12 STANDARD MUFFINS

- ³/₄ cup / 110 grams diced pitted dried dates
- 1 cup / 207 grams organic granulated sugar, divided
- ³/₄ cup / 99 grams organic all-purpose flour
- ³/₄ cup / 103 grams organic whole wheat pastry flour
- ¹/₄ cup / 39 grams organic whole cane sugar, ground in a blender until powdered
- ¹/₃ cup / 25 grams natural cocoa powder (non-alkalized)
- ¹/₄ cup / 22 grams oat flour (see page 81)
- 1 teaspoon / 5 grams baking soda
- ¹/₂ teaspoon fine sea salt
- ¹/₄ cup / 60 ml mild tasting extra-virgin olive oil or melted coconut oil
- 1 cup plus 1 tablespoon / 255 ml any nondairy milk
- 1 tablespoon / 15 ml apple cider vinegar
- 2 teaspoons / 10 ml pure vanilla extract
- ¹/₃ cup / 57 grams vegan chocolate chips
- 1 to 2 tablespoons / 15 to 30 ml maple syrup for brushing the muffins

1. Position a rack in the upper third of the oven and preheat to 375°F / 190°C. Line a 12-cup muffin tin with paper liners.

2. Put the dates into a small bowl and sprinkle with 2 tablespoons of the granulated sugar. This will help keep the dates from clumping together. Reserve until needed.

3. Place a wire mesh strainer over a medium bowl. Add the all-purpose flour, pastry flour, ³/₄ cup / 159 grams of the granulated sugar, the whole cane sugar, cocoa, oat flour, baking soda, and salt to the strainer and stir with a whisk to sift the ingredients into the bowl. (If any small bits remain in the strainer, add them to the bowl.) Whisk to aerate the mixture.

4. In another bowl, whisk the oil, nondairy milk, vinegar, and vanilla until thoroughly combined. Immediately pour into the dry ingredients and whisk until the batter is smooth. Stir in the dates and chocolate chips.

5. Divide the batter evenly between the cups, filling each about three-quarters full. Bake for 18 to 20 minutes, or until the muffins have risen and a wooden toothpick or skewer inserted in the center comes out clean or with just a few moist crumbs.

6. Set the tin on a wire rack. After 5 minutes, remove the muffins from the tin and cool on the rack.

7. When the muffins are warm but no longer hot, brush each lightly with some of the maple syrup and sprinkle with the remaining 2 tablespoons of granulated sugar. Cool to room temperature and serve.

KEEPING

Refrigerate the muffins in a tightly covered container for up to two days. The muffins can be frozen, unglazed, in an airtight container for up to one month. Defrost uncovered, glaze, and serve.

CHAPTER FOUR

Showstoppers

Welcome to a treasure trove of stunning special occasion desserts,

guaranteed to dazzle at any birthday, anniversary, or holiday party or just to add some elegance to the everyday. Many of these more elaborate desserts are built by layering cake, creams, and glazes, and these recipes are more time-consuming than most. But the good news is that nearly every component can be made ahead and refrigerated or frozen, that so you can make most of the cake (if not the whole thing) in advance. Step-by-step instructions with tips for planning ahead, assembling, and plating are included in each recipe. And once you understand the basics of building a showstopper, it's easy to make your own unique design by mixing and matching fillings and cakes—perhaps for your own birthday!

Fran's Rulebook for Successful Showstoppers

1. Carefully read Fran's Rulebook for Successful Cakes (page 64) before you begin, especially for crucial notes on measuring ingredients, checking for doneness, and cooling.

2. Read the recipe all the way through, making note of the detailed guides for planning your time and preparing the components ahead of time; many need at least a few hours to set.

3. Clear enough space in your refrigerator. Most showstoppers need to be refrigerated at more than one stage.

4. Refrigerate the cakes until cold before dividing the layers or filling and frosting. Cold cakes are easier to handle.

TROUBLESHOOTING	
Cake layer broke when being moved	"Glue" it with frosting or glaze.
One side of a layer is substantially higher than the other	Stagger thin and thicker layers and fill with more or less frosting.
Frosting or glaze is too soft	Refrigerate it longer.

THE RECIPES

Brooklyn Blackout Cake

White and Dark Chocolate Cheesecake

Chocolate Coconut Whipped Cream Cake

Chocolate Cherry Miroir Cake

Sachertorte

Chocolate Hazelnut Six-Layer Cake

Intensely Chocolate Trifle

Opera Cake

Bûche de Noël

Éclairs

Brooklyn Blackout Cake

My family moved from Brooklyn to Long Island when I was five years old, but I have vivid memories of my father regularly travelling back to Brooklyn to buy the famous Ebinger's Bakery Blackout Cake we all missed eating. I still miss it today. It is etched into my memory as the most perfect chocolate cake in the entire world. And I am hardly alone in my adoration of this iconic cake, which is named after the World War II blackouts. The all-chocolate Blackout Cake was composed of three fudgy layers, each slathered with a rich and creamy chocolate pudding, frosted with the same pudding, then showered with chocolate cake crumbs made from a fourth layer. As wonderful as it sounds, it tasted even better. When I set about creating a vegan version, I knew it had to be a perfect rendition for the New Yorkers— especially Brooklynites—who grew up eating this beloved cake. I am proud to say I've served this cake to friends who were Ebinger fans and Brooklyn natives, and they all swear it is as good as the original.

This showstopper of a cake is easy to assemble, requiring only that creamy chocolate pudding be spread between the layers and on the sides and top. There's no need to be fussy about smoothing the pudding, since it's the thick covering of crumbs that creates the final "WOW!" The cake layers can be made ahead and frozen, and the pudding can be made a day ahead and refrigerated in a covered container.

Note: I think this cake tastes best with natural cocoa powder. If you cannot find natural cocoa powder where you live, you may use Dutch-process cocoa powder, just substitute 1 teaspoon baking powder and 1 teaspoon baking soda for the 2 teaspoons baking soda.

MAKES ONE (9-INCH / 23-CM) THREE-LAYER CAKE, 12 TO 14 SERVINGS

- 2 recipes Almost-Instant Chocolate Pudding (page 179), cooled
- 2 cups / 414 grams organic granulated sugar
- 1½ cups / 198 grams organic whole wheat pastry flour
- 1½ cups / 193 grams organic all-purpose flour
- ⅔ cup / 50 grams natural cocoa powder (non-alkalized; see note about using Dutch-process cocoa powder)
- 2 teaspoons / 10 grams baking soda

- 1 teaspoon / 5 grams fine sea salt
- 2 cups / 480 ml water, at room temperature
- ⅔ cup / 160 ml mild tasting extra-virgin olive oil or organic neutral vegetable oil
- 3 tablespoons / 45 ml pure maple syrup, Grade B or dark amber
- 2 tablespoons / 30 ml apple cider vinegar
- 1 tablespoon / 15 ml pure vanilla extract
- 1 teaspoon / 5 ml chocolate extract (optional)

1. Position a rack in the middle of the oven and preheat to 350°F / 180°C. Oil the sides and bottoms of two 9 x 3-inch / 23 x 7.6-cm round cake pans. Line the bottoms with parchment circles. Do not oil the paper.

2. Place a wire mesh strainer over a large bowl. Add the sugar, whole wheat pastry flour, all-purpose flour, cocoa, baking soda, and salt to the strainer and stir with a wire whisk to sift the ingredients into the bowl. (If any small bits remain in the strainer, add them to the mixture in the bowl.) Whisk to aerate the mixture.

3. Whisk the water, oil, maple syrup, vinegar, vanilla, and chocolate extract (if using) in a separate medium bowl until completely combined. Immediately pour into the dry mixture and whisk until the batter is smooth.

(recipe continues)

4. Divide the batter between the 2 pans. Rotate the pans to level the batter and tap them lightly on the counter to eliminate air bubbles.

5. Bake on the middle rack for 30 to 35 minutes, or until the tops of the cakes are set, the sides have started to pull away from the pan, and a wooden toothpick or skewer inserted into the center comes out clean or with just a few moist crumbs.

6. Set the cakes on wire racks. After 5 minutes, run a thin knife around the sides of each cake to release the sides of the cake from the pan. Invert each cake onto a rack. Remove the pans and carefully peel off the parchment paper. It is fine to cool the cakes bottom side up.

7. When the cakes are completely cool, slide a 9-inch cardboard cake circle under each one. Wrap the layers with plastic wrap and refrigerate for about 1 hour, or until cold.

ASSEMBLE THE CAKE

1. Use a long serrated knife to slice each cake layer in half horizontally to form four layers. Crumble one of the layers into a food processor. Pulse the processor a few times to make medium-size crumbs, but stop before they get too fine. Pour the crumbs into a bowl.

2. Line a rimmed baking sheet with parchment paper. Place one of the remaining three layers, still on the cake circle, on the baking sheet. Spread with a scant cup of the pudding. Place a second cake layer on the pudding, board side up. Remove the board and spread the layer with another scant cup of pudding. Slip the board under the last layer and invert it onto the cake. Spread with another scant cup of the pudding. Refrigerate the cake and remaining pudding for 20 minutes. (It is easier to finish a cold cake.)

3. Cover the sides of the cake with the remaining pudding. Sprinkle the top and sides of the cake liberally with the cake crumbs, completely covering the pudding. Pat the crumbs lightly to make sure they adhere. Use all the crumbs, even the ones that fall onto the paper.

KEEPING

It's best to serve this cake within 24 hours, but it will hold up for a day in the refrigerator. It is not necessary to wrap the cake.

White and Dark Chocolate Cheesecake

When I was a child my family went to Lindy's, the iconic Manhattan deli known for its "legendary New York deli-style cheesecake." This particular cheesecake, perhaps the most famous in the United States in its heyday, was even immortalized in *Guys and Dolls* when Nathan Detroit and Sky Masterson sang its praises. I remember thinking each slice must have weighed five pounds, and a feeling of fullness stayed with me for hours. If the online recipes are to be trusted, those memories make sense given the cheesecake's ingredient list: two and a half cups of cream cheese, heavy cream, five eggs and a few egg yolks, and sugar.

For this cheesecake, I wanted to create one like Lindy's that was still dense and creamy, but without dairy, eggs, or white sugar. I worked very hard to get this recipe just right, since after all, I am a New Yorker. Most of the techniques will be familiar to cheesecake lovers—and even easier. Like many dairy cheesecakes, this one is baked in a water bath. But thanks to super tester Monica from Queens, New York—who proved that baking the cake in a deep cake pan works just fine—the extra (and unreliable) step of wrapping a spring-form pan in foil is eliminated. And any cake will do for the crumb crust, but since cheesecake batter is naturally gluten-free, you may want to use the gluten-free variation of the Chocolate Torte to Live For (page 69). Plan ahead: the cake needs 24 hours to chill before slicing.

Here's my suggested game plan for the components in order of how far ahead you can prepare them:

1. Make Bittersweet Chocolate Ganache Glaze (page 264), or Chocolate Coconut Ganache Glaze (page 266); refrigerate for up to five days or freeze for up to one month. Warm in a water bath until pourable (see page 28).
2. Make the tofu sour cream; refrigerate up to two days ahead.
3. Make, bake, and cool the crust; cover and store at room temperature up to a day ahead.
4. Melt the white chocolate chips and keep warm in a water bath.
5. Make the rest of the filling (starting with step 4 in Make the Cheesecake) and assemble the cake.

MAKES ONE (9-INCH / 23-CM) CHEESECAKE, 12 TO 15 SERVINGS

CRUST

1 ½ cups / 190 grams finely ground cake crumbs (any leftover cake crumbs will do; see page 68)

5 to 7 tablespoons / 75 to 105 ml maple syrup, Grade B or dark amber, as needed

CHEESECAKE

1 cup plus 2 tablespoons / 270 ml Bittersweet Chocolate Ganache Glaze (page 264), or Chocolate Coconut Ganache Glaze (page 266) plus more for serving (optional)

6 ounces / 170 grams vegan white chocolate chips (see Resources page 290)

6 ounces / 170 grams firm silken tofu (½ of a 12.3-ounce / 349-gram aseptic box)

1 tablespoon / 15 ml coconut oil, melted, or mild tasting extra-virgin olive oil

3 tablespoons / 45 ml freshly squeezed lemon juice, strained

1 scant tablespoon / 3 grams finely minced lemon zest

½ teaspoon white miso

⅜ teaspoon guar gum

Pinch sea salt

16 ounces / 454 grams vegan cream cheese, at room temperature

1 tablespoon / 15 ml pure vanilla extract

¾ cup / 83 grams confectioners' sugar, sifted twice

2 tablespoons / 14 grams tapioca or cornstarch

Boiling water

(recipe continues)

MAKE THE CRUST

1. Position a rack in the center of the oven and heat to 375°F / 190°C. Oil only the bottom of the 9 x 3-inch / 23 x 7.6-cm round pan and line with a parchment circle. Do not oil the paper.

2. Mix the crumbs and 5 tablespoons / 75 ml of the maple syrup in a small bowl until the crumbs are coated. The relative dryness of the cake crumb will determine the total amount of syrup needed. Use just enough so that the crumbs hold together when squeezed in your fingers.

3. Spread the crumbs over the bottom of the pan. Cover with a piece of plastic wrap and press into a compact layer. Pressing with the aid of the flat side of a ¼ cup measuring cup is helpful. Remove the plastic wrap and bake for 12 to 13 minutes until dry and firm. Remove from the oven and place on a wire rack.

MAKE THE CHEESECAKE

1. Position a rack in the center of the oven and preheat to 400°F / 200°C.

2. Melt the white chocolate chips in a heatproof bowl set over a saucepan containing a few inches of barely simmering water. Make sure the bottom of the bowl sits above the water. Wait until the chips are mostly melted before stirring. Keep the melted chocolate over the warm water while you make the cheesecake batter.

3. Make the tofu sour cream: Put the tofu, oil, lemon juice, zest, and miso in a food processor and pulse a few times to mix. Process the mixture for 1 minute, stopping the machine once to clean the sides of the bowl. Turn off the motor and add the guar gum directly into the mixture, *not on the blade or bowl.* Pulse once or twice, add the sea salt, and then process another minute. Keep the sour cream in the processor while you make the cheesecake batter

or transfer to a container, cover, and refrigerate for up to 2 days.

4. In the bowl of an electric mixer, beat the cream cheese with the vanilla on high speed until creamy. Stop the machine and add ¼ cup / 25 grams of the confectioners' sugar. Mix on low until incorporated. Increase speed to high and beat for 1 minute. Repeat twice until all the sugar has been added. Clean the sides of the bowl with a silicone spatula. Add the tofu sour cream and beat on high for 1 minute. Add the tapioca or cornstarch and beat for 1 minute more.

5. Turn the mixer off and add half of the melted white chocolate. Beat on low to incorporate, and then increase the speed to high and beat for 1 minute. Repeat with the remaining chocolate. The chocolate may form little clumps, but that's not a problem. Use a spatula to mix 1 cup of the ganache into the batter. Do not mix too thoroughly. A few streaks of white batter are desirable.

ASSEMBLE AND BAKE
THE CHEESECAKE

1. Brush the sides of the cake pan with oil, taking care not to drip oil on the crumb crust. Pour the batter over the crust and rotate the pan to level the top. Spoon small dollops of the remaining ganache on top and swirl into the batter using a skewer or toothpick. Place the filled 9 x 3-inch / 23 x 7.6-cm pan into a roasting pan.

2. Pour enough boiling water into the roasting pan so that it reaches halfway up the sides of the cake pan.

3. Move the roasting pan carefully onto the center oven rack. Reduce the heat to 375°F / 190°C and bake for 1 hour and 15 minutes. Use a long wooden spoon to gently push the cake pan. This cake should jiggle in the center only minimally, if at all. The top will be just firm.

4. Remove the pan from the oven. Carefully lift the cheesecake out of the water bath onto a dry kitchen towel or a few folded paper towels, then move to a wire rack.

5. Cool the cake on the rack for 3 to 4 hours until room temperature. Refrigerate the cake unwrapped for 24 hours until firm enough to remove from the pan.

6. Remove the cake from the pan: Run a thin spatula or knife around the sides of the pan to release the cake. Cover the top of the cake with a piece of parchment. Place a flat plate, large enough to hold the cake, on top and turn the whole cake over. The cake should easily release from the pan. (Pat the bottom of the pan lightly if it sticks.) Now, put another plate on the bottom of the cake and turn the cheesecake right side up. Smooth the sides with a spatula, if necessary. Refrigerate the cake for an hour before slicing.

SERVING

Cut thin slices with a long knife, wiping the knife between slices as necessary. Serve the cake slightly chilled, and pass a pitcher of ganache for drizzling.

KEEPING

The cheesecake can be covered with a piece of parchment paper and refrigerated for three days, but keep it away from strong odors. Or slice and freeze in an airtight container for up to one month. Defrost in the refrigerator.

VARIATION

Orange-Scented Chocolate Cheesecake for Thanksgiving: Add 2 tablespoons finely grated organic orange zest to the batter. Plate on a puddle of Cranberry Coulis (page 286), and serve with Chocolate Orange Glaze (page 269).

Chocolate Coconut Whipped Cream Cake

Yes, a chocolate-loving Yankee has made a classic Southern coconut cream cake vegan and chocolate—someone had to do it! Wherever you live, it's a sure bet you and your guests will swoon over this big, beautiful cake. The components need to be made ahead before the cake is assembled, which means the cake is actually quite easy as long as you plan your active time. You will likely have more Chocolate Coconut Whipped Cream than needed for the cake, but it can be refrigerated for up to 3 days to enjoy on another dessert or just eaten off a spoon.

Note: When using melted coconut oil, it is important to have all the ingredients at room temperature or the coconut oil will solidify when mixed with the other liquids. If that does happen, set the bowl of liquid ingredients over a saucepan of barely simmering water. Stir until the chunks of oil liquefy. Also note that the coconut milk will need to be refrigerated at least 24 hours and preferably two days before starting the first component.

Here's my suggested game plan for the components in order of how far ahead you can prepare them:

1. Toast the coconut; cool to room temperature and refrigerate in a container for up to 1 month.
2. Make the cake; cool and refrigerate up to a day in advance, or freeze for up to 1 month.
3. Make Chocolate Coconut Ganache Glaze; let set at room temperature until thickened, about 30 minutes, or refrigerate up to 5 days ahead. (Warm over a water bath until the cold and now-solid ganache is pourable.)
4. Make Chocolate Coconut Whipped Cream; refrigerate overnight.
5. Assemble the cake and refrigerate 2 hours before serving (or up to overnight).

MAKES ONE (9-INCH / 23-CM) TWO-LAYER CAKE

COCONUT CAKE

2/3 cup plus 6 tablespoons / 54 grams plus 36 grams unsweetened dried shredded coconut, divided

1 1/2 cups / 193 grams organic all-purpose flour

1/2 cup / 70 grams organic whole wheat pastry flour

1/4 cup / 50 grams organic granulated sugar

2 1/2 tablespoons / 22.5 grams coconut sugar, ground in a blender until powdered

1 1/4 teaspoons / 6.5 grams aluminum-free baking powder

1 1/4 teaspoons / 6.5 grams baking soda

1/2 teaspoon fine sea salt

3/4 cup plus 2 tablespoons / 210 ml pure maple syrup, Grade B or dark amber, at room temperature

3/4 cup / 180 ml coconut milk beverage, at room temperature

1/3 cup / 80 ml coconut oil, melted

1 tablespoon / 15 ml pure vanilla extract

2 teaspoons / 10 ml apple cider vinegar

1 recipe Chocolate Coconut Ganache Glaze (page 266)

1 recipe Chocolate Coconut Whipped Cream (page 280)

MAKE THE CAKE

1. Position a rack in the middle of the oven and preheat to 300°F / 150°C.

2. Toast the coconut: Spread the shredded coconut on a parchment lined rimmed baking sheet and bake until golden-brown, stirring once or twice. If the coconut is browning faster around the edges, remove the pan from the oven and stir the darker coconut into the center. Remove from the oven and cool on a wire rack.

3. Increase the oven temperature to 350°F / 180°C. Oil the sides and bottoms of two 8-inch / 20-cm round cake pans and line the bottoms with parchment paper circles or paper cut to fit. Do not oil the paper.

4. Place a wire mesh strainer over a medium bowl. Add the all-purpose flour, whole wheat pastry flour, granulated sugar, coconut sugar, baking powder, baking soda, and salt to the strainer, and stir with a whisk to sift the ingredients into the bowl. (If any small bits remain in the strainer, add them to the mixture in the bowl.) Whisk to aerate the mixture.

5. Whisk the maple syrup, coconut milk, oil, vanilla, and vinegar in a separate medium bowl until completely combined. Pour into the dry mixture and whisk until the batter is smooth.

6. Stir ⅔ cup / 52 grams of the shredded coconut into the batter and then divide the batter evenly between the 2 pans. Rotate the pans to level the batter and tap them lightly on the counter to eliminate air bubbles.

7. Bake on the middle rack for 22 to 23 minutes or until the tops of the cakes are light golden-brown, the sides have started to pull away from the pans, and a wooden toothpick or skewer inserted in the center of the cakes comes out clean or with only a few moist crumbs.

8. Set the cakes on wire racks. After 5 minutes, run a thin knife around the sides of each cake to release the sides from the pan. Invert each cake onto a rack. Remove the pans and carefully peel off the parchment paper. Invert again right side up on a rack and cool completely. (It is fine to cool the cakes bottom side up if you don't have another rack.)

9. When the cakes are completely cool, slide a 9-inch cardboard circle under each one. Wrap the layers with plastic wrap, and refrigerate for about 1 hour or until cold before assembling the cake. The wrapped cakes can be refrigerated overnight or frozen for up to 2 months. To freeze, slip the wrapped cakes into a zipper-lock bag and seal, or overwrap the plastic-wrapped cakes in foil. Defrost unwrapped.

ASSEMBLE THE CAKE

1. Use a long serrated knife to level the top layer, if it is domed. (Save the excess cake for snacking.)

2. Place one of the layers, still on the board, on a cake plate or decorating turntable. Tuck strips of parchment paper or waxed paper under the outside edge of the cake.

3. Spread the layer with 5 tablespoons / 75 ml of the Chocolate Coconut Ganache Glaze. Wait a few minutes for the ganache to set (or refrigerate briefly), then spread with about ¾ cup / 180 ml of the Chocolate Coconut Whipped Cream. Sprinkle 2 tablespoons / 10 grams toasted coconut over the cream.

4. Remove the cake board from the other layer and place topside up on the cake. Press down lightly. Spread with another 5 tablespoons / 75 ml of the ganache. When the ganache is set, spread about ¾ cup / 180 ml of the whipped cream on top of the cake, swirling as you go. Use more if you like, or reserve the remaining cream for snacking.

5. Frost the sides with about ½ cup / 120 ml of the ganache, or more as needed to cover. Reserve any extra ganache for serving or another time. Sprinkle some of the remaining toasted coconut on the top and sides of the cake.

6. Refrigerate the cake for at least 1 hour, or until ready to serve. For the neatest slices, cut the cake when it is cold, but wait 10 to 15 minutes for the cake to come to room temperature before serving.

VARIATION

Chocolate Caramel Coconut Whipped Cream Cake: Drizzle the top of the cake with about ¼ cup / 60 ml of Chocolate Dulce de Leche (page 239) and swirl using a skewer, or pass a pitcher of warmed Dulce with the cake.

Chocolate Cherry Miroir Cake

There is nothing quite as glamorous as a *miroir*, which is a layered dessert that is assembled in a cake ring. To make a traditional miroir, genoise cake is cut to fit snugly into the cake ring. A thick layer of mousse or cream is spread over the cake. A gelled "Nappage," which is as shiny as a mirror, is poured over the top. The glass-like glaze is thrilling, but it is made with gelatin, which vegans do not use. I found that substituting agar, the seaweed that gels, creates an effect that is just as dramatic and delicious. The rest of my vegan adaptation mostly follows the same basic steps for making any miroir, but I assemble the cake in a more versatile springform pan. The effect of the dark Magic Chocolate Mousse layered with plump dried cherries, Vanilla Custard Cream Filling, and the "mirror" topping is breathtaking. The fact that the cake can be completely assembled up to two days ahead and refrigerated makes it a stress-free, show-stopping party cake. For a completely gluten-free dessert, use the gluten-free variation of the Chocolate Torte to Live For (page 69).

Notes: The cake is baked in a 9-inch pan but is cut to fit an 8-inch springform pan after chilling; the cake shrinks as it cools, creating a gap between the cake and 9-inch springform. Cutting it to fit a smaller pan creates a tight fit for pouring the miroir topping.

It is essential that the agar glaze be applied as soon as it is no longer hot so it will set on the cake and not in the measuring cup. Pour the glaze slowly to avoid bubbles, but if some appear, just pop them with a skewer.

Here's my suggested game plan for the components in order of how far ahead you can prepare them:

1. Bake and cool the cake; refrigerate up to 1 day ahead or freeze for up to 1 month. (Defrost uncovered.)
2. Soak the cashews for the Vanilla Custard Cream Filling for 4 hours, or refrigerate up to a day ahead.
3. Make the Vanilla Custard Cream Filling; refrigerate for 4 hours or up to a day ahead.
4. Make the Magic Chocolate Mousse; use immediately (preferred) or refrigerate up to a day ahead.
5. Soak the dried cherries in juice for 20 to 30 minutes.
6. Assemble the cake; refrigerate until cold while you make the Miroir Glaze. (The cake can be refrigerated at this point a day ahead.)
7. Make the Chocolate Cherry Miroir Glaze; cool to lukewarm and pour over the cake.
8. Refrigerate the cake for 2 hours until glaze is set, or up to a day ahead.

MAKES ONE (8-INCH / 20-CM) CAKE, 10 TO 12 SERVINGS

²/₃ cup / 110 grams sulfite-free dried pitted cherries

¹/₃ cup / 80 ml cherry juice

1 recipe Bittersweet Ganache–Glazed Chocolate Torte to Live For (page 68) or any chocolate cake in Chapter Three, baked in 9 x 3-inch / 23 x 7.6-cm springform pan, refrigerated or frozen and unglazed

ASSEMBLE THE CAKE

1. Plump the dried cherries in the cherry juice for 20 to 30 minutes. (The time will depend on the relative dryness of the fruit.) Drain and reserve the cherries and the liquid separately. (Use the reserved soaking liquid to make the Magic Chocolate Mousse recipe.)

2. Remove the cake from the refrigerator. Cut the cake with a sharp knife to fit snugly inside an 8 x 3-inch / 20 x 7.5-cm springform pan. Refrigerate the cake in the pan until ready to assemble.

(recipe continues)

1 recipe Vanilla Custard Cream Filling
(page 282), at room temperature

1 recipe Magic Chocolate Mousse
(page 182), made with ½ cup
plus 1 tablespoon/135 ml cherry
juice instead of water and 1 table-
spoon/15 ml kirsch or framboise
(substitute 1 additional tablespoon
juice, optional)

CHERRY FILLING

¼ cup / 60 ml any cherry jam
or preserves

1 tablespoon/ 15 ml kirsch or
framboise (optional, or use
1 teaspoon fresh lemon juice,
strained)

**CHERRY CHOCOLATE MIROIR
GLAZE**

1 recipe Creamy Chocolate Cupcake
Frosting (page 270), made with
¾ cup plus 2 tablespoons/210 ml
cherry juice instead of water, and
prepared through step 6

1 cup / 140 grams fresh cherries on
the stem, dipped in chocolate (see
page 222) for garnish (optional)

3. Make sure the Magic Chocolate Mousse and the Vanilla Custard Cream are at room temperature. Spoon the mousse into a medium bowl. Stir the custard and add ½ cup / 120 ml of the custard to the mousse in two additions, mixing hard with a silicone spatula after each addition. (You will have some Vanilla Custard Cream remaining.)

4. Spread the mousse over the cake, pushing the mousse to the edges, and level the top with an offset spatula.

5. Make the cherry filling by mixing the jam and liquor, if using, in a small bowl. Spoon and spread over the mousse. Sprinkle the drained plumped cherries on top, pressing lightly.

6. Spread the remaining Vanilla Custard Cream over the cherry filling and level with a spatula. Refrigerate for 2 hours or a day ahead before making and applying the miroir topping.

MAKE THE CHOCOLATE CHERRY MIROIR GLAZE

1. Pour the Creamy Chocolate Cupcake Frosting into a 2-cup/500-ml or larger measuring cup and stir slowly but frequently until it is lukewarm, but not so long that it cools and sets (do not cool and process the glaze.)

2. Pour the glaze slowly over the cake, half at a time, rotating the pan if necessary to create an even layer. If any bubbles appear in the glaze, pop them using a skewer.

3. Refrigerate for about 2 hours until the glaze is set, or up to 2 days ahead.

SERVING

Insert a small sharp knife between the top ½ inch / 12 mm of the cake pan and the cake. Slowly release and remove the sides of the springform pan. Smooth the sides of the cake with a metal spatula if necessary. The cake is rich so serve thin slices. Cut with a long thin knife, wiping the knife between slices. Garnish each slice with a few chocolate-covered cherries, if using.

KEEPING

Refrigerate the assembled cake for up to 2 days, covered with parchment paper.

VARIATION

Embellished Chocolate Cherry Miroir Cake: Use 1¼ cups of the miroir glaze for the cake. Pour the rest into a shallow dish. When the glaze is gelled, cut into hearts or stars, for example, and place on the cake or serving plates.

Sachertorte

The legend of the Sachertorte—a chocolate cake filled with a thin layer of apricot jam and covered in a shiny chocolate glaze—dates to 1832. That's when Prince von Metternich of Austria instructed his chef to create a new dessert for a VIP guest, but when the chef took ill, he passed the task to his sixteen-year-old apprentice, Franz Sacher. Sacher created his namesake torte and his son Eduard, a trained pastry chef, perfected the recipe at both the Hotel Sacher and Demel's Bakery. Subsequently, a nine-year legal battle raged over the rights to use the words "The Original Sachertorte" and ended with the hotel calling it the "Orginal Sachertorte" and Demel's "Eduard Sachertorte." Despite the history and hype that continues today, legions of the Sacher-obsessed who have taste tested both are often disappointed, using words like "dry" and "austere" to describe the Sachers. No doubt this is why the cakes are served with whipped cream. No one would ever describe my Sachertorte this way. Moist and chocolaty, it has a healthy layer of apricot jam spread over a layer of ganache that adds flavor and texture while guarding against soggy cake. The entire cake is coated in two layers of Bittersweet Chocolate Ganache Glaze. Apricot-cognac sauce is swirled into Vanilla Custard Cream, which is served as a complement, not a necessity, as is writing "Sacher" on the cake—a nice touch but certainly optional. No matter which cake you use as the basis, this is an easy, elegant Showstopper.

Note: For a completely gluten-free dessert, use the gluten-free variation of the Chocolate Torte to Live For.

Here's my suggested game plan for the components in order of how far ahead you can prepare them:

1. Make and cool the cake layers; refrigerate until cold or up to 1 day ahead, or freeze for up to 1 month. Use cold, but not frozen.
2. Make the Bittersweet Chocolate Ganache Glaze; allow to set until thick enough to pour, or refrigerate up to 5 days or freeze up to 1 month. Warm in a water bath until pourable (see page 28).
3. Soak the cashews for the Vanilla Custard Cream, if making, for 4 hours, or refrigerate up to a day ahead.
4. Make the Vanilla Custard Cream, if using; refrigerate until needed, up to a day ahead.
5. Glaze and assemble the cake layers, then glaze the cake; refrigerate to set the glaze.
6. Prepare the apricot-cognac sauce, if using.

MAKES ONE (8-INCH / 20-CM) CAKE, 8 TO 10 SERVINGS

2 recipes Chocolate Torte to Live For (page 68), refrigerated until cold, divided

1 recipe Bittersweet Chocolate Ganache Glaze (page 264), warmed in a water bath until pourable

⅓ cup / 80 ml good-quality apricot preserves, plus ¼ cup / 60 ml for apricot-cognac sauce (optional), divided

4 ounces / 113 grams dark chocolate (any percentage), tempered (see page 28), for writing "Sacher " (optional)

2 teaspoons / 10 ml cognac (optional) (substitute 1 teaspoon / 5 ml freshly squeezed and strained lemon juice)

½ recipe Vanilla Custard Cream (page 282), for serving (optional)

(recipe continues)

ASSEMBLE THE CAKE

1. Place the first cake layer on a cardboard cake circle that is exactly the same size or slightly smaller than the cake.

2. Spread a thin layer (about ¼ cup / 60 ml) of Bitter-sweet Chocolate Ganache Glaze on the layer. Allow the glaze to set.

3. Spread ⅓ cup / 80 ml of apricot preserves over the glaze.

4. Spread the second layer of cake with ¼ cup / 60 ml of the ganache glaze and refrigerate until set.

5. Place the second layer, glaze side down, on the apricot-coated layer.

6. Glaze the entire cake: Place the cake on a wire rack set over a parchment-lined baking sheet. Pour 1 cup / 240 ml of the Bittersweet Chocolate Ganache Glaze into a measuring cup with a spout. Holding the cup at about the center of the cake, pour the glaze onto the cake. Coax the glaze to the edges and down the sides by tilting the baking sheet, or by using an offset spatula. Use the spatula to spread the glaze onto the sides.

7. Allow the glaze to set undisturbed for 15 minutes, and then refrigerate the cake for 10 minutes.

8. Refill the measuring cup with the remaining ½ cup / 120 ml of glaze, and add another coating on the top of the cake. This time, try not to move the glaze around with the spatula after it has been applied. Doing so will mar the finish. Refrigerate to set the glaze.

9. To write in chocolate: Place a small round (Wilton size 4, 5, or 6) pastry tip into a small pastry bag and fill the bag halfway with some of the tempered chocolate. Write "Sacher" on top of the cake. (Refill the bag if more chocolate is needed.) Refrigerate briefly until the chocolate is set.

10. Make the apricot-cognac sauce: Mix ¼ cup/60 ml of the apricot preserves and the cognac together in a small bowl and refrigerate until needed. For an alcohol-free sauce, mix 1 teaspoon fresh lemon juice into the spread.

SERVING

For the neatest slices, cut the cake while it is cold but serve at room temperature. If desired, spoon about ¼ cup / 60 ml per serving of the Vanilla Custard Cream next to each slice. Stir 1 tablespoon / 15 ml of apricot-cognac sauce or alcohol-free apricot glaze into each portion of cream. Alternatively, omit the cream and serve with a puddle of sauce.

KEEPING

The glazed cake can be refrigerated for up to 2 days, unwrapped or in a cake box. (Keep the cake away from strong odors).

Chocolate Hazelnut Six-Layer Cake

This may be the fastest showstopper in the book—just fill and frost six thin layers of with Chocolate Hazelnut Butter and Bittersweet Chocolate Ganache Glaze—but it still has all of the "Wow!" You can even make the three components ahead of time (highly encouraged) and freeze the fully assembled cake. Then, all you'll have left to do before serving is defrost the cake for about two hours and arrange whole roasted hazelnuts on top. The cake also travels well—mine made it to Philadelphia for Thanksgiving. I was concerned it had defrosted too much along the way (delayed train), but my family didn't leave behind a single crumb.

Note: Hazelnuts vary in flavor from "these look like hazelnuts but don't have any flavor" to the sensational Freddy Guys hazelnuts from Portland, Oregon. It's worth mail-ordering some from Freddy for this and any recipe (see Resources page 290).

Here's my suggested game plan for the components in order of how far ahead you can prepare them:

1. Bake the cake; cool and chill 1 day ahead or freeze up to 1 month.
2. Make the Bittersweet Chocolate Ganache Glaze; refrigerate at least 30 minutes until thick enough to glaze or up to 5 days, or freeze up to 1 month.
3. Make the Chocolate Hazelnut Butter; refrigerate 4 hours or up to 5 days.

MAKES ONE 7 1/2-INCH X 3 1/2-INCH / 19-CM X 9-CM CAKE, 12 TO 14 SERVINGS

1 cup / 240 ml almond milk, plus optional 2 tablespoons / 30 ml, divided

2 teaspoons / 10 ml apple cider vinegar, divided

1 cup / 129 grams organic all-purpose flour

1/4 cup / 34 grams organic whole wheat pastry flour

3/4 cup / 159 grams organic granulated sugar, finely ground in a blender

1 tablespoon / 6 grams arrowroot

3/4 teaspoon / 3.75 grams aluminum-free baking powder

1/2 teaspoon baking soda

1/2 teaspoon fine sea salt

1/4 cup plus 1 tablespoon / 75 ml mild tasting extra-virgin olive oil or organic neutral vegetable oil

2 teaspoons / 10 ml pure vanilla extract

3/4 teaspoons / 3 3/4 ml hazelnut extract (optional)

1/2 cup plus 2 tablespoons / 63 grams hazelnut meal

1 recipe Chocolate Hazelnut Butter (page 232)

1/4 cup / 60 ml hazelnut liqueur (optional), divided

1/2 recipe Bittersweet Chocolate Ganache Glaze (page 264)

1/4 cup / 50 grams roasted chopped hazelnuts for garnish, optional

1. Position a rack in the middle of the oven and preheat to 350°F / 180°C. Oil the sides and bottom of an 18 x 13-inch / 46 x 33-cm rimmed baking sheet, and line the bottom with parchment paper cut to fit. Do not oil the parchment.

2. Pour 1 cup of the almond milk into a small bowl. Add 1 1/2 teaspoons / 7.5 ml of the vinegar and set aside for 7 to 8 minutes to clabber.

3. Place a wire mesh strainer over a medium bowl. Add the all-purpose flour, pastry flour, granulated sugar, arrowroot, baking powder, baking soda, and salt to the strainer and stir with a whisk to sift the ingredients into the bowl. (If any small bits remain in the strainer, add them to the mixture in the bowl.) Whisk to aerate the mixture.

4. Whisk the oil, vanilla and hazelnut extracts, and the clabbered milk in a separate medium bowl until completely combined. Immediately pour into the dry mixture and whisk until the batter is smooth. Stir the hazelnut meal and the remaining ½ teaspoon / 2.5 ml of vinegar into the batter. The batter will be thin enough to pour easily.

5. Pour the batter into the prepared pan. Rotate the pan to level the batter and tap it lightly on the counter to eliminate air bubbles.

6. Bake on the middle rack for 15 to 16 minutes until the top of the cake is set, the sides have started to pull away from the pan, and a wooden toothpick or skewer inserted in the center of the cake comes out clean or with only a few moist crumbs.

7. Set the cake on a wire rack. After 5 minutes, run a thin spatula around the sides of the cake to release the sides of the cake from the pan.

8. Refrigerate the cake in the pan until cold. Cut the cake lengthwise into 3 equal strips, about 4 inches / 10 cm wide each. Cut the long strips in half to make 6 pieces of equal size. Do not stress about being exact; the cake will be trimmed. Chill or freeze the cake strips again until very cold (it's easier to frost a cold cake).

9. Warm the Chocolate Hazelnut Butter to come to room temperature for 15 minutes before using. If the butter is too thick to spread easily on the cake, thin with the additional tablespoons of almond milk, or add 1 tablespoon / 15 ml of the liqueur, a little at a time, until the desired consistency is reached.

10. Warm the Bittersweet Chocolate Ganache Glaze over a water bath until spreadable, if it has been made ahead. Add 1 tablespoon / 15 ml of the liqueur, if you wish.

ASSEMBLE THE CAKE

1. Cover a flat surface (at least 6 x 8 inches / 15 x 20 cm) with plastic wrap wide enough to eventually wrap the stack of cake layers. Slip a wide spatula under 1 piece of cake and set it on the plastic wrap. Spread with about ¼ cup / 60 ml of the Chocolate Hazelnut Butter. Repeat with the other 5 pieces of cake, lining the edges up as neatly as possible.

2. Chill the cake for about 10 minutes. Remove from the refrigerator. Spread the 2 long sides with Bittersweet Chocolate Ganache Glaze.

3. Refrigerate until the glaze is set. Move the cake to the freezer and wait until the spread and ganache are no longer tacky before wrapping tightly in plastic wrap.

SERVING

Cut a thin slice, about ¼ inch / 0.6 cm, off each of the short ends of the cake. (Baker's treat!)

Sprinkle chopped hazelnuts along the long sides of the cake, pressing them lightly into the frosting.

Cut the cold cake with a thin long knife into ½-inch / 1.3-cm slices. Allow the cake to come to room temperature before serving to bring out the flavor of the hazelnuts. This will take only about 10 minutes.

KEEPING

The cake may be completed and refrigerated up to two days ahead of time or frozen, tightly wrapped, for one month. Defrost unwrapped in the refrigerator.

Intensely Chocolate Trifle

Classic English trifles—layered desserts composed of cake, cooked fruits, and vanilla custard—are wonderfully decadent. Spike them with liquor (usually rum or sherry), and those trifles become what the English call "Tipsy Cakes." Tipsy or not, chocolate makes everything better so this trifle starts with a chocolate cake or brownie and adds two of my other favorite ingredients: vegan vanilla custard and a sweet cranberry sauce. But this is an infinitely customizable recipe, so bake any of the chocolate cakes or brownies in the book, defrost cakes you have in your freezer, or use leftovers. (I once used a cake that broke coming out of the pan.) Then, layer the cake with any custard or creams and the fruit of your choice. If you want to "tipsy the trifle," add 1 to 2 tablespoons of a liquor to the custard. Make the components ahead and assemble up to two hours before serving.

Note: The custard can actually be cooked to a boil with the agar and oil in a high-speed blender. If you are using a standard blender, you will cook the agar and oil into the custard in a skillet. Instructions for both methods are included in the vanilla custard directions.

Here's my suggested game plan for the components in order of how far ahead you can prepare them:

1. Bake the cake or brownies; refrigerate or freeze until cold before cutting.
2. Make the Bittersweet Chocolate Ganache Glaze; refrigerate up to 5 days or freeze up to 1 month. Use at room temperature.
3. Make the Maple Cranberry Sauce; use when cool, or refrigerate up to 4 days.
4. Soak the cashews for the Vanilla Custard Cream Filling for 4 hours up to overnight.
5. Make the Vanilla Custard Cream Filling; refrigerate 4 hours to a day ahead before using.
6. Make the Almost Instant Chocolate Pudding; use when cool, or refrigerate up to 1 day ahead.

MAKES A LARGE TRIFLE, 10 TO 12 SERVINGS

½ recipe (1 layer) Brooklyn Blackout Cake (page 94), 1 recipe Very Fudgy Chocolate Chip Brownies (page 128), or 1 recipe Gluten-free Brownie Bites (page 126)

1 recipe Bittersweet Chocolate Ganache Glaze (page 264), at room temperature, warmed in a water bath until pourable

1 recipe Almost-Instant Chocolate Pudding (page 179) made with an additional 3 tablespoons / 45 ml of milk or water

1 recipe Vanilla Custard Cream Filling (page 282)

2 tablespoons / 30 ml liquor like rum, sherry, framboise, or Kahlua (optional)

1 recipe Maple Cranberry Sauce (page 286)

2 ounces / 57 grams dark chocolate (any percentage), finely chopped or shaved, for garnish

ASSEMBLE THE TRIFLE

1. Use a serrated knife to cut enough cubes of cake to cover the bottom of a clear glass serving bowl (preferably a trifle bowl—see Sidebar) plus another layer. The amount needed depends on the size of the bowl.

2. Place half of the cake in the bottom of the bowl.

3. Pour ²/₃ cup / 160 ml of the Bittersweet Chocolate Ganache Glaze over the cake. Refrigerate for 10 to 15 minutes until the glaze is no longer liquid.

4. Add the Almost-Instant Chocolate Pudding and smooth the top.

5. Add another layer of cake. Pour ²/₃ cup / 160 ml of the glaze over the cake. Refrigerate until the glaze is no longer liquid.

6. Stir the Vanilla Custard Cream Filling and add the optional liquor if using. Spread about two-thirds of the custard cream on the cake and smooth the top.

7. Reserve a few tablespoons of the cranberries from the Maple Cranberry Sauce for garnish and spoon the rest on the custard. Drizzle with the remaining glaze. Refrigerate until the glaze is no longer liquid.

SERVING

Up to 1 hour before serving, spoon or pipe the remaining custard cream around the sides. Garnish the trifle with the reserved cranberries. Sprinkle with the chopped chocolate.

KEEPING

The trifle can be assembled up to two hours before serving.

VARIATION

Gluten-Free Intensely Chocolate Trifle: Use the Gluten-Free Brownie Bites (page 126) or the gluten-free version of the Chocolate Torte to Live For (page 69) to make a completely gluten-free dessert.

Trifle Bowls

A trifle may be a make-it-work-with-what-you-have dessert, but it is a showstopper. Use any glass bowl, like a punch or mixing bowl, and the trifle will look elegant and elaborate. Better yet: Get a trifle bowl, which is deeper than it is wide, with straight sides to show off the layering.

Opera Cake

There is some disagreement about the origin of the Opera Cake. It might date back to the Clichy Cake, a dessert unveiled by Louis Clichy at the 1903 *Exposition Culinaire* in Paris, while the legendary Parisian store *Le Maison Dalloyau* claims creation of the original *L'Opéra* in 1955. But there is no controversy about the taste and stunning look of this rich-yet-light "Wow!" of a cake. Classic Opera Cake is composed of three layers of almond cake, coffee syrup, espresso-flavored buttercream, dark chocolate ganache, and chocolate glaze. It is often finished with a piece of shimmering gold leaf. You will find these components in this updated vegan *L'Opéra*. The recipe can be doubled to make an impressive 10-inch / 25-cm square cake for a big party.

Here's my suggested game plan for the components in order of how far ahead you can prepare them:

1. Make the Almond Sheet Cake; cool to room temperature, then refrigerate until cold up to a day ahead, or wrap and freeze it for up to 1 month.
2. Make the Espresso Concentrate; cool to room temperature or refrigerate for up to 1 week in a covered container before using.
3. Make the Espresso Ganache Glaze; refrigerate for up to 5 days or freeze for up to 1 month.
4. Make the Mocha Cream; refrigerate for at least 4 hours until set or up to a day ahead before using, or freeze for up to 2 weeks.
5. Make the Coffee Syrup; cool to room temperature and refrigerate for 1 hour or up to a week.
6. Make the Chocolate Transfers (optional).
7. Assemble the cake.

MAKES ONE (5-INCH / 12.5-CM SQUARE) 3-LAYER CAKE, 12 TO 14 SERVINGS

ALMOND SHEET CAKE

1 cup / 240 ml almond milk or soymilk, vanilla or plain

2 teaspoons / 10 ml apple cider vinegar, divided

¾ cup / 99 grams organic all-purpose flour

½ cup / 70 grams organic whole wheat pastry flour

½ cup / 111 grams organic granulated sugar, ground in a blender until superfine

¼ cup / 39 grams organic whole cane sugar, ground in a blender until powdered

1 tablespoon / 6 grams arrowroot

¾ teaspoon / 3.75 grams aluminum-free baking powder

½ teaspoon baking soda

½ teaspoon fine sea salt

¼ cup plus 1 tablespoon / 75 ml mild tasting extra-virgin olive oil or organic neutral vegetable oil

2 teaspoons / 10 ml pure vanilla extract

1 teaspoon / 5 ml almond extract

½ cup plus scant 3 tablespoons / 80 grams finely ground almonds, divided

ESPRESSO CONCENTRATE

¼ cup / 60 ml boiling water

¼ cup / 60 ml instant espresso powder

MOCHA CREAM

1 recipe Basic Thick Cashew Cream (page 284)

½ cup / 111 grams organic granulated sugar, ground until superfine in a blender

¼ cup / 60 ml Espresso Concentrate

1 ounce / 28 grams dark chocolate (70 to 72%), finely chopped

1 teaspoon / 5 ml pure vanilla extract

ESPRESSO GANACHE GLAZE

1 recipe Bittersweet Chocolate Ganache Glaze (page 264), warmed in a water bath until softened

1 tablespoon / 15 ml Espresso Concentrate

COFFEE SYRUP

½ cup / 120 ml agave syrup

½ cup / 120 ml pure maple syrup, Grade B or dark amber

Pinch salt

1 tablespoon / 15 ml Espresso Concentrate

1 to 2 tablespoons / 15 to 30 ml cognac (optional)

1 transfer sheet with gold musical note pattern (optional)

5 ounces / 142 grams tempered chocolate (see page 28) for transfer sheet, kept liquid and at proper temperature

MAKE THE CAKE

1. Position a rack in the middle of the oven and preheat to 350°F / 180°C. Oil the sides and bottom of a rimmed quarter baking sheet (13 x 9½ inches / 33 x 24 cm) and line the bottom with parchment paper cut to fit. Do not oil the parchment.

2. Pour the milk into a 1-cup measure. Add 1½ teaspoons / 7.5 ml of the vinegar into the milk and set aside for 7 to 8 minutes to clabber.

3. Place a wire mesh strainer over a medium bowl. Add the all-purpose flour, pastry flour, granulated sugar, whole cane sugar, arrowroot, baking powder, baking soda, and salt to the strainer and stir with a whisk to sift the ingredients into the bowl. (If any small bits remain in the strainer, add them to the mixture in the bowl.) Whisk to aerate the mixture.

4. Whisk the oil, vanilla and almond extracts, and the clabbered milk in a separate medium bowl until completely combined. Immediately pour into the dry mixture and whisk until the batter is smooth. Stir ½ cup plus 2 tablespoons / 73 grams of the ground almonds and the remaining ½ teaspoon / 2.5 ml of vinegar into the batter. The batter will pour easily.

5. Pour the batter into the prepared pan. Rotate the pan to level the batter and tap it lightly on the counter to eliminate air bubbles.

6. Bake on the middle rack for 21 to 22 minutes until the top of the cake is set, the sides have started to pull away from the pan, and a wooden toothpick or skewer inserted in the center of the cake comes out clean or with only a few moist crumbs.

7. Set the pan on a wire rack. After 10 minutes, sprinkle the remaining tablespoon of ground almonds over the top of the cake and press down lightly. Cover with another piece of parchment, and with the aid of another baking sheet or cutting board, flip the pan over. Remove the pan and carefully peel off the parchment paper. The underside may be slightly damp. Cool to room temperature.

8. Wrap the cake tightly in plastic wrap and refrigerate until cold before cutting and assembling. The cake can be wrapped in aluminum foil and frozen for up to 1 month. Defrost unwrapped.

MAKE THE ESPRESSO CONCENTRATE

1. Pour the boiling water over the espresso in a small bowl. Whisk until the espresso is dissolved.

2. Strain the concentrate through a fine mesh sieve. Cool to room temperature and reserve until needed. Whisk before using. (The concentrate can be made up to 1 week in advance and refrigerated in a covered container.)

(recipe continues)

MAKE THE MOCHA CREAM

1. Pour the Cashew Cream into a medium saucepan with a heavy bottom. Warm over the lowest heat, whisking frequently.

2. Add the sugar and cook over low heat, whisking frequently until the cream is hot and thick bubbles are visible around the sides, about 1 minute. The bottom of the pan may be lightly coated with the cream.

3. Add ¼ cup / 60 ml of the Espresso Concentrate and cook, whisking frequently, for 1 minute. Don't worry if the cream becomes lumpy as it heats. It will smooth as you whisk.

4. Remove the pan from the heat. Add the chopped chocolate and vanilla and stir with a silicone spatula until the chocolate is melted.

5. Spoon the filling into a bowl. Cool to room temperature, then cover and refrigerate until needed. Stir before using. (The filling can be made a day ahead and can be frozen for up to 2 weeks.

MAKE THE ESPRESSO GANACHE GLAZE

1. Mix the Bittersweet Ganache Glaze and 1 tablespoon / 15 ml of the Espresso Concentrate in a medium bowl. Taste and add additional concentrate if you like stronger coffee flavor, reserving at least 1 tablespoon of the concentrate for the coffee syrup (next recipe). Set aside until needed.

MAKE THE COFFEE SYRUP

1. Pour the agave and maple syrups and salt into a medium saucepan. (Cooking syrups expand and climb the sides of the pan, so always use a much larger pan than the volume would suggest is needed.) Cook over medium heat to a boil. Reduce the heat and simmer for 1 minute.

2. Stir the Espresso Concentrate into the syrups and remove the saucepan from the heat. Whisk until the syrup stops bubbling. Add the cognac, if using. Cool to room temperature and refrigerate in a covered jar until needed. The syrup will thicken as it cools.

MAKE THE CHOCOLATE TRANSFERS (IF USING)

Refer to Decorating with Chocolate (page 29) for making chocolate transfer sheet decorations.

ASSEMBLE THE OPERA CAKE

1. Cut the Almond Sheet Cake into two (5 x 5-inch / 12 x 12-cm) squares and two (5 x 2½-inch, 12 x 6-cm) rectangles (placed side by side, the rectangles make the square middle layer). The pieces do not have to be exactly square. The assembled cake will be trimmed.

2. Spread the bottom square of the cake with a scant 4 tablespoons / 60 ml of Espresso Ganache Glaze. Spread the other pieces with slightly less ganache, about 3 tablespoons / 45 ml, just to cover. (The ganache adds flavor and texture, and protects against soggy cake.) Chill the squares for about 10 minutes to set the glaze.

3. Spread the chilled bottom square with a scant ¼ cup / 60 ml of Mocha Cream. Place the rectangles side by side on top of the bottom layer to form a square, ganache side down. Spread the top of the rectangles with a thin layer of ganache. Chill for about 10 minutes to set.

4. Spread the top with a scant ¼ cup / 60 ml of Mocha Cream. Place the last square of cake ganache side down on the cream and press lightly. Spread with a thin layer of ganache and chill for about 10 minutes to set.

5. Spread the cake with a scant ¼ cup / 60 ml of Mocha Cream and smooth the top. Chill the cake for about 30 minutes.

6. Spread the remaining ganache over the top of the cake with an offset spatula. Refrigerate the cake for at least 2 hours or overnight.

7. Before serving, use a long thin knife to carefully trim and square the sides of the cake. This will remove any ganache that has dripped over the sides. (This is the baker's treat—enjoy!)

8. Attach chocolate transfers on 2 sides of the cake if desired, using the remaining Mocha Cream or ganache as glue.

SERVING

Slice the cake cold with a long thin knife, wiping the knife between cuts. Serve slightly chilled or at room temperature. Garnish each serving with some Mocha Cream if you like, and then drizzle the plate or cake with Coffee Syrup.

Bûche de Noël

Bûche de Noël is the French name for a Christmas cake shaped like a Yule log. Traditionally, this is a rolled cake, but I have learned that unless the cake contains an unthinkable amount of fat, a rolled vegan cake will be greasy (and exceptionally unhealthy). Still, I wanted a holiday log complete with mushrooms shaped from marzipan and cocoa "dirt"—all dusted with confectioners' sugar "snow." Once I thought differently, this *bûche* materialized. It is made from a simple sheet cake that is cut into long layers to resemble a log, filled with Chocolate Cranberry Cream (page 283) and frosted thickly with Bittersweet Chocolate Ganache Glaze (page 264). With a knot in the log made from cake and the glaze combed to look like bark, your *bûche* will be the talk of the table, if not the town. You will also have the satisfaction of knowing you did not have to tap into your 401(k) to buy one at the tonier pastry shops.

Here's my suggested game plan for the components in order of how far ahead you can prepare them:

1. Bake and cool the Bittersweet Chocolate Sheet Cake; refrigerate a day ahead or freeze for up to 1 month.
2. Make the Marzipan Mushrooms; refrigerate for up to 1 week.
3. Make the Bittersweet Chocolate Ganache Glaze; allow to thicken at room temperature for about 30 minutes, refrigerate for up to 5 days, or freeze for up to 1 month. Use at room temperature or warm briefly in a water bath until spreadable.
4. Make the Chocolate Cranberry Cream Filling; refrigerate for at least 4 hours or up to 1 day ahead.

MAKES ONE (10-INCH / 25-CM) LOG-SHAPED CAKE

1 recipe (1 ¾ cups / 420 ml) Bittersweet Chocolate Ganache Glaze (page 264)

1 recipe Marzipan (page 289), plus 1 ounce / 28 grams dark chocolate (any percentage) for making mushrooms

1 recipe Chocolate Cranberry Cream Filling (page 283)

BITTERSWEET CHOCOLATE SHEET CAKE

1 cup / 129 grams organic all-purpose flour

½ cup / 70 grams organic whole wheat pastry flour

1 cup / 207 grams organic granulated sugar, ground in a blender until superfine

3 ½ tablespoons / 17.5 grams natural cocoa powder (non-alkalized)

1 teaspoon / 5 grams baking soda

½ teaspoon fine sea salt

⅓ cup / 80 ml mild tasting extra-virgin olive oil

1 tablespoon / 15 ml apple cider vinegar

2 teaspoons / 10 ml pure vanilla extract

1 cup / 240 ml water, at room temperature

MAKE THE CAKE

1. Position a rack in the center of the oven and preheat to 375°F / 190°C. Oil the sides and bottom of a 13 x 9 ½ x 1-inch / 33 x 24 x 2.5-cm quarter sheet pan and line with parchment paper. Do not oil the paper.

2. Place a wire mesh strainer over a medium bowl. Add the all-purpose flour, pastry flour, sugar, cocoa powder, baking soda, and salt to the strainer and stir with a whisk to sift the ingredients into the bowl. (If any small bits remain in the strainer, add them to the mixture in the bowl.) Whisk to aerate the mixture.

3. Whisk the oil, vinegar, and vanilla in a separate medium bowl. Add the water slowly and whisk until combined. Immediately pour into the dry mixture and whisk until the batter is smooth.

4. Pour the batter into the prepared pan. Rotate the pan to level the batter and tap it lightly on the counter to eliminate air bubbles.

5. Bake the cake on the center rack for 22 to 23 minutes, or until the top of the cake is set, the sides have started to pull away from the pan, and a wooden toothpick or skewer inserted in the center of the cake comes out clean or with only a few moist crumbs.

(recipe continues)

6. Set the cake on a wire rack. After 5 minutes, run a thin spatula around the sides of the cake to release the cake from the pan. Cool the cake in the pan. Refrigerate or freeze until cold before cutting.

MAKE THE MARZIPAN MUSHROOMS

1. Form the caps of your marzipan mushrooms by rolling about three-quarters of the marzipan into dime- to quarter-size balls. Roll and press into a mushroom cap shape and press the bottoms flat. Roll the remaining marzipan into stubby stems, roughly ½ inch long x ¼ inch wide / 12 mm long x 6 mm wide for your mushrooms. Natural, uneven mushrooms are just fine here. Make a depression in the flat side of each mushroom cap—the flat side of a chopstick is perfect for this task.

2. Melt the chocolate. Fill each mushroom cap with a little bit and insert a stem. Repeat until all the mushrooms are made. Set the mushroom on their sides in a flat dish and refrigerate until the chocolate hardens. The marzipan should make 8 to 10 (1- to 1½-inch / 2.5 to 4-cm) mushroom caps and stems.

3. Store the mushrooms in a covered container in the refrigerator. The marzipan will become oily; don't worry.

SHAPE AND ASSEMBLE THE CAKE

1. Cut the frozen or refrigerated cake lengthwise into 3 strips as follows: 1 piece just under 3 inches / 7.5 cm wide, a second piece about 2¾ inches / 7 cm wide, and a third piece about 2½ inches / 6 cm wide.

2. Place the 3-inch-wide strip of cake on a serving platter and spread with ½ cup / 120 ml of the Chocolate Cranberry Cream Filling.

3. Place the next widest piece on top and press down lightly. Spread with another ½ cup of the cranberry filling.

4. Place the last piece of cake on top and press down lightly. The cake should now resemble a log that is widest at the bottom and tapers slightly toward the top, mimicking the curve of a rolled cake. Refrigerate the cake for 10 minutes before proceeding.

5. Spread the top and sides of the cake with about ⅔ cup / 160 ml of the ganache glaze. Use a fork to make wavy lines to simulate bark. Refrigerate the cake to set the glaze. Repeat with another ⅔ cup / 160 ml of glaze and refrigerate for about 10 minutes until set.

6. Cut a small diagonal slice off one end of the cake. This will be the knot. Freeze the piece before glazing. Glaze the knot with enough ganache to cover and affix it to the top of the cake off-center to resemble a knot on a tree. The glaze will be the glue. Use more if needed. Keep the cake refrigerated until ready to serve.

TO FINISH THE CAKE

Up to 30 minutes before serving, dry the marzipan mushrooms with paper towels and dust with confectioners' sugar or cocoa. Arrange the mushrooms on the cake log, pushing them lightly onto the frosting.

SERVING

A long skinny wooden cake board shows off the cake wonderfully, but any platter will be fine.

Before serving, dust the cake with confectioners' sugar "snow" and cocoa "dirt." Slice and serve.

KEEPING

The cake can be assembled and refrigerated for up to 2 days, lightly covered with parchment. Do not add the mushrooms until ready to serve. Finish the cake and serve slices with any of the chocolate sauces in Chapter Eleven.

Éclairs

The idea for this éclair came to me when I was proposing a Better Old-Fashioned Snack Cake class for the Institute of Culinary Education, after reading yet another blog post about my wildly popular Organic Vegan Twinkie. I developed my version of the famous snack cake for the 2007 book launch of *Twinkie, Deconstructed* by Steve Ettlinger. My version won the unofficial taste test at the party, and ABC's *Nightline* and Better TV filmed me making the treats. I basked in my Twinkie-inspired fifteen minutes of fame, and then moved on. Fast forward to 2012: the pandemonium surrounding the shutting down of Hostess, who makes Twinkies, led to another round of interest, articles, and interviews at the same time I was finishing this book. I realized I just had to include one of my most beloved creations with a chocolate twist. What started as vegan junk food has now become an elegant pastry to share with your office for an unforgettable afternoon coffee break.

MAKES 16 ÉCLAIRS

1 cup / 129 grams organic all-purpose flour

1 cup / 128 grams organic whole wheat pastry flour

¼ cup plus 2 tablespoons / 76 grams organic granulated sugar

1 teaspoon / 5 grams aluminum-free baking powder

1 teaspoon / 5 grams baking soda

½ teaspoon fine sea salt

⅓ cup / 80 ml mild tasting extra-virgin olive oil or organic neutral vegetable oil

¾ cup plus 2 tablespoons / 210 ml maple syrup, Grade B or dark amber

¾ cup / 180 ml any nondairy milk

2 tablespoons / 30 ml pure vanilla extract

2½ teaspoons / 12.5 ml apple cider vinegar

1 recipe White Chocolate Cream Filling (page 281) or 1 recipe Vanilla Custard Cream Filling (page 282)

½ recipe (1 cup / 240 ml) Bittersweet Chocolate Ganache Glaze (page 264), warmed in a water bath until softened

1. Position a rack in the middle of the oven and preheat to 350°F / 180°C. Oil the cups of 2 Twinkie pans or cream canoe pans. (These pans need a heavy coating or spray of oil.)

2. Place a wire mesh strainer over a medium bowl. Put the all-purpose flour, pastry flour, sugar, baking powder, baking soda, and salt in the strainer and stir with a whisk to sift the ingredients into the bowl. (If any small bits remain in the strainer, add them to the mixture in the bowl.) Whisk to aerate the mixture.

3. Whisk the oil, maple syrup, nondairy milk, vanilla, and vinegar in a medium bowl until completely combined. Immediately pour into the dry mixture and whisk until the batter is smooth.

4. Fill each cup about one third full (about 3 tablespoons / 45 ml of batter). Bake for 16 to 17 minutes, until the cakes are golden and a wooden toothpick or skewer inserted in the center of the cake comes out clean or with only a few moist crumbs.

5. Set the cake pans on a wire rack. After 5 minutes, run a thin knife between the cakes and the inside of the cups and lift each onto the rack to cool completely. Refrigerate or freeze until cold before filling and glazing.

ASSEMBLE THE ÉCLAIRS

1. Using a serrated knife, split each cake in half horizontally. Spread the bottom piece with about 2 tablespoons / 30 ml of the cream

(recipe continues)

filling. Replace the top half of each cake, pressing lightly. Chill briefly to set.

2. Put the cakes on a parchment-lined sheet pan (so any chocolate that drips off the cakes onto the paper can be reused). Spoon about 2 tablespoons / 30 ml of the ganache glaze on top of each cake. Refrigerate for 10 to 15 minutes to set the glaze.

KEEPING

Éclairs can be assembled a day ahead. The unfilled cakes can be refrigerated in a covered container for two days and frozen in an airtight container for a month. Defrost uncovered.

CHAPTER FIVE

Cookies, Bars, and Little Bites

Big or small, crunchy or chewy, as a snack or set into a simple bowl of pudding or ice cream to create a "plated dessert," there's always room for a cookie. Personally, I don't consider a meal complete until I've eaten a crunchy cookie. This chapter features cookies, bars, and little bites to suit every taste and time, including Moon Pies, Brownies, and Magic Cookie Bars. There are authentic tasting—but no fat added—100% whole wheat flour Chocolate Chip Almond Biscotti. You'll learn the technique for making real graham crackers that taste so much better than the boxed kind and the secret to making crispy-yet-chewy Passover-style macaroons egg-free. Every one of these recipes can be baked ahead and frozen, so if you plan accordingly, you'll always have a batch of cookies or bars at the ready.

Are the Cookies Done?

When cookies smell done, they usually are, but pay attention! Check the bottom of a cookie by turning it over with an offset spatula. (Hot cookies are soft and may break—that's the baker's treat.) The bottom should be lightly browned or, if it's supposed to be pale, look set and dry. Under-baked cookies can be returned to the oven, even after they have cooled.

Fran's Rulebook for Successful Cookies and Bars

1. Read the recipe all the way through and plan your time for all the components. *Note:* Bars bake more like cakes so review Fran's Rulebook for Successful Cakes (page 64) before baking them.

2. Prepare your *mise en place*: gather the equipment, prepare the pans, grind the sugar, chop or melt the chocolate, soak or roast the nuts, warm the rice syrup.

3. Position the oven racks correctly (cookies are baked on the middle rack).

4. Unless you have several ovens, bake cookies in batches. If your oven has hot spots, rotate the pan halfway through baking.

5. Preheat the oven and allow enough time for it to reach the correct temperature. An oven thermometer is essential.

6. Use the right pan! Do not bake cookies on dark or insulated pans—the bottoms will burn or won't bake properly. (The recipes are written for shallow, rimmed baking sheets because that is what I use; if you use rimless cookie sheets just bake a minute or two less.)

7. Use parchment, not silicone liners like Silpat, to line the baking sheet. (Silicone liners get too hot for most of the cookies in this chapter.)

8. Measure the ingredients carefully using the correct measuring utensil and method. The recipes in this book use the *"whisk, dip, and sweep"* method of measuring dry ingredients unless otherwise noted (see Sidebar page 63).

9. Portion and shape the dough as uniformly in size and thickness as possible so the cookies bake evenly.

10. Check the cookies for doneness. One extra minute of baking can be the difference between a good cookie and one that is dry (see Troubleshooting).

11. Cool the cookies on the pan on an elevated wire rack so the bottoms don't get soggy.

12. Only use airtight glass jars or metal tins to keep crisp cookies and BPA-free plastic containers or zipper-lock bags for softer cookies. Store in the freezer; they defrost quickly.

TROUBLESHOOTING	
Dry cookies	Brush warm cookies with maple syrup and water, mixed $2/3$ to $1/3$.
Under-baked cookies	Put them back into the oven briefly, even after they have cooled.
I want my chocolate chunk cookies melty	Warm them in a low oven (200˚F / 90˚C) for a few minutes.

THE RECIPES

Gluten-Free Brownie Bites

Very Fudgy Chocolate Chip Brownies

Blondies

Chocolate Chip Almond Biscotti

Chocolate-Dipped Coconut Macaroons

Graham Crackers

S'mores

Moon Pies

Magic Cookie Bars

Gluten-Free Chocolate Chunk Cookies

Double Chocolate Chunk Cookies

Gluten-Free Brownie Bites

You don't need to be gluten-free to love these fudgy, deeply chocolate brownies. None of my tasters or testers could tell the difference between these and fudge brownies made with wheat. The brownies taste best to me after a half-hour in the refrigerator, but you might like them better at room temperature. Fans of dense, chewy brownies will love them straight out of the freezer. Baking the brownies in individual tins gives each piece nice chewy edges—along with built-in portion control.

Many of the gluten-free mixes contain bean flour, and if you are new to baking with gluten-free flours, you may find the "beany" smell of the batter alarming. Don't worry: the odor bakes out. It is very important to read the label on that gluten-free mix and check whether xanthan gum is one of the ingredients. If xanthan gum is not listed, add the optional quarter teaspoon of xanthan gum to the recipe.

MAKES 24 MINI BROWNIES

½ cup plus 2 tablespoons / 103 grams gluten-free
　　all-purpose baking mix

¼ cup / 25 grams Dutch-process cocoa powder

¼ cup / 50 grams organic granulated sugar

3 ½ tablespoons / 32 grams organic whole cane sugar,
　　ground in a blender until powdered

¾ teaspoon / 4 grams aluminum-free baking powder

¼ teaspoon baking soda

½ teaspoon fine sea salt

¼ teaspoon xanthan or guar gum (if needed,
　　see headnote)

¼ cup / 60 ml mild tasting extra-virgin olive oil

¼ cup / 60 ml any nondairy milk

¼ cup / 60 ml Homemade Sweetened Prune Purée
　　(recipe follows) or a 2-ounce jar of organic baby food
　　plums or prunes

1 tablespoon / 15 ml pure vanilla extract

¼ teaspoon chocolate extract (optional)

¼ cup / 46 grams mini gluten-free vegan chocolate
　　chips

1. Position a rack in the center of the oven and preheat to 325˚F / 160˚C. Oil the cups of one 24-cup or two 12-cup mini muffin tins or use a non-stick cooking spray.

2. Place a wire mesh strainer over a medium bowl. To measure the baking mix, put a flat-sided, dry ½-cup measuring cup on a sheet of parchment. Spoon the flour into the cup, filling it to overflowing. Level the flour by gently sweeping a knife or offset spatula across the top. Do not pack or shake the cup. Put the baking mix into the strainer. Measure the additional 2 tablespoons of baking mix in the same manner, using metal measuring spoons, and add them to the strainer. Use the parchment to pour the excess mix back into the bag.

3. Add the cocoa powder, granulated sugar, whole cane sugar, baking powder, baking soda, and salt to the strainer. If your mix does not include xanthan or guar gum, add the ¼ teaspoon now. Stir with a whisk to sift into the bowl. (If any small bits remain in the strainer, add them to the mixture in the bowl.) Whisk to aerate the mixture.

4. In a small bowl, whisk the oil, nondairy milk, prune purée, and vanilla and chocolate extracts until thoroughly combined. Immediately pour the liquid ingredients into the dry ingredients and mix with a rubber spatula until no traces of dry ingredients are visible. Expect the batter to be thick. Stir the chocolate chips into the batter.

5. Fill each baking cup about two-thirds full using a small (1 table-spoon) ice cream scoop or ordinary tablespoons. (If you are using spoons, scoop the batter with one spoon, and push it off the spoon into the tin with another.)

6. Bake for 12 to 13 minutes, or until the brownies have risen and feel set when lightly tapped. Do not overbake if your brownies are still fudgy. A wooden toothpick or skewer inserted into the center of a couple of brownies should look sticky but not wet.

7. Set the pan on a wire rack. After 5 minutes, use a small offset spatula to lift each brownie onto the wire rack. (Warm brownies are soft, but should be easy to lift out from the tins.) Cool completely. For the best flavor, refrigerate the brownies for an hour.

What Are Prunes Doing in My Brownie?

Prunes and chocolate are frequently paired in traditional chocolate recipes, and these fudge brownies are no exception. In addition to enhancing the flavor of the chocolate, prune purée adds a healthy dose of fiber and replaces some of the fat.

SERVING

The brownies taste great at room temperature, cold, or straight from the freezer—whatever way you like them best!

Homemade Sweetened Prune Purée

Eric, a very meticulous graduate of my Vegan Baking Boot Camp Intensive®, sent me an email saying it was easier to make the smooth prune purée for his much-requested fudge brownies with an immersion blender. When I questioned his technique, Eric replied, "Chef Fran, you know I have high standards!" He does. I tried Eric's method and never looked back, but any blender will work fine.

MAKES ABOUT 1 CUP

½ cup / 3 ounces / 85 grams pitted dried plums (prunes), coarsely chopped

1 cup / 240 ml boiling water, or more as needed

2 tablespoons / 30 ml pure maple syrup, Grade B or dark amber

1. Put the prunes into a small saucepan. Pour the boiling water over the prunes and let them soak for 5 minutes. Bring the liquid to a boil over high heat. Reduce the heat to low and simmer for 10 minutes. Check the prunes. They are ready to be drained when they are very soft. Simmer as long as it takes to get the prunes to an almost falling-apart stage. Note that the length of cooking time and amount of water is variable, depending on the dryness of the prunes.

2. Set a small mesh strainer over a heatproof cup and drain the prunes. Reserve ⅓ cup / 80 ml of the cooking liquid to make the purée.

3. Purée the prunes, the maple syrup, and ¼ cup / 60 ml of the reserved cooking liquid with an immersion blender in the saucepan or in a blender. Add more of the cooking liquid, a little at a time if needed, until the purée is absolutely smooth with no bits of prune skin. The finished purée should be the consistency of a thick mayonnaise.

KEEPING

Refrigerate the purée for up to 1 week in a covered container, or freeze for up to 2 months.

Very Fudgy Chocolate Chip Brownies

You'll get plenty of "brownie points" for these soft, fudgy, and rich chocolate treats studded with chocolate chunks or chips. Walnuts add crunch and cut the sweetness, but if you like a brownie unencumbered by nuts, just say no to this option. No matter what you prefer, these brownies will stay fudgy when frozen, making them the perfect cake for ice cream sandwiches or any of the frozen desserts in Chapter Eight. Make a Blow Them Away Brownie Sundae (page 206), or just dip into some of the Thick Fudge Sauce (page 277). Just watch out: These brownies are not low-fat or low-sugar: a small square should satisfy.

Note: If using coconut oil as the fat, make sure the other ingredients are at room temperature, or the oil will harden into clumps during mixing.

MAKES ONE (8 X 8-INCH / 20 X 20-CM) SQUARE PAN

½ cup plus 1 tablespoon / 73 grams organic all-purpose flour

½ cup / 70 grams organic whole wheat pastry flour

½ cup / 58 grams Dutch-process cocoa powder

½ cup minus 1 tablespoon / 98 grams organic granulated sugar

¼ cup / 38 grams organic whole cane sugar, ground in a blender until powdered

2 tablespoons / 12 grams arrowroot or organic cornstarch (14 grams)

1 teaspoon / 5 grams aluminum-free baking powder

½ teaspoon fine sea salt

¼ cup plus 2 tablespoons / 90 ml mild tasting extra-virgin olive oil or organic neutral vegetable oil

½ cup / 120 ml pure maple syrup, Grade B or dark amber

¼ cup / 60 ml any nondairy milk

2 teaspoons / 10 ml pure vanilla extract

½ teaspoon chocolate extract (optional)

Heaping ½ cup / 85 grams vegan chocolate chips or mini chunks

⅓ cup / 43 grams lightly toasted walnuts or mixed nuts, coarsely chopped (optional)

1. Position a rack in the middle of the oven and preheat to 350°F / 180°C. Oil an 8 x 8-inch / 20 x 20-cm square pan and then line the bottom with parchment paper. Do not oil the paper.

2. Place a wire mesh strainer over a medium bowl. Add the all-purpose flour, pastry flour, cocoa, granulated sugar, whole cane sugar, arrowroot or cornstarch, baking powder, and salt to the strainer and stir with a whisk to sift the ingredients into the bowl. (If any small bits remain in the strainer, add them to the mixture in the bowl.) Whisk to aerate the mixture.

3. Whisk the oil, maple syrup, nondairy milk, vanilla, and chocolate extract, if using, in a separate medium bowl until completely combined. Pour into the dry ingredients and mix with a silicone spatula until the batter, which will be thick, is smooth. Allow the batter to rest for ten minutes.

4. Stir the chocolate chips and nuts, if using, into the batter. Spoon the batter into the prepared pan, and spread into an even layer with a metal spatula.

5. Bake for 23 minutes until the top is set and dry and the sides have pulled just slightly away from the pan.

6. Remove the pan from the oven and set on a cooling rack. Immediately insert a wooden tester diagonally into the brownies. The tester will be coated with batter, but not wet. If necessary, bake for another minute.

7. Cool to room temperature. The middle of the cake will sink as it cools; don't worry. Once cold you can push the sides down to level the cake if you like. Refrigerate until very cold before cutting into squares.

KEEPING

Refrigerate the brownies in a covered container, in layers separated by parchment, for up to three days, or freeze for up to one month. Defrost unwrapped or eat straight out of the freezer.

Blondies

Brownies without chocolate in the batter are considered Blondies! These moist bar cookies are made with brown sugar, which is their defining flavor. As conventional brown sugar is just white sugar with the molasses added back in, I prefer to use organic whole cane sugar from which the molasses has never been removed. You can vary this recipe as you would a brownie recipe—for example, add a half-cup of chopped nuts or spread with Thick and Glossy Fudge Frosting (page 271). For a party, double the recipe and bake it in a 13 x 9-inch / 33 x 23-cm pan.

Note: If you are using coconut oil, make sure the other liquid ingredients are at room temperature, or the coconut oil will harden into clumps during mixing.

MAKES ONE (8 X 8-INCH / 20 X 20-CM) SQUARE PAN

½ cup plus 6 tablespoons / 210 ml canned
 unsweetened full-fat coconut milk, well-stirred
 (do not use light), divided
1 teaspoon / 5 ml apple cider vinegar
½ cup / 64 grams organic all-purpose flour
½ cup / 70 grams organic whole wheat pastry flour
3 tablespoons / 27 grams coconut flour
½ teaspoon aluminum-free baking powder

¼ teaspoon ground cinnamon
¼ teaspoon fine sea salt
¼ cup plus 2 tablespoons / 90 ml coconut oil, melted,
 or mild tasting extra-virgin olive oil
1 cup plus 1 tablespoon / 169 grams organic whole cane
 sugar, ground in a blender until powdered
1 tablespoon / 15 ml pure vanilla extract
½ cup / 85 grams vegan dark chocolate chips

1. Position a rack in the middle of the oven and preheat to 350°F / 180°C. Oil the sides and bottom of the pan and line the bottom with parchment cut to fit. Do not oil the parchment.

2. Mix ½ cup / 120 ml of the coconut milk with the vinegar and set aside for 30 minutes to clabber.

3. Place a wire mesh strainer over a medium bowl. Add the all-purpose flour, pastry flour, coconut flour, baking powder, cinnamon, and salt to the strainer and stir with a whisk to sift the ingredients into the bowl. (If any small bits remain in the strainer, add them to the mixture in the bowl.) Whisk to aerate the mixture.

4. Beat the oil and sugar in a separate medium bowl with electric beaters on low speed for 2 minutes until thoroughly combined. Increase the speed to medium and beat another minute. Add the clabbered coconut milk and beat on low until the mixture is smooth.

5. Add the sifted ingredients to the liquid ingredients in thirds, mixing on low between each addition. Add the remaining 6 tablespoons / 90 ml of coconut milk and the vanilla and beat on low until the batter is smooth.

6. Stir the chocolate chips into the batter. Pour the batter into the pan and level the top.

7. Bake for 21 to 22 minutes, or until a wooden toothpick inserted in a few spots near the center comes out mostly clean and not sticky. Cool on a wire rack.

SERVING

For the neatest slices, refrigerate or freeze the Blondies before cutting. Serve at room temperature or chilled.

KEEPING

The Blondies can be refrigerated for up to two days in an airtight container or frozen for up to one month in a tightly sealed container. Defrost uncovered at room temperature.

Chocolate Chip Almond Biscotti

Bravissimo for better biscotti made with all whole wheat pastry flour and no oil at all! Alessandra, my Italian-born culinary school intern, insists that any biscotti fan will enjoy eating these crunchy, lightly anise-scented biscotti. Twice baked like all biscotti, the chocolate-chip-studded slices beg to be dipped in a caffè latte. So steam up your favorite nondairy milk and dunk away anytime of the day, even at breakfast. But you will need to plan ahead to have the biscotti ready for that latte: The dough is refrigerated for an hour before the logs are shaped, and the logs are refrigerated for an hour before they are baked. After baking, the logs are sliced while warm and baked a second time. Since the logs can be frozen unbaked or baked, I almost always make a double recipe and divide the dough into four portions, guaranteeing future biscotti without fuss!

MAKES ABOUT 28 BISCOTTI

2 tablespoons / 12 grams anise seeds

½ cup / 59 grams ground roasted unpeeled almonds (see chapter 1 page 19)

1 cup / 128 grams organic whole wheat pastry flour

¼ cup plus 2 tablespoons / 57 grams organic whole cane sugar, ground in a blender until powdered

¼ teaspoon aluminum-free baking powder

¼ teaspoon baking soda

⅛ teaspoon fine sea salt

3 tablespoons / 45 ml pure maple syrup, Grade B or dark amber

3 tablespoons / 45 ml water, at room temperature

2 teaspoons / 10 ml pure vanilla extract

1 teaspoon / 5 ml almond extract

Scant ½ cup / 85 grams vegan chocolate chips

1. Toast the anise seeds over low heat in a small dry skillet, stirring constantly until just fragrant, about 5 minutes. Let the seeds cool and then finely grind them in a coffee or spice grinder.

2. Place a wire mesh strainer over a medium bowl. Add the flour, sugar, baking powder, baking soda, and salt and stir with a whisk to sift the ingredients into the bowl. (If any small bits remain in the strainer, add them to the mixture.) Stir in the almonds and anise seed with a whisk to combine and aerate the mixture.

3. In a small bowl, whisk the maple syrup, water, and vanilla and almond extracts until well blended. Pour into the flour mixture and stir with a silicone spatula until the dough holds together. The dough will be firm and a little sticky, but not wet. Stir the chocolate chips into the dough with a large silicone spatula. Allow the dough to rest in the bowl for 10 minutes.

4. Divide the dough into two equal pieces. Shape each into a short, fat log. Wrap each separately in plastic wrap and refrigerate for at least 1 hour, or up to 4 hours, before shaping into thinner logs to bake: the dough needs time to absorb the liquid.

5. Shape the logs: Unwrap one piece of dough and place it on a piece of parchment paper or onto a silicone baking mat. (The dough rolls more easily on a baking mat.) Roll the dough into a skinny log about 12 inches long and 1 ½ inches wide / 30.5 cm long x 4 cm wide. You may have to push and roll at the same time. Clean your hands if they get too sticky. Smooth any tears or gaps in the log and push in any wayward chocolate chips if necessary. Repeat with the other piece of dough.

6. Rewrap the logs in plastic or roll them up in parchment paper and place them on a cookie sheet, taking care not to distort the shape. Refrigerate again for an hour, or up to 24 hours, before baking. (This allows for the dough to firm up.)

7. When you are ready to bake the biscotti, position one oven rack in the middle of the oven, and the other just below it. Preheat the oven to 350°F / 180°C. Line a baking sheet with parchment paper. (Do not use silicone mats. The mats can get hotter in the oven than parchment, and the bottoms of the logs will be in danger of burning.)

8. Remove the logs from the refrigerator and unwrap. Place them on the lined baking sheet, spacing them 4 inches / 10 cm apart. Set the baking sheet on the middle rack of the oven and bake for 35 to 38 minutes, or until the logs are lightly golden-brown and feel firm when lightly tapped with your fingertip.

9. Remove the baking sheet from the oven and place on a wire rack. Cool for 10 minutes, and then carefully slide the logs off the baking sheet and directly onto the rack. Cool for 5 minutes longer before slicing. Leave the parchment paper on the baking sheet for the second baking.

10. Place a warm log on a cutting board. Cut ½-inch / 12-mm slices, using a long serrated knife to saw diagonally through the log, almost to the bottom, then pressing the knife straight down to make the cut. You may have to experiment to see what creates the neatest slices. Place the slices cut-side down, ¼ inch / 6 mm apart, on the parchment-lined baking sheet. Brush the crumbs off the cutting board and repeat with the second log.

11. Bake the slices on the lower oven rack for 12 minutes. Remove the baking sheet from the oven and place it on a wire rack. Carefully turn 1 or 2 slices over to check the color. They should be very lightly browned. If they are not, bake for another 2 to 3 minutes. When finished, remove from the oven and turn each slice over using tongs. Let cool on the sheet for 10 minutes. Move the slices to the wire rack and cool completely.

KEEPING
The biscotti will stay fresh for up to one week in an airtight tin and can be frozen in an airtight container for up to two months. Unbaked logs can be frozen and baked at another time. Wrap the logs tightly in plastic wrap and then in aluminum foil. The foil will protect the shape of the logs, which are rather soft at this point. Defrost the logs unwrapped at room temperature. Bake them while they are still chilled starting from step 7.

VARIATION
Chocolate-Dipped Biscotti: Melt 3 to 4 ounces / 85 to 113 grams of dark chocolate (66 to 70%). Use an offset spatula to spread some of the melted chocolate over one side of each slice. Alternatively, dip the biscotti halfway into the melted chocolate. Put the biscotti on a parchment-lined baking sheet and refrigerate until the chocolate hardens. You may also dip biscotti in the Chocolate Olive Oil Glaze on page 222.

Chocolate-Dipped Coconut Macaroons

Passover, like all of my family's gatherings, was food-centric, and dessert was no exception. After dinner, we always had two kinds of Passover macaroons on the table: a bakery version and a canned version. The ones from the bakery were certainly better than the canned, but I admit to favoring the latter as a child. Today, I make a delicious, preservative-free version of that canned cookie that appears on virtually every Seder table. But it wasn't easy. Replacing the egg whites found in every macaroon recipe proved a tough puzzle to solve. Commercial egg replacer and starches made a cookie that tasted powdery with a texture not even close to what I was after. One afternoon, wondering what to do with the bowl of white chia gel I was whisking, I thought, "Egg white!" In short order, I had made a cookie too good to eat only on Passover, and one that you certainly don't have to be Jewish to enjoy.

Note: 1½ teaspoons / 4.5 grams whole white chia seeds yield the 1 tablespoon ground seeds needed for the recipe, but that is too small a quantity to grind. Grind at least 3 tablespoons / 30 grams and store the ground chia in a small covered jar in the refrigerator for up to 6 months.

**MAKES 24 TO 26
SMALL MACAROONS**

**7 tablespoons plus 2 teaspoons /
99 grams organic granulated sugar,
divided**

**1 tablespoon / 10 grams ground white
chia seeds**

**3 tablespoons / 45 ml water, at room
temperature**

¼ cup / 33 grams coconut flour

**¼ teaspoon aluminum-free baking
powder**

**½ cup plus 2 tablespoons / 52 grams
toasted shredded coconut, divided**

**3 tablespoons / 45 ml vanilla coconut
milk beverage**

½ teaspoon pure vanilla extract

**3 ounces / 85 grams dark chocolate
(62 to 72%), melted and kept warm
in a water bath, for dipping**

1. Position a rack in the center of the oven and preheat to 375°F / 190°C. Line a rimmed baking sheet with a sheet of parchment paper.

2. Lightly grind 7 tablespoons / 91 grams of the sugar in a blender and set aside until needed.

3. Put the ground chia in a small bowl. Pour the water over the chia. Set aside for 5 minutes undisturbed and then whisk hard. The chia gel will be lumpy at first but will smooth out as it hydrates. Whisk a few more times while you sift the dry ingredients. (You can make the gel ahead of time and refrigerate for up to 3 days. Whisk vigorously before using.)

4. Place a wire mesh strainer over a medium bowl. Add the coconut flour, the 7 tablespoons of ground sugar, and the baking powder to the strainer and stir with a whisk to sift the ingredients into the bowl. (If any small bits remain in the strainer, add them to the mixture in the bowl.) Stir ½ cup / 40 grams of the shredded coconut into the dry ingredients.

5. Whisk in the chia gel. Use a silicone spatula or your hands, if necessary, to get the gel thoroughly mixed into the flour mixture. Add the coconut milk beverage and the vanilla extract and mix with a silicone spatula, pushing hard on the dough until it holds together when squeezed in your fingers.

6. Form the macaroons. Use a 1-teaspoon measure to scoop out rounded teaspoons of dough. Squeeze the dough hard in the palm of your hand so that it sticks together, and then roll into balls.

7. Coat the macaroons. In a small bowl, mix the remaining 2 tablespoons / 12 grams of coconut and 2 teaspoons of sugar. Roll the dough balls in the coconut-sugar mixture. Press each ball on the baking sheet to flatten the bottoms.

8. Place the baking sheet on the middle rack of the oven and immediately reduce the heat to 350°F / 180°C. Bake for 14 minutes until the bottom of the macaroons are lightly browned.

9. Set the baking sheet on a wire rack. After 3 to 4 minutes, lift the macaroons off the baking sheet onto the rack. Cool the macaroons to room temperature and then refrigerate until cold before dipping the bottoms.

10. Dip the bottoms of the cold macaroons in the melted chocolate. Set the coated macaroons on an acetate sheet or parchment-lined tray and refrigerate until the chocolate is set.

KEEPING

Freeze the macaroons in an airtight container for up to one month. These little cookies defrost fast.

VARIATION

Chocolate-Covered Macaroon: Dip the entire macaroon in chocolate.

Chocolate Chip Coconut Macaroons: Add 6 tablespoons mini gluten-free vegan chocolate chips to the dough before coating.

Almond Coconut Macaroons: Add ¼ cup plus 2 tablespoons / 73 grams ground and roasted unpeeled almonds and 2 teaspoons / 10 ml almond extract to the dough.

Graham Crackers

Most people buy graham crackers from a box in the store, but making homemade grahams is tasty and fun, and requires relatively few ingredients. Plus, it's hard to find healthy authentic vegan graham crackers in stores. Make your own and say hello to vegan Moon Pies (page 141), Magic Cookie Bars with a graham cracker crust (page 142), or S'mores (page 139) for all-around good snacking.

Toasting the whole wheat pastry flour gives these cookies the traditional graham taste without using the less widely available graham flour. The flour can be toasted and cooled ahead of time and stored in an airtight container or bag in the freezer until needed.

MAKES 24 (2 X 2-INCH / 5 X 5-CM) SQUARE COOKIES, 18 (2-INCH / 5-CM) ROUNDS, OR 2 CUPS / 250 GRAMS FINE CRUMBS

1½ cups / 198 grams organic whole wheat pastry flour

⅓ cup / 49 grams organic whole cane sugar, ground in a blender until powdered

¼ teaspoon baking soda

½ teaspoon ground cinnamon

¼ teaspoon fine sea salt

¼ cup / 60 ml mild tasting extra-virgin olive oil or organic neutral vegetable oil

3 tablespoons / 45 ml pure maple syrup, Grade B or dark amber

2½ teaspoons / 12.5 ml pure vanilla extract

2 to 4 tablespoons / 30 to 60 ml water, at room temperature, as needed to adjust dough

1. Toast the flour: Position a rack in the center of the oven and preheat to 350°F / 180°C. Line a rimmed baking sheet with parchment paper. Spread the flour on the parchment paper and toast in the oven for 10 minutes, stirring a few times. Cool the flour before continuing. (You can reuse the parchment to roll out the dough later.)

2. Place a wire mesh strainer over a medium bowl. Add the flour, sugar, baking soda, cinnamon, and salt to the strainer and stir with a wire whisk to sift the ingredients into the bowl. (If any small bits remain in the strainer, add them to the mixture in the bowl.) Whisk to aerate the mixture.

3. Whisk together the oil, maple syrup, and vanilla in a small bowl until completely combined. Immediately pour over the dry ingredients and mix with a silicone spatula until the mixture holds together. (It will be too dry to form a pliable ball of dough at this point.)

4. Mix 2 tablespoons / 30 ml of the water into the dough. Set aside for 5 minutes to allow the flour to absorb the liquid. Add additional water as needed until the dough is pliable when formed into a ball. It should be glossy but not wet.

5. Roll the dough: Wipe any flour dust from the parchment. Flip it over and move it to the counter. Place the dough on the center of the parchment and use the palm of your hand to pat and press it into a rough rectangle. The shape does not need to be perfect. Cover the dough with a second piece of parchment and use a rolling pin to roll the dough to about 14 x 10 inches (35.5 x 25 cm) and ¼ inch (6 mm) thick. The thickness matters more than the size for the crackers to bake evenly.

(recipe continues)

6. Remove the top sheet of parchment paper and trim the edges with a sharp knife to make a neat rectangle. Cut 2-inch / 5-cm) square pieces by making vertical and then horizontal cuts all the way across the dough. Using a fork or skewer, poke holes all over the top of the dough. (Think boxed grahams.) Gather the scraps of dough together, press into a ball, and then roll, trim, and prick.

7. Transfer the dough, still on the parchment, to the baking sheet. Run a small sharp knife over the cuts once more. Bake on the middle rack for 11 to 12 minutes, or until the tops are uniformly dry and the bottoms are lightly browned. (Turn one over to check.)

8. Place the baking sheet on a wire rack. Allow the crackers to cool to room temperature before breaking them into pieces. The crackers will be soft when they are hot and crisp as they cool.

KEEPING

The graham crackers can be made up to four days ahead and stored in an airtight tin, or they can be frozen for up to one month in a freezer-proof airtight container.

VARIATION

Round Graham Crackers: Starting close to the outside edge of the dough, cut crackers with a 2-inch / 5-cm round cookie or biscuit cutter, making the cuts as close together as possible. You will get at least 15 crackers. Gather the scraps of dough together, press into a ball, and then reroll and make another 1 or 2 crackers. Using a toothpick or skewer, prick rows of dots in the crackers. Pricking the dough is necessary for the grahams to bake right, but you don't need to break out a ruler, since these are homemade.

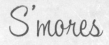

S'mores

I can't make a campfire in my apartment or in the park across the street. I can't eat conventional marshmallows because they contain bovine gelatin and I can't just eat most boxed graham crackers because they contain honey. What's a s'mores lovin', former Girl Scout-turned-vegan city dweller supposed to do? The answer is simple: I sandwich mini vegan marshmallows from Sweet and Sara (see Resources page 290) and squares of my favorite dark chocolate bar between two homemade Graham Crackers (page 136). What are you waiting for?

MAKES 8 S'MORES

16 (2 inch / 5 cm) Graham Crackers (page 136)

5 to 6 ounces / 142 to 170 grams any favorite dark chocolate bar, broken into small pieces

16 to 20 mini vegan marshmallows

1. Position a rack in the upper third of the oven and preheat to 425°F / 220°C. Line a baking sheet with parchment paper.

2. Lay half the graham crackers on the baking sheet. Cover the grahams with pieces of chocolate, leaving a small border. Warm in the oven for 2 to 3 minutes, until the chocolate is just beginning to melt.

3. Remove the baking sheet from the oven: Be careful—the baking sheet is hot! Press enough of the mini marshmallows over the chocolate to cover. The marshmallows will adhere to the melty chocolate.

4. Return the baking sheet to the oven and bake until the marshmallows and chocolate are soft and gooey, about 5 minutes.

5. Remove from the oven and top with the remaining graham crackers, pressing down slightly to make a sandwich.

SERVING

Serve immediately with plenty of napkins.

VARIATION

Chocolate-Covered Graham Cracker S'mores: Spread the top graham of each s'more with about a tablespoon of one of the chocolate ganache glazes (pages 264-269) to cover.

Moon Pies

Moon pies are an American classic dating back to the 1920s. Manufactured commercially in Chattanooga, these childhood favorites are made by sandwiching round graham crackers around a marshmallow filling. The sandwiches are then dipped in chocolate and chilled until the chocolate is set. This version is an accurate copy of the original, but far healthier. I'm confident you'll think they taste better, too! Variations follow the recipe, but don't call them Moon Pies if you serve them to strident fans of the original. (RC Cola was—or still is—the traditional accompaniment to Moon Pies in some southern towns!)

MAKES 8 MOON PIES

**1 recipe Graham Crackers (page 136),
cut into 2-inch / 5 cm rounds,
baked and cooled**

**2 cups / 480 ml Rice Mallow Cream
(see Resources page 290) or use an
alternative filling (see Variations)**

**5 ounces / 142 grams dark chocolate
(66 to 70%), melted**

ASSEMBLE THE MOON PIES

1. Spread the bottoms of half of the graham cracker cookies with 3 to 4 tablespoons / 45 to 60 ml of marshmallow cream. Top each with another cookie, bottom side down, and press together lightly.

2. Spread or pour enough melted chocolate to cover the top of each cookie and allow it to run down the sides (about 2 tablespoons / 30 ml). Refrigerate the Moon Pies for 10 to 15 minutes, or until the chocolate hardens.

SERVING

The Moon Pies are ready to eat as soon as the chocolate hardens. Serve with plenty of napkins.

KEEPING

Assembled Moon Pies can be refrigerated in an airtight container for up to three days. Eat them cold or at room temperature.

VARIATIONS

Instead of marshmallow cream, fill the Moon Pies with 2 to 3 tablespoons of jam or any nut butter, or Vanilla Custard Cream Filling (page 282).

Magic Cookie Bars

This recipe was a personal challenge for me. While working in my first pastry kitchen, I made hundreds of the popular traditional Magic Cookie Bars (a.k.a. Seven-Layer Bars) weekly using the requisite base of sweetened condensed milk. I never felt well after snacking frequently on these overly sweet bars throughout my shift, but I can't deny their popularity. I wanted to make a vegan version that would be true to the original but without the cloying sweetness. After many unsuccessful attempts to replace the sweetened condensed milk, I found that my Basic Thick Cashew Cream worked perfectly, and my testers enthusiastically agreed. The bars freeze beautifully, so you can store them for whenever you have a craving or have a whole pan ready for the next bake sale.

Notes: The Graham Crackers and Cashew Cream are best made ahead of time. (Both can be frozen.)

MAKES ONE (8 X 8-INCH / 20 X 20-CM) PAN

CRUMB CRUST

1½ cups / 200 grams fine graham cracker crumbs from 1 recipe Graham Crackers (page 136) or use any boxed vegan graham crackers

½ cup / 111 grams organic granulated sugar

¼ cup plus 1 tablespoon / 75 ml mild tasting extra-virgin olive oil

2 tablespoons / 30 ml pure maple syrup, Grade B or dark amber

1 teaspoon / 5 ml vanilla extract

BARS

1½ cups / 360 ml Basic Thick Cashew Cream (page 284)

1 cup / 113 grams toasted walnut halves, broken or coarsely chopped into rather large pieces

1 cup / 170 grams vegan chocolate chips, divided

1¼ cups / 104 grams toasted coconut (see page 19)

MAKE THE CRUST

1. Position a rack in the center of the oven and preheat to 350°F / 180°C. Lightly oil the bottom only of an 8 x 8-inch / 20 x 20-cm baking pan. Line the bottom with parchment cut so that the parchment extends up two of the sides of the pan. This will help with the removal of the bars from the baking pan.

2. Mix the graham cracker crumbs and the sugar in a medium bowl.

3. Mix the maple syrup, oil, and vanilla in a small bowl. Pour over the crumbs and use a silicone spatula to mix until the crumbs are thoroughly moistened.

4. Pour the moistened crumbs into the prepared pan. Place a piece of plastic wrap directly on the crust and use a flat-bottomed glass or cup to press the dough into an even, compact layer on the bottom of the pan.

5. Bake the crust on the center rack for 10 minutes. Cool on a wire rack to room temperature before filling. Increase the oven temperature to 375°F / 190°C.

MAKE THE BARS

1. Pour the cashew cream evenly over the cooled crust.

2. Sprinkle the nuts evenly over the cream, then sprinkle ¾ cup / 128 grams of the chocolate chips over the nuts. Sprinkle the toasted coconut evenly over the top.

3. Using a piece of parchment or plastic wrap, lightly press the top of the bars before baking.

4. Place the pan on the middle rack. Reduce the oven temperature to 350°F / 180°C and bake for 25 minutes until the coconut is lightly browned and there are some brown spots on the edges.

5. Cool the pan on a wire rack. Press down lightly with a spoon on any areas where the coconut does not look anchored. Scatter the remaining chocolate chips on top. Cool completely. Place the pan in the freezer for about 30 minutes, until cold, before cutting.

SERVING

Release the sides of the cookie from the pan with a thin knife. Lift the cookie out of the pan and onto a cutting board with the help of the long pieces of paper. Cut into quarters. Cut each quarter into six squares.

KEEPING

Refrigerate the cookies in a covered container for up to two days or freeze for up to two months. Defrost at room temperature.

Gluten-Free Chocolate Chunk Cookies

Can gluten-free chocolate chunk cookies possibly be any good? Yes! This chocolate chunk cookie will make any and all cookie lovers happy. Similar in texture to the soft and gooey studded Double Chocolate Chunk Cookie, nobody will think these easy-to-make cookies are anything but delicious, even though they use gluten-free all-purpose baking mix (my favorite is from Bob's Red Mill) and gluten-free chocolate chunks (I like those from Enjoy Life or simply chop up any gluten-free chocolate bar).

Note: You don't need skill but you do need extra time to make these cookies: Make sure you allow 30 minutes for whisking and allowing the dough to thicken. And remember when using melted coconut oil, all the other ingredients need to be at room temperature or the oil will harden into lumps during mixing.

MAKES 1 DOZEN COOKIES

½ cup plus 1 tablespoon / 87 grams all-purpose gluten-free baking mix

3 tablespoons / 18 grams Dutch-process cocoa powder

⅜ teaspoon ground cinnamon

⅜ teaspoon fine sea salt

¼ teaspoon aluminum-free baking powder

3 to 4 grinds of black pepper, optional

1 tablespoon/ 6 grams ground chia seeds

2 tablespoons / 30 ml hot water

2 tablespoons / 30 ml nondairy milk

2 tablespoons / 30 ml pure maple syrup, Grade B or dark amber

2 teaspoons / 10 ml pure vanilla extract

5 tablespoons organic granulated sugar / 65 grams, plus ⅓ to ½ cup / 64 to 111 grams for shaping

2½ tablespoons / 37.5 ml coconut oil, melted

⅓ cup / 52 grams gluten-free chocolate chunks

1. Position a rack in the middle of the oven and preheat to 375°F / 190°C. Line a baking sheet with parchment paper.

2. Place a wire mesh strainer over a medium bowl. Add the baking mix, cocoa, cinnamon, salt, and baking powder to the strainer and stir with a whisk to sift the ingredients into the bowl. (If any small bits remain in the strainer, add them to the mixture in the bowl.) Add the pepper if using; whisk to aerate the mixture, and set aside.

3. Make the chia gel: Put the ground chia seeds into a small bowl. Pour the hot water over the chia and set aside for 1 minute. Whisk for 30 seconds. (The paste will be thick.)

4. Whisk the nondairy milk into the chia paste until combined. Let sit for 5 minutes and whisk again. Whisk in the maple syrup and vanilla until combined. Let sit for 5 minutes and whisk again.

5. Add 5 tablespoons of the sugar and whisk vigorously for 1 minute to "cream" the sugar. Add the coconut oil and whisk until thoroughly incorporated. Add to the dry ingredients and mix with a silicone spatula until no traces of dry ingredients remain.

6. Mix the chocolate chunks into the dough—it will be shiny and thick but soft. Set aside for 15 to 20 minutes at room temperature to allow the dough to thicken, stirring every five minutes.

5. Shape the cookies: Put ⅓ cup of the remaining sugar into a shallow dish. Scoop the dough in a measuring tablespoon and push off into the sugar with a teaspoon. Roll the pieces in the sugar until thoroughly coated. Add more sugar as needed. Lift the cookies onto the parchment-lined baking sheet, placing them 2 inches (5 cm) apart. Press to flatten.

6. Place the baking sheet into the oven; immediately reduce the heat to 350°F / 180°C, and bake for 11 minutes until the cookies are puffed and set. The cookies are soft when they come out of the oven but will firm as they cool.

7. Place the baking sheet on a wire rack. Wait 10 minutes until the cookies are cool, then run a spatula underneath to release.

SERVING
Cold cookies offer up the crunch of hardened chocolate chunks, and warm cookies are gooey.

KEEPING
Store the cookies in a covered tin or jar, layers separated by parchment, for up to two days. Freeze for up to one month.

Double Chocolate Chunk Cookies

After what seemed like unending tests, I finally got the chewy, soft, chocolate chunk–studded chocolaty cookie I was dreaming about. Using coconut oil in solid form is important to the success of these cookies, which fairly beg for an ice-cold glass of your favorite nondairy milk. I can eat just one of these cookies, but it is not especially easy. If you do not have mini chunks, use regular size vegan chocolate chips: mini chips will not work. My assistant Megan's boyfriend Marty named these the "eat every day forever" cookies.

MAKES ABOUT 16 (1-INCH / 2.5-CM) COOKIES

1 ½ teaspoons / 3 grams ground chia

1 tablespoon / 15 ml water, at room temperature

¼ cup plus 1 tablespoon / 42 grams organic all-purpose flour

¼ cup plus 1 tablespoon / 44 grams organic whole wheat pastry flour

¼ cup / 25 grams Dutch-process cocoa powder

¼ teaspoon / 1.25 grams aluminum-free baking powder

⅛ teaspoon fine sea salt

¼ cup / 54 grams coconut oil, solid

¼ cup / 50 grams organic granulated sugar

¼ cup / 39 grams organic whole cane sugar or coconut sugar, ground in a blender until powdered

1 teaspoon / 5 ml pure vanilla extract

2 tablespoons / 30 ml pure maple syrup, Grade B or dark amber

Heaping ½ cup / 103 grams vegan mini chocolate chunks or vegan chocolate chips

1. Position a rack in the center of the oven and preheat to 350°F / 180°C. Line a baking sheet with parchment paper.

2. Put the ground chia in a small bowl. Pour the water over the chia. Set aside for 5 minutes undisturbed and then whisk hard. The chia gel will be lumpy at first but will smooth out as it hydrates. Whisk a few more times while you sift the dry ingredients.

3. Place a wire mesh strainer over a medium bowl. Add the all-purpose flour, pastry flour, cocoa, baking powder, and salt to the strainer and stir with a whisk to sift the ingredients into the bowl. (If any small bits remain in the strainer, add them to the mixture in the bowl.) Whisk to aerate the mixture.

4. In a deep mixing bowl, beat together the coconut oil and both of the sugars with an electric mixer, starting on low speed then moving to high. Beat until no solid oil remains. (If the oil is very cold, this can take a few minutes.) Whip the chia gel with a fork and add to the bowl with the vanilla. Beat until thoroughly combined.

5. Add about one third of the dry ingredients to the bowl and beat on low until combined. Repeat with the remaining thirds until all the dry ingredients are incorporated.

6. Stir the maple syrup and chocolate chunks into the batter with a silicone spatula.

7. Scoop the dough into a measuring tablespoon and pack tightly. Roll between your hands into a ball. (This will get messy!) Wipe your hands on paper towels as needed. Drop the cookies onto the parchment-lined baking sheet

and press to about 2 inches / 5 cm in diameter. Bake on the middle rack for 9 minutes for a softer cookie and 10 minutes for a crisper but still chewy cookie. The cookies are soft when they come out of the oven but will firm as they cool.

8. Place the baking sheet on a wire rack. Cool the cookies to room temperature.

KEEPING

Store the cookies in a covered tin or jar at room temperature for up to two days. Freeze for up to one month.

CHAPTER SIX

Pies and Tarts

There's nothing like a homemade pie—except a homemade tart! The good news is that both are as easy as pie when you follow my step-by-step instructions for tender vegan pastry dough made with heart-healthy extra-virgin olive oil. This new recipe produces a crust that is tender and flaky and features a much simpler technique for getting the dough into the pie pan—a method that has revolutionized my pie making. The recipes in this chapter run the gamut from the unabashedly sweet, rich, and gooey Chocolate Pecan Pie, to the fresh and tart Bittersweet Chocolate and Lemon Tartlets, to the decadent "lost recipe" Nesselrode Pie made with chestnut purée. Most of the components for these and all the pies and tarts can be made ahead and some can even be frozen, too.

Fran's Rulebook for Successful Pies and Tarts

Note: The same techniques apply for pastry crusts made in a pie or tart pan.

1. Read the recipe all the way through and plan your time: make note of the detailed guides for preparing the components ahead of time, especially making and resting the pastry dough.

2. Prepare your *mise en place*: gather the equipment and prepare the pans, chill the oil and water, grind the sugar, chop or melt the chocolate, soak or roast and cool the nuts, soak the agar.

3. Position the oven racks correctly for pie crusts (start on bottom rack, move to the middle) and cookie crusts (middle rack).

4. Preheat the oven and allow enough time for the oven to reach the correct temperature. An oven thermometer is essential.

5. Measure ingredients carefully using the correct measuring utensil and method. The recipes in this book use the *"whisk, dip, and sweep"* method of measuring dry ingredients unless otherwise noted (see Sidebar page 63).

6. Handle the pastry dough as little as possible.

7. Finish the edges of your pie crust.

8. Bake, cool, and store pie crusts following the directions in each recipe exactly.

TROUBLESHOOTING	
The blind-baked pie dough cracked	Brush with some melted chocolate to glue
A piece broke off the side of the cookie crust	Lean it on your piece of pie

THE RECIPES

Tender Olive Oil Pastry Dough

Almond Cookie Crust

Raw Nut Crust

Chocolate Pecan Pie

Nesselrode Pie

Raw Chocolate Fudge and Mandarin Orange Tart

Raspberry Chocolate Silk Tart

Chocolate Coconut Cream Pie

Bittersweet Chocolate and Lemon Tartlets

Black Bottom Banana Cream Pie

Tender Olive Oil Pastry Dough

This update to my classic flaky pastry dough resulted from experiments with my favorite mild-tasting olive oil. I was delighted to discover that icy cold olive oil, just enough ice water, and two rest periods in the refrigerator to relax the gluten—this is where the magic happens!—created perfect pastry dough for sweet or savory pies and tarts. This crust is not difficult to make, but proper handling and careful attention to the directions are essential to its success.

A tender pie crust requires oil that is icy-cold but still liquid. Measure the amount of oil you need at room temperature and pour it into a small freezer-proof container. Cover and freeze for 20 to 25 minutes, or until the oil has become slightly thicker. Check the oil as it chills; you do not want it to get so cold that it solidifies. Don't be fooled by the consistency: frozen, solidified oil will not mix into the flour mixture properly. If the oil has chilled too long and is solid, allow it to liquefy at room temperature (this will take 20 minutes, more or less) and chill it again. Remember to set a timer!

Note: After the ingredients are mixed, the dough rests for 45 minutes to 4 hours—but after 4 hours the dough will be too greasy to use and will have to be discarded.

MAKES ONE (9 TO 9½-INCH / 23 TO 24-CM) PIE CRUST, TART CRUST, OR FREEFORM TART

¾ cup plus 1 tablespoon / 108 grams organic all-purpose flour

¾ cup / 103 grams organic whole wheat pastry flour

½ teaspoon fine sea salt

¼ cup plus 1 tablespoon / 75 ml mild tasting extra-virgin olive oil, ice-cold, plus more at room temperature to grease the pie pan

1 teaspoon / 5 ml apple cider vinegar

2 to 2½ tablespoons / 30 to 38 ml ice water

1. Place a wire mesh strainer over a medium bowl. Whisk the flours in their containers to aerate, and measure the all-purpose flour and pastry flour into the strainer using the *"whisk, dip, and sweep"* method (page 63). Add the salt to the strainer and stir with a wire whisk to sift the ingredients into the bowl. (If any small bits remain in the strainer, add them to the mixture in the bowl.) Whisk to aerate the mixture.

2. Drizzle the cold oil over the flour mixture. Using a silicone spatula, toss until the oil is coated with flour. Do not break up the irregular fat pieces that form. These lumps are equivalent to the solid shortening used in conventional recipes and help to create a flaky crust.

3. In a small dish, stir the vinegar into 2 tablespoons of the ice water. Drizzle the liquid over the mass of dough and shake the bowl; this will get the water into the dough without extra handling—handling as little as possible is one of the important rules of making pie dough. Toss gently, using the spatula, until all the flour is moistened and a rough mass of dough holds together. Do not over mix. It is unlikely that more water will be needed, but if it is, use only as much as needed so that the dough holds together. Do not squeeze or press the dough into a round at this point.

4. It's easier to roll half the dough at a time (and easier to find refrigerator space for 2 smaller pieces.) Turn half the dough at a time onto a large

(recipe continues)

piece of plastic wrap. Enclose the dough lightly, allowing enough space for it to move freely. Pass a rolling pin over the dough until it is about 1 inch / 2.5 cm thick. Repeat with the other half. If you have extra-wide plastic wrap, you may wrap the dough in one piece. Rest the wrapped dough in the refrigerator for 45 minutes or up to 4 hours.

5. Shape the crust: Unwrap the dough but do not discard the plastic wrap. Cut off small pieces of dough with a sharp knife. (The pieces do not have to be uniform in size.) Scatter the pieces over the bottom of the pan and on the sides.

6. Cover the pan with a piece of plastic wrap. Flatten the pieces of dough with your fingertips by spreading them out until they form an even layer that covers the bottom and sides of the pan. Patch with extra dough as needed. Even out the dough by pressing on it with a flat-bottomed ½-measuring cup.

7. If using a pie pan, flute the edges. If using a tart pan, press the dough straight up the sides. Press lightly on the top edges of the pan with the cup to smooth the top ridge. Clean the outside of the pan of any dough. Wrap the dough in the pan lightly in plastic and refrigerate for 40 minutes or up to 4 hours before baking. Set a timer, and don't let it go longer than 4 hours.

8. Blind bake the crust: Preheat your oven to 425°F / 220°C while the pie dough rests in the refrigerator. Position one rack in the lower third of the oven and another in the center.

9. Put the pie or tart pan on a baking sheet and remove the plastic wrap. Do not prick the dough. Cut a square of parchment paper slightly larger than the pie pan. Crumple the paper to make it more flexible, and place it on the pie dough. Put a piece of heavy duty foil on top of the parchment paper, shiny side down, and fill with pie weights or dried beans used for this purpose.

10. Bake on the lower rack for 17 minutes. Remove the baking sheet from the oven and very carefully remove the beans in the foil and the parchment. Unless the dough is completely dry, without any shine of oil, return the dough to the oven for 5 minutes. Do not bake longer or the crust will crack. (Should this happen, brush a little melted chocolate over the cracks to seal when the pie crust is cooled.) Remove the pan from the oven and cool completely on a wire rack before filling.

KEEPING

The baked crust can be kept loosely wrapped overnight at room temperature.

Almond Cookie Crust

Combine finely ground nuts with flour, sweetener, and flavorings; bind the mixture with just enough fat; press the crumb into a removable-bottom tart pan; bake, and let cool. That's all you need to do before you can load this tender crust up with any unbaked creamy filling or even ice cream. Using a removable-bottom tart pan makes the prettiest presentation, but you can bake the crust in a well-oiled pie pan instead.

MAKES ONE (9 TO 9½-INCH / 23 TO 24-CM) CRUST OR SIX (4-INCH / 10-CM) TARTS

½ cup / 64 grams organic all-purpose flour

½ cup / 70 grams organic whole wheat pastry flour

½ teaspoon ground cinnamon

¼ teaspoon fine sea salt

¾ cup / 106 grams whole unpeeled almonds, toasted and cooled (page 19)

¼ cup / 60 ml mild tasting extra-virgin olive oil or organic neutral vegetable oil

¼ cup / 60 ml pure maple syrup, Grade B or dark amber

1½ teaspoons / 7.5 ml pure vanilla extract

⅛ teaspoon almond extract

1. Line a baking sheet with parchment. Place a 9-inch / 23-cm tart pan with a removable bottom on a baking sheet. A nonstick pan is highly recommended; and it still needs to be lightly oiled. If using a regular pan, coat thoroughly with oil or cooking spray.

2. Place a wire mesh strainer over a medium bowl. Add the all-purpose flour, pastry flour, cinnamon, and salt to the strainer and stir with a whisk to sift the ingredients into the bowl. (If any small bits remain in the strainer, add them to the mixture in the bowl.) Whisk to aerate the mixture.

3. Grind the almonds to a fine meal in a food processor. Do not process longer or the nuts will be oily. Stir the ground almonds into the flour mixture.

4. Whisk the oil, maple syrup, and vanilla and almond extracts in a small bowl until completely combined. Pour over the dry mixture and mix with a silicone spatula until the crumbs are evenly moistened and a small amount squeezed between your fingers sticks together. In the unlikely case that it does not, add a little more maple syrup. If it is still too dry, add a little more oil.

5. Spoon the dough into the tart pan. Place a piece of plastic wrap directly on the crust and use a flat-bottomed glass or cup to press the dough into an even layer on the bottom and up the sides of the pan, making the bottom a little thicker than the sides. Refrigerate for 15 minutes. While it chills, position a rack in the center of the oven and preheat the oven to 375°F / 190°C.

6. Place the baking sheet on the center rack, and immediately reduce the temperature to 350°F / 180°C. Bake for 15 to 18 minutes, or until the sides are lightly browned and the bottom looks evenly dry. The crust may puff up in a few spots, but do not be concerned. Just push the high spots down lightly after the crust is removed from the oven.

7. Set the baking sheet on a wire rack. Do not touch the sides of the crust—they are soft and easily broken when hot, but become firm as the crust cools.

8. Release the sides after 5 minutes: Holding the sides with a dry kitchen cloth, lift the tart pan onto a jar or can. The sides will slip right off. Carefully move the tart crust to the wire rack and cool to room temperature. Refrigerate or freeze until cold before filling.

Raw Nut Crust

I never expected a raw nut crust to become one of my favorite crusts, but the ease of making this one and its lovely flavor converted me. This flourless crust is not baked. It is simply formed and pressed into a removable bottom tart pan using the same method as the Almond Cookie Crust (page 155). Instead of baking, you freeze the crust until it is firm. For a truly raw option, use alcohol-free vanilla extract.

    Note: It is essential to use a tart pan with a removable bottom. A pan with a nonstick finish does not need to be oiled.

MAKES ONE (9 TO 9½-INCH / 23 TO 24-CM) CRUST OR SIX (4½-INCH / 11-CM) TARTS

5 ounces / 142 grams walnuts (or use another nut)

3 ounces / 85 grams raw unpeeled whole almonds

¼ cup / 60 ml agave syrup or pure maple syrup, Grade B or dark amber

1 tablespoon / 15 ml coconut oil, melted

1 teaspoon / 5 ml pure vanilla extract

½ teaspoon ground cinnamon

½ teaspoon fine sea salt

1. Place a 9 to 9½-inch / 23 to 24-cm tart pan with a removable-bottom on a parchment-lined sheet pan. The parchment will catch any dough that may spill over when you press the crust. It is much easier to move a removable-bottom pan when it is on a sheet pan.

2. Chop the walnuts and almonds coarsely in a food processor by pulsing the processor on and off a few times, then process to a fine meal. Do not process longer or the nuts will get oily.

3. Add the maple syrup, oil, vanilla, cinnamon, and salt and process just long enough for the ingredients to become moistened. Press a small amount in your fingers; it should stick together. If not, process again very briefly.

4. Spoon the dough into the tart pan. Place a piece of plastic wrap directly on the crust and use a flat-bottomed glass or cup to press the dough into an even layer on the bottom and up the sides of the pan, making the bottom a little thicker than the sides. Use about 4½ tablespoons / 70 ml of crumb for each 4½-inch / 11-cm tart pan. Freeze the crust before filling.

Chocolate Pecan Pie

Pecans, which are native to North America, are one of the healthiest nuts. But the typical filling of the classic American pecan pie is super-sweet and made with a trifecta of ingredients we are increasingly determined to avoid: eggs, sugar, and corn syrup. Pour them into a pie crust made with saturated fats and we are confronted with a dessert that is as unhealthy as the pecans are healthy. What to do? I started by looking at the best for inspiration—the exemplary chocolate pecan pie in Maida Heatter's *Book of Great Chocolate Desserts*—and eventually created this recipe for a tender, cholesterol-free pie crust that holds a thick and chewy, chocolate-laced, abundantly nutty filling sweetened with maple and rice syrups. Miraculously, the pie even tastes fresh after three days in the refrigerator, and it freezes beautifully, too. You will need to plan ahead, since the pie crust is baked and cooled before it is filled and the nuts roast slowly for thirty-five minutes in a low oven. (This can be done ahead of time; see Sidebar.) The pie filling takes about twenty-five minutes of cooking, and you do need to pay attention.

MAKES ONE (9-INCH / 23-CM) PIE, 8 TO 12 SERVINGS

- ½ cup / 120 ml brown rice syrup, warmed in the jar until liquid (page 23)
- 1 cup / 240 ml pure maple syrup, Grade B or dark amber
- 1 tablespoon / 15 ml freshly squeezed and strained lemon juice
- ³/₈ teaspoon fine sea salt
- 3 tablespoons / 52 grams smooth cashew butter
- ¼ cup plus 1 tablespoon / 31 grams Dutch-process cocoa powder, sifted
- 2 tablespoons / 30 ml almond milk, soymilk, or coconut milk beverage
- 2½ ounces / 71 grams dark chocolate (66 to 70%), finely chopped
- 3½ cups / 364 grams slow-roasted pecans, cooled (see Sidebar, page 159)
- 1 teaspoon / 5 ml pure vanilla extract
- 1 teaspoon / 5 ml almond extract
- 1 Tender Olive Oil Pastry Dough pie crust, blind baked and cooled (page 152)

1. Make the filling. Pour the rice syrup and the maple syrup into a large heavy-bottomed saucepan with high sides. Bring the syrups to a boil over medium heat, stirring with a long silicone spatula. Syrups expand and climb the sides; be careful to avoid a boil-over mess on your stovetop or a serious burn. Reduce the heat to low, but expect the syrups to continue to bubble. Adjust the heat as needed so that small bubbles rise to the surface almost continuously. You do not need to be concerned about the mixture reaching a particular temperature, but it needs to boil slowly for 6 minutes.

2. Add the lemon juice and then the salt. The syrups will bubble furiously when the salt is added, so be careful. Simmer on the lowest heat for 1 minute. Adjust the heat as needed and cook at a low boil for 8 minutes.

3. Put the cashew butter into a small heatproof bowl. Add ¼ cup / 60 ml of the hot syrup mixture to the nut butter and stir vigorously until combined. Repeat with another 2 tablespoons / 30 ml of the hot syrup mixture. Set aside the now-tempered nut butter.

4. Whisk half of the cocoa powder into the remaining hot syrup until dissolved and then whisk in the other half until dissolved. Adjust the heat so that the mixture boils very gently for 6 minutes.

5. Position the oven racks so one rack is in the lowest third and the other is in the top third of the oven; preheat to 425ºF / 220˚C.

6. Whisk half of the tempered nut butter into the syrup. The mixture may appear curdled but will become smooth as you whisk. Repeat with the rest of the tempered nut butter.

(recipe continues)

7. Add the nondairy milk and simmer 5 minutes. Add the chopped chocolate. Wait a minute for the chocolate to melt. Add the nuts and stir with a silicone spatula until the spatula is coated.

8. Remove the saucepan from the heat and stir in the vanilla and almond extracts. Pour the filling into a heatproof shallow dish and cool on the counter for about 10 minutes, or until it is barely warm. Don't refrigerate the filling or it will become too thick to spread into the crust.

9. Place the pre-baked crust on a baking sheet to make moving the pie in and out of the oven easy. The bottom of the pie crust will set fastest on a dark sheet, making it a great choice for baking pies (and a poor choice for baking cookies, as the bottoms will burn).

10. Spoon the filling into the crust. Spread the filling—it will be thick and sticky—with a small offset spatula or spoon. Make sure the pecans are distributed evenly. You can move them around with a fork if need be.

11. Bake the pie on the lower oven rack for 15 minutes. Reduce the heat to 400°F / 200°C and move the baking sheet to the upper rack. Bake for 15 to 20 minutes, or until the filling is bubbling. (The filling will appear soft, but will become firm as it cools.)

12. Remove the baking sheet from the oven and set it on a wire rack. Wait 10 minutes before moving the pie pan directly onto a wire rack.

SERVING

It might be hard to wait, but the pie needs to cool completely before slicing. This will take about 2 hours. Slice and serve the pie at room temperature. If the pie has been refrigerated or frozen, allow it to come to room temperature. It will be fudgy after about 10 minutes. Or, warm the pie first in a low (225°F / 110°C) oven if you like yours a little gooey. Any way you choose, it tastes rich enough to be served without any accompaniment.

KEEPING

Cover the pie in plastic wrap and refrigerate for up to three days, or wrap tightly in two layers of plastic wrap and freeze for two months. While a room temperature pie slices easily, you will get the neatest slices when the pie is cold.

Slow-Roasted Pecans

Slow-roasting pecans for 35 minutes in a 275°F / 140°C oven takes far longer than the standard directions for roasting nuts (see page 19), but you will be rewarded with a more concentrated pecan flavor. Slow roast the pecans in quantity. Cool to room temperature. Put the nuts into a zipper-lock bag and close tightly. Slip the bag into a second bag and seal, pressing out all the air. Freeze the nuts for up to four months.

Nesselrode Pie

Until I was in culinary school, the only chestnuts I ever had were mixed into holiday stuffing at the home of my Italian friends, the Melottis. When I first tried them in a dessert—chestnut crêpes stuffed with a chocolate-chestnut purée— I fell in love with the starchy *castagna*. I had forgotten about those crêpes until an unyielding desire to make a chocolate chestnut pie led me to the fascinating lore surrounding the Nesselrode, a "lost recipe" no longer available in bakeries or restaurants. According to *Larousse Gastronomique*, Nesselrode is a chestnut-based pudding named after the nine-teenth-century Russian Count Nesselrode, but there is no mention of the pie: a Bavarian cream pie flavored with candied chestnuts, rum, and mixed candied fruit ("tutti-frutti"). Prior to World War II, Hortense Spier made Nesselrode Pie for her brownstone restaurant right in my neighborhood, New York City's Upper West Side. I never got to taste her pie but can imagine it clearly. What follows is my take on this elusive, fabulous dessert, veganized and chocolate-enhanced.

Note: There are quite a few components but all can be made in advance and the result is worth the time and expense. And, if you don't want to make a pie—make Nesselrode Pudding!

Here's my suggested game plan for the components in order of how far ahead you can prepare them.

1. Make the Bittersweet Chocolate Ganache Glaze; refrigerate up to 5 days ahead or freeze for up to 1 month. Warm in a water bath if made ahead.
2. Make the Vegan Orange Blossom Honey; refrigerate up to 2 weeks ahead.
3. Make the Basic Thick Cashew Cream; refrigerate up to 2 days ahead.
4. Make the Chestnut Purée; refrigerate up to 2 days ahead. (The purée is used to make both the White and Dark Chocolate Chestnut Creams.)
5. Make the White Chocolate Cream Filling; refrigerate up to a day ahead.
6. Make the White Chocolate Chestnut Cream (1 cup / 240 ml White Chocolate Cream Filling plus 1 cup / 240 ml Chestnut Purée); refrigerate for 1 hour or up to 2 days.
7. Make the Dark Chocolate Chestnut Cream (1/2 cup / 120 ml of Chestnut Purée plus 1/2 cup / 120 ml of Bittersweet Chocolate Ganache); refrigerate for 1 hour or up to 2 days.
8. Make the Tender Olive Oil Pastry Dough pie crust up to a day ahead; keep wrapped at room temperature up to 1 day ahead

MAKES ONE 9-INCH / 23-CM PIE

1 recipe (2/3 cup / 160 ml) Vegan Orange Blossom Honey (page 287)

9 ounces / 255 grams roasted and shelled chestnuts, divided

1/2 cup / 120 ml Basic Thick Cashew Cream (page 284)

2 tablespoons / 30 ml rum (optional)

1 recipe White Chocolate Cream Filling (page 281)

1 recipe Bittersweet Chocolate Ganache Glaze (page 264), warmed in a water bath until liquefied

1 Tender Olive Oil Pastry Dough pie crust (page 152), blind baked and cooled

MAKE THE CHESTNUT PURÉE

1. Pour 2/3 cup / 160 ml of the honey into a medium saucepan and warm gently over low heat until liquefied. Add the

chestnuts and stir until coated. Raise the heat to medium and bring to a boil. Reduce the heat to low and cover the saucepan. Simmer for 10 minutes.

2. Uncover the pan and use a fork to break the chestnuts into smaller pieces. Cook over medium-low heat for 5 minutes, adjusting the heat as needed to keep the mixture at a low boil.

3. Reduce the heat to low and add the cashew cream. Cook until the mixture returns to a low boil and remove from the heat.

4. Spoon the mixture into a food processor. Process until almost but not completely puréed. (Some small pieces of chestnuts are desirable.) Add the rum if using. Spoon the purée into a bowl, and refrigerate until needed. You should have about 1½ cups / 360 ml.

5. Mix 1 cup / 240 ml of the Chestnut Purée into 1 cup / 240 ml of the White Chocolate Cream Filling until incorporated. Reserve the remaining White Chocolate Cream Filling for garnish. Refrigerate the White Chocolate Chestnut Cream in a covered container for at least 3 to 4 hours to allow the flavors to develop. The cream will thicken and can be made up to 2 days ahead.

6. In a small bowl, mix ½ cup / 120 ml of the Bittersweet Chocolate Ganache into the remaining ½ cup / 120 ml of the Chestnut Purée. (It is fine if you don't have exactly ½ cup; use all that remains.) Set aside or refrigerate until needed.

ASSEMBLE THE PIE

1. Spread 1¼ cups / 300 ml of the Bittersweet Chocolate Ganache on the bottom and up the sides of the prepared pie crust. Refrigerate briefly until the ganache is set, about 10 minutes.

2. Spoon about half of the White Chocolate Chestnut Cream into the crust.

3. Spoon the Dark Chocolate Chestnut Cream over the white cream and smooth the top.

4. Spoon the remaining White Chocolate Chestnut Cream on top, mounding the cream higher in the center.

5. Drizzle the top of the pie with the remaining ¼ cup / 60 ml of the Bittersweet Chocolate Ganache. Refrigerate the pie for at least 4 hours before serving.

SERVING

For the neatest slices, cut the pie when it is cold. For the best flavor, serve at room temperature. Add a dollop of the reserved ½ cup / 120 ml of White Chocolate Cream Filling to each serving.

KEEPING

Refrigerate the pie, loosely covered, up to one day ahead of serving.

VARIATION

Nesselrode Pudding: To make a Nesselrode pudding instead of a pie, just skip the crust and layer the components in one large serving dish or individual parfait glasses.

Raw Chocolate Fudge and Mandarin Orange Tart

Raw chocolate fillings often taste like date paste–flavored cocoa, which can be fine, but is certainly not a rich and silken chocolate fudge. This filling is different. Luxuriously smooth and definitely chocolate, I'm betting that whether or not you are a raw enthusiast, this recipe will find its way into your file of favorite chocolate fillings. The filling can be spread into the baked Almond Cookie Crust, too, for a change of pace, and Dutch-process cocoa can be used. It won't be a raw recipe, but it will be very good.

Note: As is the case with all dried fruits, the relative dryness is variable so the amount of liquid needed to hydrate the fruit and the quantity of purée is not absolute.

MAKES ONE (9 TO 9½-INCH / 23 TO 24-CM) TART

5 ¼ ounces /149 grams pitted Medjool dates (about 9 large)

½ cup / 120 ml hot water, or more if the dates are very dry

3 ounces / 85 grams cocoa butter, chopped into small pieces (substitute coconut oil)

2 teaspoons / 10 ml freshly squeezed lemon juice, strained

¾ cup plus 1 tablespoon / 60 grams raw cacao powder

¼ cup plus 2 tablespoons / 90 ml pure maple syrup, Grade B

¼ cup plus 2 tablespoons / 105 grams cashew butter, jarred or homemade

2 tablespoons / 30 ml agave syrup, or use an additional 2 tablespoons of maple syrup

2 teaspoons / 10 ml alcohol-free vanilla extract

¾ teaspoon / 3.75 ml tamari or nama shoyu (unpasteurized soy sauce)

1 Raw Nut Crust (page 156), prepared in a removable-bottom tart pan and frozen

6 to 7 mandarin oranges, for garnish

⅛ teaspoon lemon salt or any flaked finishing salt, for garnish

1. Rinse the dates and soak them in the hot water for 20 minutes. (The dates can soak overnight in the refrigerator if this is more convenient.) When the dates are very soft, mash them with a fork to a paste. Remove any skins that slip off easily.

2. While the dates soak, melt the cocoa butter: Put the cocoa butter into a small heatproof bowl. Fill a small skillet with enough very hot water so that it will reach about one third of the way up the side of the bowl. Carefully place the bowl into the skillet and stir the cocoa butter until it is melted. Be careful not to splash even a single drop of water into the melting cocoa butter. If using coconut oil, use the same method. Keep the cocoa butter warm.

3. Purée the dates, any remaining soaking liquid, and the lemon juice in a food processor until smooth. Measure out 6 tablespoons of date paste and refrigerate any extra for another use. Return the 6 tablespoons of paste to the processor.

4. Add the melted cocoa butter, cacao powder, maple syrup, cashew butter, agave syrup, vanilla, and tamari. Process for 2 to 3 minutes, until the filling is absolutely smooth, stopping the machine a few times to clean the sides.

5. Spread the filling in the tart crust and smooth the top. Refrigerate the tart for about 2 hours until the filling is firm.

FINISH THE TART

Remove the tart from the refrigerator. Peel the mandarins, removing all the white pith. Separate the oranges into their natural sections. Arrange the slices over the filling in concentric circles, so that most of the filling is covered but some of the chocolate peeks through. Sprinkle with the lemon salt or other finishing salt if you wish.

SERVING

Slice the tart cold for the neatest slices. Serve at room temperature.

KEEPING

The tart can be refrigerated without the orange segments for up to three days or loosely wrapped overnight with the fruit.

Freeze the tart without the oranges, tightly wrapped, for up to one month. Defrost unwrapped in the refrigerator. Add the oranges before serving.

Raspberry Chocolate Silk Tart

Raspberries and dark chocolate look beautiful together and taste even better, especially if you follow my few caveats to ensure the chocolate will not overpower the raspberry flavor. I don't cook the raspberries, and I use frozen unsweetened berries instead of fresh—even in season—when making the purée (called a coulis). Mixing a good-quality seedless raspberry jam or straining the seeded kind into the purée adds even more raspberry flavor. Save the fresh seasonal berries for the top of the tart, using a mix of golden and red berries for a stunning presentation.

You have two crust options for this tart: The Tender Olive Oil Pastry Dough, which makes a more delicate tart, and the Almond Cookie Crust, which I prefer for its crunch. Both crusts can be made ahead, as can the raspberry filling, which can be refrigerated and warmed very gently until pourable.

MAKES ONE 9 TO 9½-INCH / 23 TO 24-CM TART

7 ounces / 198 grams dark chocolate (66 to 70%), finely chopped

³⁄₄ cup / 180 ml canned unsweetened full-fat coconut milk, well-stirred (do not use light)

¼ cup / 50 grams organic granulated sugar

¼ teaspoon fine sea salt

½ cup / 61 grams frozen raspberries

3 tablespoons plus ¼ cup / 105 ml seedless raspberry jam, divided

1 tablespoon / 15 ml framboise (optional)

1 tablespoon / 15 ml mild tasting extra-virgin olive oil

1 teaspoon / 5 ml pure vanilla extract

1 Tender Olive Oil Pastry Dough pie crust (page 152), blind baked in a tart pan with a removable bottom and cooled, or 1 Almond Cookie Crust (page 155), baked in a tart pan with a removable bottom and cooled

½ to 1 pint / 250 to 500 ml fresh raspberries, red and golden, for garnish (optional)

2 to 3 tablespoons / 12 to 18 grams organic confectioners' sugar for garnish (optional)

1. Put the chocolate into a medium heatproof bowl and set aside until needed.

2. In a small saucepan, bring the coconut milk, sugar, and salt to a low boil over medium heat, stirring a few times as the milk heats. Strain the hot milk through a fine mesh strainer directly into the chocolate. Swirl the bowl to ensure the chocolate is submerged. Cover the bowl with a plate and set aside undisturbed for 4 minutes.

3. While the chocolate mixture sits, make the raspberry coulis: Mash the frozen raspberries with a fork and press them through a small fine mesh sieve into a small bowl (you should have about 3 tablespoons / 45 ml of purée). Stir 3 tablespoons / 45 ml of the raspberry jam and the framboise (if using) into the purée and set aside until needed. The coulis (purée) can be made ahead; use at room temperature.

4. Uncover the bowl of chocolate and whisk from the center out until the ganache is smooth. Stir the raspberry coulis, olive oil, and vanilla into the ganache.

ASSEMBLE THE TART

Mix the remaining ¼ cup / 60 ml of the raspberry jam and ⅓ cup / 80 ml of the ganache in a small bowl and spread over the crust. Chill briefly until the ganache is set. Pour the remaining raspberry ganache into the tart crust, and slowly rotate the tart to level the top. Chill until the filling is set.

SERVING

Garnish the tart with fresh raspberries and a sprinkling of confectioners' sugar if you like. For the neatest slices, cut the tart cold, but serve at room temperature.

KEEPING

The assembled tart can be refrigerated for up to two days. Add the fruit and sugar garnish just before serving.

Chocolate Coconut Cream Pie

My dad, Sonny, liked all desserts, but his favorite was pie, specifically any coconut cream pie served in a Greek diner. Dad was proud when I became a "cook," and since he liked chocolate too, I am sure he would have been okay with my "messing" with his beloved pie. In fact, Dad, who cooked in a homeless shelter when he was in his eighties, might have even baked this pie for the people he served; proudly telling everyone it was his daughter's recipe. If so, I'd tell him what I tell you: Start the pie the day before you plan to serve it, since both of the cream components need to be refrigerated overnight. The pie crust needs to be baked and cooled before being filled, but can be made in advance and frozen until needed. The Blender Coconut Cream component of this recipe was inspired by Elizabeth Falkner's recipe for Magic Coconut Cream.

Here's my suggested game plan for the components in order of how far ahead you can prepare them:

1. Bake and cool the Almond Cookie Crust. Refrigerate overnight or freeze for up to 1 month.

2. Make the Blender Coconut Cream and refrigerate overnight

3. Make the base for the Chocolate Coconut Cream Filling, and refrigerate overnight

4. Combine the two creams, and refrigerate for 2 hours before assembling the pie

MAKES ONE 9-INCH / 23-CM PIE OR TART

1 recipe Almond Cookie Crust (page 155)

BLENDER COCONUT CREAM

2/3 cups / 160 ml canned unsweetened full-fat coconut milk, well-stirred (do not use light)

3 tablespoons / 27 grams coconut sugar or organic granulated sugar

3/8 teaspoon guar gum

Pinch fine sea salt

CHOCOLATE COCONUT CREAM FILLING

1 can (13.5 to 14-ounce / 400 to 414-ml) unsweetened full-fat coconut milk, at room temperature (do not use light)

2 tablespoons / 14 grams organic cornstarch

1 1/4 teaspoons / 3 grams agar powder

1/4 cup plus 1 tablespoon / 63 grams organic granulated sugar

3 tablespoons / 45 ml coconut oil, divided

1/8 teaspoon fine sea salt

1 tablespoon / 15 ml pure vanilla extract, divided

7 ounces / 198 grams dark chocolate (66 to 71%) finely chopped, divided

1/2 cup / 38 grams toasted shredded coconut, plus more for garnishing the pie

MAKE THE BLENDER COCONUT CREAM

1. Put the coconut milk, coconut sugar, guar gum, and salt in a blender on low for 30 seconds. Increase the speed to high (or full power) and blend for 2 minutes.

2. Pour into a container. Cover and refrigerate for at least 5 hours or overnight. The cream will thicken slightly as it chills. (Think melted marshmallow cream.)

MAKE THE CHOCOLATE COCONUT CREAM FILLING

1. Pour the coconut milk into a medium saucepan and whisk until the milk is thoroughly mixed.

2. Pour ½ cup of the coconut milk from the saucepan into a small bowl. Add the cornstarch and agar and whisk until dissolved. This is called a slurry. Set aside until needed.

3. Add the sugar, 1 tablespoon / 15 ml of the coconut oil, and the salt to the coconut milk in the saucepan and whisk to combine. Cook over low heat, whisking a few times until you see a few wisps of steam.

4. Whisk the cornstarch-agar slurry to release any starch that may have settled to the bottom. Whisking constantly, add the slurry to the saucepan.

5. Cook to a boil over medium-low heat, whisking constantly. Adjust the heat as needed so that the mixture boils slowly for 1 minute. The mixture will be thick.

6. Remove the saucepan from the heat. Stir in 1 teaspoon of the vanilla. Pour the cream base into a 3 to 4-cup shallow container and cool to room temperature.

7. Cover and refrigerate for at least 5 hours (or up to 2 days) before proceeding. The cream should be quite firm.

8. Remove the cream base from the refrigerator. Spoon the cream base into a food processor and pulse on and off a few times. Add 1 teaspoon / 5 ml of the vanilla and process until the cream is perfectly smooth, but not longer.

9. Spoon the cream into a 3 to 4-cup bowl. Cover and refrigerate for 15 to 30 minutes while you prepare the chocolate. The cream can be refrigerated overnight at this point if you wish to finish later.

10. Put a small heatproof bowl into a skillet and pour enough water into the skillet so that the water reaches halfway up the bowl. Put 5 ounces of the chocolate and the remaining coconut oil into the bowl.

11. Bring the water to a simmer over medium-low heat. Reduce the heat to low, adjusting the heat as needed to keep the water at a bare simmer. Stir the chocolate and the coconut oil with a silicone spatula a few times until the chocolate is smooth. The melted chocolate will be relatively liquid.

12. Stir the remaining teaspoon of vanilla into the chocolate. Remove the bowl from the skillet and dry the bottom.

13. Remove the cream base from the refrigerator. Fold the melted chocolate into the cream. A few streaks of white are fine.

14. Fold the Blender Coconut Cream into the Chocolate Coconut Cream Filling. Again, a few streaks of the white cream remaining are fine. Fold in the toasted coconut. Refrigerate the cream for an hour to set or up to overnight.

ASSEMBLE THE PIE

Melt the remaining 2 ounces of chocolate following the procedure in step 10. Spread a thin layer of the chocolate on the bottom and halfway up the sides of the pie crust. Refrigerate the crust for about 10 minutes until the chocolate hardens. Spoon the filling into the prepared pie crust, mounding it higher in the center, and sprinkle with more of the toasted coconut to garnish. Refrigerate the pie for 1 hour before serving.

SERVING

For the neatest slices, cut the pie when it is cold, but serve at room temperature for the best flavor.

KEEPING

Refrigerate the pie loosely wrapped for up to one day.

Bittersweet Chocolate and Lemon Tartlets

Almonds and dark chocolate are a favorite combination of mine and are the foundation of these tartlets. The crunchy Almond Cookie Crust is glazed with lemon olive oil ganache, which is made from the Lemon Olive Oil Truffle recipe. (I told you ganache is versatile!) The rich yet light lemon filling is nestled between bottom and top coatings of ganache.

Notes: The refreshingly tart filling is made with both lemon juice and zest. Use a Microplane zester to make very fine zest from non-sprayed or organic lemons (see Sidebar page 21). Follow the recipe for the Lemon Olive Oil Truffles, but use the still-pourable ganache instead of allowing the ganache to set for making truffles. However, if you have more ganache than is needed to paint the crust and glaze the tart, well, make some truffles to serve with the tart.

Here's my suggested game plan for the components in order of how far ahead you can prepare them.

1. Make the Lemon Olive Oil Truffle recipe; do not shape into truffles; refrigerate for up to 3 days or freeze up to 1 month ahead.

2. Make and cool the Almond Cookie Crust (6 tartlets or 1 tart); refrigerate up to 2 days ahead.

3. Spread a thin layer of ganache, (about a tablespoon for the tartlets and ⅓ cup for a 9-inch / 23-cm tart) on the bottom of the crust. More ganache will be spread over the filling. Refrigerate up to 2 days ahead.

4. Make the Lemon Cream, and as soon as the cream is no longer hot, pour into the crusts.

MAKES SIX (4 TO 4½-INCH / 10 TO 11-CM) TARTLETS OR ONE (9 TO 9½-INCH / 23 TO 24-CM) TART

1 recipe Lemon Olive Oil Truffles (page 44: make the ganache but do not form truffles)

1 recipe Almond Cookie Crust (page 155), blind baked and cooled

2 tablespoons / 5.5 grams agar flakes

½ cup plus ⅓ cup / 220 grams canned unsweetened full-fat coconut milk, well-stirred (do not use light)

½ cup / 111 grams organic granulated sugar

1½ tablespoons / 4.5 grams finely grated lemon zest, divided

Pinch fine sea salt

⅛ teaspoon turmeric (optional, for color)

2 tablespoons / 14 grams arrowroot

¼ cup / 60 ml fresh lemon juice, unstrained

¼ teaspoon pure vanilla extract

2 ounces / 57 grams whole almonds, chopped, for garnish (substitute plump berries)

1. Measure the agar into a medium saucepan. Pour ½ cup / 120 ml of water over the agar, but do not stir or heat. Set aside for 15 minutes or longer to allow the agar to soften. This will help the agar dissolve thoroughly and easily.

2. Warm the ganache, if necessary, until liquefied in a water bath. Spread the crusts with a thin layer of ganache. Refrigerate until the ganache is set.

3. Bring the agar-water to a boil over medium heat, stirring a few times. Reduce the heat to low. Cover the saucepan and simmer for 5 to 6 minutes, stirring a few times to release any bits of agar that may be stuck on the bottom of the pan. Check a spoonful of liquid for specks of agar. Cover and simmer longer, if necessary, until the agar is completely dissolved.

(recipe continues)

4. Add the coconut milk, sugar, half the zest, salt, and turmeric if using. Cover the pan and simmer for 10 minutes.

5. In a small bowl, dissolve the arrowroot in ¼ cup / 60 ml of water. Whisking continuously, add the dissolved arrowroot to the saucepan. Cook just until the mixture boils and immediately remove from the heat. The mixture will be thick.

6. Stir the remaining zest, lemon juice, and vanilla into the cream. Pour into a shallow bowl, stirring a few times until the cream is not hot but still warm. The cream sets up fast. Pour into the ganache-glazed tart crust.

7. After about 10 minutes, the filling should be soft but not set. Pour enough of the ganache over the cream to cover each tartlet (1 ½ to 2 tablespoons / 22.5 to 30 ml), but let a bit of the bright yellow cream peek through. (Alternatively, you can drizzle the ganache decoratively.)

SERVING

Paint a line of ganache on each serving plate. Set a tartlet or slice alongside. Sprinkle with chopped almonds.

KEEPING

The tarts can be refrigerated, with or without glaze, for up to two days, but the sheen on the ganache will be nicest if it is applied shortly before serving. Cover lightly with parchment once the glaze has set.

Black Bottom Banana Cream Pie

Layer thick fudge sauce, slices of ripe banana, and a creamy chocolate filling in a baked pie crust, top with more sliced bananas and a hearty drizzle of fudge sauce, and you have a dessert that looks and tastes like it came from a magazine. All the components can be made ahead, so you need only to assemble, chill, and serve.

MAKES ONE (9-INCH / 23-CM) PIE

1 can (13.5 to 14 ounces / 400 to 414 ml) unsweetened full-fat coconut milk, well-stirred (do not use light)

½ cup / 111 grams organic granulated sugar

¼ cup / 28 grams organic cornstarch

¼ teaspoon ground cinnamon

¼ teaspoon fine sea salt

Pinch freshly grated nutmeg

½ cup / 120 ml water, at room temperature, plus more for coconut milk (see step 1)

2 teaspoons / 5 grams agar powder

1½ ounces / 45 grams vegan chocolate chips

2 teaspoons / 10 ml pure vanilla extract

1½ recipes (1½ cups / 360 ml) Thick Fudge Sauce (page 277)

1 recipe Tender Olive Oil Pastry Dough (page 152) blind baked in a 9-inch / 23-cm pie pan and cooled, or 1 Almond Cookie Crust (page 155)

2 to 3 ripe (but not overripe) bananas

1. Add enough water to the coconut milk to make 2 cups / 480 ml and set aside.

2. Sift the sugar, cornstarch, cinnamon, salt, and nutmeg into a medium saucepan. Stir the coconut milk into the mixture.

3. Add ½ cup / 120 ml of the water and the agar powder and cook over medium heat, whisking frequently until the mixture boils. Reduce the heat as needed so that the pudding cooks at a low boil for a full minute to allow the taste of the raw cornstarch to cook out and thicken the pudding.

4. Add the chocolate chips and vanilla extract to the pudding, stirring gently until the chocolate melts.

5. Spoon the pudding into a bowl and cool completely at room temperature before assembling the pie.

ASSEMBLE THE PIE

1. Spread 1 cup / 240 ml of the Thick Fudge Sauce over the prepared pie crust.

2. Slice 2 of the bananas into rounds and arrange over the fudge sauce, pressing them down lightly.

3. Spoon the cooled pudding over the bananas and smooth the top.

4. Slice the remaining banana on the diagonal and arrange the slices on top of the pie. Drizzle with the remaining Thick Fudge Sauce. Refrigerate the pie for 3 or 4 hours to set.

SERVING

For the neatest slices, cut the pie while it is cold. Serve slightly chilled or at room temperature.

KEEPING

Refrigerate the pie loosely wrapped for up to two days.

CHAPTER SEVEN

Creams, Puddings, and Gels

Some of these desserts are light and some are rich, a few are gelled, and only two require turning on the oven, but all of them are creamy—even though no cream or eggs are used. In this chapter, learn how gelatinizing agents like agar, arrowroot, tapioca, and organic cornstarch combine with tofu, avocado, nondairy milks, and nuts to make impossibly smooth, velvety, and satisfying desserts like Chocolate Panna Cotta (an elegant and light company dessert) and Chocolate Chunk Banana Bread Pudding (that makes brunch a special occasion). And who doesn't like Almost-Instant Chocolate Pudding? As a rule, creams and mousses benefit from advance preparation and often need time to set up properly. Nearly every recipe can be made ahead and refrigerated or frozen.

Fran's Rulebook for Successful Creamy Desserts

1. **Read the recipe all the way through and plan your time for all the components.**

2. **Prepare your *mise en place*: gather the equipment, grind the sugars, chop or melt the chocolate, soak the dates, chia seeds, or nuts, drain the tofu, soften the agar, make a starch slurry.**

3. **Measure the ingredients carefully using the correct utensil and method.**

4. **Always test the consistency of the cream or mousse before finishing the recipe, and adjust as needed.**

TROUBLESHOOTING	
The cream or pudding is softer than intended	Call it custard and serve in small bowls. Next time do the recommended test.
The cream or pudding tastes gritty or lumpy	Cook the sugar into the liquid until dissolved. Next time make sure to use finely ground sugar. Make sure the starch slurry is thoroughly dissolved before being added to the saucepan.
The texture is stringy	Do not substitute starches, and stir and boil only as directed.

THE RECIPES

Chocolate Panna Cotta

Almost-Instant Chocolate Pudding

Coconut Milk Black Rice Pudding

Warm Chocolate Cashew Cream Pudding

Magic Chocolate Mousse

White Chocolate and Matcha Mousse Pudding

Mocha Crème Brûlée

Chocolate, Date, and Coconut Chia Pudding

Chocolate Chunk Banana Bread Pudding

Chocolate Jello Shots

Chocolate Panna Cotta

I still remember marveling at the silken texture of the first *panna cotta* ("cooked cream" in Italian) I ate in Italy more than twenty-five years ago. Ever since, I have been meaning to create a vegan version that eliminates the heavy cream or half-and-half and gelatin of traditional versions, but without too many flavors to interfere with the delicate texture. After much experimentation, I'm delighted with the results.

It is a good idea to review how to work with agar before you begin. Measeure it carefully and follow the directions exactly in Chapter One, page 15, to get a creamy dessert and not a ramekin of rubbery Jell-O. Soaking the agar and then simmering it in a small amount of water instead of the coconut milk ensures it will dissolve. (If you prefer a softer, more pudding-like panna cotta, cut the agar by ½ teaspoon.) Simmering the sugar and the cocoa will dissolve the sugar and rid the cocoa of any powdery uncooked taste. Covering the saucepan ensures that the liquid will not boil away, creating a too-firm gel. Finally, testing the final texture before filling and refrigerating the ramekins takes only 10 minutes, and in my recipes, like in my classes, testing is never optional.

You may find it convenient to cook the panna cottas early in the day, unmold them, and leave them at room temperature for up to two hours before serving. This is possible with this recipe because agar gels do not melt at room temperature.

MAKES 4 SERVINGS

3 ½ teaspoons / 3.5 grams agar flakes

½ cup / 120 ml water, at room temperature

1 ½ cups / 360 ml canned unsweetened full-fat organic coconut milk, well-stirred (do not use light)

¼ teaspoon ground cinnamon

Pinch fine sea salt

2 tablespoons / 18 grams organic whole cane sugar, ground in a blender until powdered

¼ cup / 25 grams Dutch-processed cocoa powder, sifted

2 tablespoons / 30 ml pure maple syrup, Grade B or dark amber, or agave syrup

½ ounce / 14 grams dark chocolate (66 to 70%), finely chopped

¾ teaspoons / 3.75 ml pure vanilla extract

¾ cup fresh berries or any other seasonal fresh fruit, for serving

½ to ⅔ cup / 120 to 160 ml All-Purpose Chocolate Syrup (page 274), for serving

1. Set four 3-ounce / 89-ml ramekins on a tray or small baking sheet.

2. Measure the agar into a medium saucepan. Pour the water over the agar, but do not stir or heat. Set aside for 15 minutes or longer to allow the agar to soften. This will help the agar dissolve thoroughly and easily.

3. Bring the liquid to a boil over medium heat, stirring a few times. Reduce the heat to low. Cover the saucepan and simmer 5 to 6 minutes, stirring a few times to release any bits of agar that may be stuck on the bottom of the pan. Check a spoonful of liquid for specks of agar. There should be none or very little. Cover and simmer on lowest heat if necessary, until the agar is completely dissolved.

4. Slowly whisk the coconut milk into the dissolved agar. Add the cinnamon and salt and cook covered over low heat for 2 minutes, raising the lid and whisking a few times. Raise the heat slightly and bring to a gentle boil.

5. Reduce the heat to the lowest simmer and add the sugar. Simmer for 1 minute. Add the cocoa powder 1 tablespoon at a time, whisking until dissolved after each addition. Simmer covered for 4 minutes. Add the maple syrup and reduce the heat as needed to allow the mixture to cook at a low boil for 1 minute. Add the chocolate and stir until it has melted

6. Remove the saucepan from the heat and add the vanilla extract.

7. Test the texture of the panna cotta: Spoon a scant tablespoon of the liquid panna cotta into a small cup and refrigerate for 10 minutes. Keep the saucepan covered, but whisk the mixture a few times while the test is chilling. If the panna cotta tastes too firm, add a small amount of water (as little as 1 tablespoon, or more as needed) and repeat the test until you are satisfied with the texture.

8. Pour the panna cotta into the ramekins. Refrigerate the ramekins for 15 to 30 minutes, until the panna cotta is set, or up to a day ahead of time. (Panna cotta does not have to be served molded. Pour the still-liquid panna cotta into wine glasses and top with All-Purpose Chocolate Syrup and berries.)

SERVING

Unmold the panna cottas: Run a thin knife around the sides of the ramekins to release the panna cotta. Dip the bottom of one ramekin at a time in very hot water for about 30 seconds. Cover with a small serving plate, invert the plate and the ramekin, and the panna cotta should release. If it does not, dip the ramekin in hot water again. After unmolding, spoon a few tablespoons of All-Purpose Chocolate Syrup around the panna cottas and garnish with berries.

Almost-Instant Chocolate Pudding

I grew up eating my mom's chocolate pudding from a boxed mix. It was a bit lumpy and thick, with rubbery chocolate pudding skin (I have permission from my dear mother to tell this story), but it was warm and chocolate and homemade, and I liked it. On the East Coast there was only one brand worth knowing: My-T-Fine, the premium pudding. It wasn't exactly instant, since the mix had to be cooked with milk, and somewhere along the way Mom decided cooking pudding and washing the pot was not worth the effort. We moved over to Jell-O brand—really instant pudding: put the mix in a bowl, add milk, and mix with a rotary egg beater. Still, if the bowl wasn't deep enough (especially if I was doing the mixing) it spattered, and then there were still beaters to wash. And the finished pudding was cold! That's why I love this recipe so much: in the same time it took my mom to make sad chocolate pudding, you can make Almost-Instant Chocolate Pudding that is real chocolate pudding the way we always wanted it to be: warm, thick, and chocolaty.

Note: The cornstarch is crucial to get the right texture for this pudding. Using another starch thickener, such as my usual first choice arrowroot, would result in pudding with a soft and unpleasant texture.

MAKES 2¼ CUPS / 540 ML
FOR 3 TO 4 SERVINGS

½ cup / 111 grams organic granulated sugar

¼ cup / 28 grams organic cornstarch (do not use arrowroot, see Note)

¼ cup / 25 grams Dutch-process cocoa powder

¼ teaspoon fine sea salt

1½ cups plus 6 tablespoons / 450 ml vanilla soymilk, vanilla almond milk, or vanilla coconut milk beverage

1½ ounces / 43 grams dark chocolate (59 to 62%), chopped into small pieces

1 teaspoon / 5 ml pure vanilla extract

1. Sift the sugar, cornstarch, cocoa powder, and salt through a wire mesh strainer into a medium saucepan. Slowly stir in the milk. Keep stirring until no trace of any of the dry ingredients is visible. The idea is to make sure the cornstarch is completely dissolved before you turn on the heat.

2. Cook over medium-high heat, whisking frequently, until the mixture begins to thicken and is close to a boil. This can take as long as 12 minutes. Adjust the heat as needed to get a full boil, but don't let it be so high that the bottom scorches. As soon as the pudding starts to boil, it will thicken to pudding consistency. Immediately lower the heat and boil gently for another minute, stirring frequently with a silicone spatula.

3. Remove the saucepan from the heat. Gently stir in the chocolate with the silicone spatula until the chocolate is melted and incorporated. Stir in the vanilla.

4. Spoon the pudding into a bowl. It will be set and ready to use in about 30 minutes at room temperature, but it can be refrigerated for up to 24 hours. If you refrigerate it, cover the surface with plastic wrap, making sure the wrap adheres to the pudding to prevent a skin from forming.

Coconut Milk Black Rice Pudding

Chinese black rice, coconut milk, and sugar are the main ingredients in Southeast Asian breakfast puddings. But you do not need to be in Southeast Asia to find any of the ingredients. I have enjoyed the taste and texture of Chinese black rice, which is also called forbidden rice, on the Upper West Side of Manhattan for years. (The rice turns purple when it cooks and stays toothsome.) Its abundant antioxidants are another bonus. Soak the rice in room temperature water for a day to shorten the initial cooking time, or make some extra plain black rice for your next meal and use the leftovers for this recipe, as I did. One day, I opened a container of black leftover rice and was sure I heard it say, "I'd rather be a creamy chocolate coconut milk pudding!" A recipe was born.

MAKES 2 CUPS / 480 ML
FOR 2 TO 4 SERVINGS

½ cup / 119 grams black rice, rinsed

1 ¾ cups / 420 ml boiling water

½ teaspoon / 3 grams fine sea salt

1 can (13.5 to 14-ounce / 400 to 414-ml) unsweetened full-fat coconut milk (do not use light)

½ cup / 111 grams organic granulated sugar

¼ cup plus 1 tablespoon / 31 grams Dutch-process cocoa powder (or use natural)

2 tablespoons / 18 grams organic whole cane sugar, ground in a blender until powdered

1 tablespoon / 15 ml pure vanilla extract

½ cup / 60 grams roasted pistachio nuts (salted or unsalted), shelled and peeled

1 cup / 100 grams mango (about ½ a large mango), diced in ½ inch pieces

1. Rinse the rice in a sieve under cold running water. Bring the rice, water, and salt to a boil in a heavy medium saucepan, uncovered, over medium-high heat. Stir, cover, and reduce the heat to low. Cook for about 30 minutes or until the rice is just tender and most of the water has been absorbed. Remove from the heat and let stand, covered, for 10 minutes.

2. Add the coconut milk, granulated sugar, cocoa powder, and whole cane sugar to a blender and blend on high for 1 minute.

3. Pour the chocolate coconut milk into the rice and cook over medium-low heat until bubbles appear around the sides. Adjust the heat up or down so that the liquid bubbles slowly around the sides and on the surface. Stir frequently with a silicone spatula until the liquid has thickened and reduced, about 30 to 40 minutes. The pudding will look like a soupy chili but will thicken as it cools. Remove from the heat and stir in the vanilla.

4. Cool to room temperature, then spoon into a container and refrigerate for 2 hours and up to 24 hours before serving.

SERVING

Mix half the pistachios and half the mango into the pudding. Sprinkle the rest of the mango and nuts over the top.

Warm Chocolate Cashew Cream Pudding

Because cashew cream reduces faster than heavy cream when it is cooked, this creamy chocolate pudding is pot-to-bowl in about five minutes (assuming you have my Basic Thick Cashew Cream already made and stored in the refrigerator or freezer as I recommend).

MAKES 3 TO 4 SERVINGS

1 recipe (about 1 3/4 cups) / 420 ml Basic Thick Cashew Cream (page 284)

2 tablespoons / 12 grams Dutch-process cocoa powder, sifted

2 tablespoons / 26 grams organic granulated sugar

2 ounces / 57 grams dark chocolate (62 to 68%), finely chopped, or use vegan chocolate chips for a sweeter pudding

1 teaspoon / 5 ml pure vanilla extract

Dark chocolate shavings, for garnish (optional)

1. In a small saucepan, heat the cashew cream gently over low heat until just warm to the touch. Add the cocoa powder and sugar, and stir until dissolved. Remove the saucepan from the heat.

2. Add the chocolate and the vanilla and stir until the chocolate is melted.

SERVING

Spoon the warm pudding into small dishes and serve immediately garnished with some chocolate shavings.

KEEPING

The pudding can be made ahead and refrigerated in a covered container for up to three days. It tastes good chilled or at room temperature.

Magic Chocolate Mousse

I first attempted making a chocolate mousse just after I was married. The women in my circle of friends were all cooking from Julia Child's *Mastering the Art of French Cooking*, and although I was an absolute novice in the kitchen, I somehow decided to make Julia's *Mousseline au Chocolat*—the one known for its velvety texture and for using *every* pot in the house—as dessert for my in-laws. (My mother-in-law, Wini, was a very accomplished cook.) What a production! This nervous bride in her tiny kitchen sweated the big and small stuff—Julia's mousse is based on butter instead of heavy cream and specifies beating separated egg whites over hot water—and I remember little more than being exhausted . . . and getting compliments.

Later, I learned the vegan version of chocolate mousse—basically tofu and melted chocolate chips—and knew it could be vastly improved. I always stress the importance of keeping water and chocolate apart, but this recipe is one exception. Years ago, I began teaching a chocolate-water glaze and mousse. Both were splendid, and velvety smooth *when* the recipe worked, but too often the result was a bowl of gritty chocolate. Since the outcome was unpredictable, I took the recipe out of class and put it into a "figure it out" folder. My hunch was that the problems stemmed from the variations in percentage and quality of chocolate I was given to use in class, as well as over-stirring and overheating the chocolate. This can happen easily when too many cooks stir the pot. When last year I saw a similar recipe on Food52, from Hervé This, the author of *Molecular Gastronomy: Exploring the Science of Flavor*, my hunches were confirmed and my recipe updated. Since the mousse is made with water instead of milk or cream, the chocolate taste is very pronounced: be sure to choose one you love!

Note: If the mousse is whisked too vigorously and it becomes grainy, set the bowl over a water bath and stir a few times until it is it liquid again. Whisk again over the bowl of ice, more slowly and for a shorter time. Stop whisking when the mousse is soft; it thickens as it sets.

MAKES 6 TO 8 SERVINGS

1 cup plus 2 tablespoons / 270 ml water, at room temperature, or fruit juice

12 ounces / 340 grams high-quality dark chocolate (68 to 70%), finely chopped

⅛ teaspoon fine sea salt

1 tablespoon / 15 ml liqueur (optional) or fruit juice

1 tablespoon / 15 ml mild tasting extra-virgin olive oil

2 teaspoons / 10 ml pure vanilla extract

Berries or toasted nuts for serving

1. Have 2 bowls ready, one large filled about halfway with ice cubes, and one medium that fits inside the large bowl with the ice. Set the bowls aside (don't nest them yet) while you melt the chocolate into the water.

2. Pour the water into a saucepan. Add the chocolate and salt, and whisk over medium-low heat until the chocolate is completely melted into a smooth sauce. Stir in the liqueur or additional water. Stir in the olive oil. Pour the chocolate sauce into the medium bowl and set it into the ice-filled bowl.

3. Add the vanilla. Whisk *only* until the chocolate has lightened in color and has thickened enough so that tracks from the whisk are visible, then stop. The mousse will be soft at this point, like soft chocolate whipped cream, but will become more dense as it sets. This happens quickly.

4. Spoon into small cups. Allow the mousse to set for 10 minutes or longer, until the texture is just right for your taste.

SERVING

Garnish each serving with some berries or chopped nuts, or a dollop of any of the creams in Chapter Eleven.

KEEPING

Cover with plastic wrap and refrigerate for up to 2 days. Serve at room temperature. Whisk to lighten if the texture has become too firm for your taste.

White Chocolate and Matcha Mousse Pudding

The tart citrus flavor of the kumquat is a good foil for the rich, sweet unusual cream, and the pistachios add crunch and color. A chewy crispy mochi waffle is an optional but delightful component. The matcha adds an astringent note, but the pudding is sweet. Small portions are the way to go.

Note: Vegan white chocolate chips, which can be purchased in most kosher stores and from many online shops (see Resources page 290) do not fit into the category of high-quality chocolate, but sometimes these chips are the only thing that will do. Like most chocolate chips, they will take longer to melt, so the procedure for melting the chocolate in this recipe does not follow the standard water bath procedure. Dissolving matcha in boiling water makes it taste bitter, so use very hot water instead.

MAKES 4 TO 6 SMALL SERVINGS

6 ounces / 171 grams vegan white chocolate chips or another vegan white chocolate

¼ cup / 60 ml almond milk or coconut milk beverage

4 ounces / 116 grams silken tofu (one third of a 12.3-ounce/ 349 gram aseptic box), drained

1 tablespoon / 3 grams matcha

2 tablespoons / 30 ml very hot water (steaming, not boiling)

½ teaspoon pure vanilla extract

4 to 6 (1-inch / 2.5-cm) pieces mochi, for garnish (optional)

2 to 3 thinly sliced kumquats, for serving

2 to 3 tablespoons / 28 grams chopped pistachio nuts, for serving

MAKE THE PUDDING

1. Put a small heatproof bowl into a skillet and pour enough water into the skillet so that the water reaches halfway up the bowl. Put the chocolate into the bowl.

2. Bring the water to a simmer over medium-low heat. Reduce the heat to low, adjusting the heat as needed to keep the water at a bare simmer. When the chocolate looks softer and glossy, stir with a silicone spatula until it is completely melted and smooth.

3. Add 1 tablespoon of the almond milk or coconut milk beverage, stirring slowly and constantly until incorporated. The chocolate may look curdled as the milk is added but will smooth out as you stir. Repeat with the remaining milk. Turn off the heat. Keep the bowl of white chocolate in the skillet while you prepare the other ingredients.

4. Put the tofu into a small bowl and mash with a fork.

5. In a separate small bowl, dissolve the matcha in the hot water. Pour the dissolved matcha over the mashed tofu and stir to combine. Add the tofu mixture and the vanilla to the melted white chocolate.

6. Using an immersion blender, purée the white chocolate-tofu mixture in the bowl until absolutely smooth. Stir to check for any orphan pieces of tofu and purée again if necessary.

7. Pour the pudding into individual 4-ounce / 120-ml glasses (you will have enough for 4 to 6 glasses) and refrigerate for at least 4 hours or overnight until softly set. The flavor of the matcha will continue to develop as the pudding chills.

MAKE THE MOCHI GARNISH (OPTIONAL)

Cut the mochi into squares. Heat a waffle iron. Place each square of mochi on the waffle iron, leaving 2 inches between each piece so the waffles stay separate. Close the cover and cook until the waffles are crisp on the outside and lightly browned. The waffles will release easily from the iron when they are ready. (Alternatively, cook the mochi squares on a parchment-lined sheet pan in a 450°F / 230°C oven for 8 to 10 minutes until puffed.)

SERVING

Garnish each pudding with sliced kumquats and a sprinkling of the chopped pistachio nuts. Set a piece of mochi waffle, if using, into each glass on an angle.

KEEPING

Refrigerate in the individual serving glasses or in a covered container for up to three days.

CREAMS, PUDDINGS, AND GELS
185

Mocha Crème Brûlée

The rich custard underneath the crispy caramelized sugar shell of a traditional *Crème Brûlée* is made with egg yolks, heavy cream, and white sugar and baked in a water bath. The rich custard underneath the crispy caramel of this vegan version is not baked and is far easier to make. Cashew cream and agar powder are the secret agents.

Notes: The crème part of the recipe is made in a high-speed blender, such as a Vitamix. The mixture will actually boil. If you do not have a high-speed blender, see the stovetop variation that follows (page 188). You will need a blowtorch to make the *brûlée* topping. A propane torch can be bought at your local hardware store and smaller ones are available at most housewares shops. If you don't have a torch, you can caramelize the topping under the broiler set on high, but watch very carefully to ensure that the sugar does not burn.

MAKES 4 SERVINGS

1½ cups / 360 ml Basic Thick Cashew Cream (page 284)

¼ cup / 60 ml pure maple syrup, Grade B or dark amber, or agave syrup

3 tablespoons / 39 grams organic granulated sugar

2 tablespoons plus 1 teaspoon / 14 grams Dutch-process cocoa powder

2 tablespoons / 9 grams instant coffee or espresso granules

⅜ teaspoon agar powder

Pinch fine sea salt

1 teaspoon / 5 ml pure vanilla extract

Organic granulated sugar, ground superfine in a blender, for the *brûlée* (use enough to make a 1/4-inch coating for each layer)

1. Combine the cashew cream, maple syrup, sugar, cocoa, instant coffee, agar, and salt in the high-speed blender in the order listed. Blend on low to start, and then increase the speed to high. Blend 2 to 3 minutes until the mixture boils. Open the cap in the cover and you will see a lot of steam. The mixture will sputter since it is thick when it boils. The container is hot. Be careful.

2. Add the vanilla extract and blend low for 15 seconds.

3. Pour into four 3-ounce / 89-ml ramekins or other heatproof dishes. Cool to room temperature uncovered. A very thin skin will form. This is desirable.

4. Cover with plastic wrap but do not allow the wrap to directly touch the surface. Refrigerate until ready to add the brûlée topping, which should be done no more than 30 minutes before serving.

TO BRÛLÉE

1. Be very careful when using a blowtorch: Don't hold the ramekins in your hands. Place the ramekins on a flameproof surface, such as a baking sheet. Sprinkle a thin, even layer of superfine sugar over the surface.

2. Use a blowtorch to dissolve and caramelize the sugar, constantly moving the flame over the surface. Don't hold the blowtorch too close to the surface or the sugar will burn.

3. If a thicker layer of caramelized sugar is desired, it's better to do two separate layers rather than one thick one.

(recipe continues)

SERVING

Wait 5 to 10 minutes before serving.

KEEPING

The crème brûlées can be made ahead and refrigerated without the sugar topping for up to three days.

VARIATION

Stovetop Brûlée: Mix the maple syrup, ¼ cup water, sugar, instant coffee, agar, and salt in a small saucepan and bring to a boil over medium heat, whisking frequently.

Reduce the heat to low and add the cocoa. Whisking constantly, cook until the cocoa is dissolved.

Add the cashew cream. Increase the heat to medium and cook to a boil, stirring frequently with a silicone spatula. Make sure to stir the bottom of the saucepan. Remove from the heat and add the vanilla.

Pour into four 3-ounce / 89-ml (about 3-inch-wide) ramekins and set aside to cool. When the pudding is cool, add enough of the granulated sugar (about 1 tablespoon per each ramekin for a ¼-inch / 6-mm layer) and brûlée.

Chocolate, Date, and Coconut Chia Pudding

No Chia Pet jokes here, friends, just the facts about a healthy chocolate breakfast or anytime pudding. Chia is an edible seed that comes from the desert plant *Salvia hispanica*. The seeds are even richer in Omega-3 fatty acids than flax seeds, and since chia is so rich in antioxidants, the seeds can be stored for long periods without becoming rancid. Furthermore, unlike flax, chia seeds do not have to be ground to make their nutrients available to the body. Chia seeds provide a healthy dose of fiber as well as calcium, phosphorus, magnesium, manganese, copper, iron, molybdenum, niacin, and zinc. When mixed with liquid, the seeds form a gel, hence the creamy texture of this pudding. The chia softens into tapioca-like pearls with a slight crunch. If you like a thinner pudding, add more nondairy milk. If you like a sweeter pudding, add more maple syrup. You may be tempted to ignore the instructions to stir several times, but stirring is the difference between a hit-or-miss chia pudding and one that is so good, you may want to double the recipe.

MAKES 3 TO 4 SERVINGS

2 ounces / 60 grams pitted Medjool dates (about 4 large) or an equal amount of another variety of date

⅓ cup / 80 ml very hot water

1¼ cups / 300 ml almond milk or coconut milk beverage, divided

¼ cup plus 1 tablespoon / 26 grams dried shredded coconut, divided, plus more for garnish

2 tablespoons / 12 grams Dutch-process cocoa powder

Pinch fine sea salt

3 tablespoons / 45 ml pure maple syrup, Grade B or dark amber

¼ cup / 40 grams chia seeds, white or black

1. Put the dates in a small bowl. Pour the water over the dates and set aside for 15 minutes or until very soft.

2. While the dates soak, purée ½ cup / 120 ml of the milk, 3 tablespoons of the coconut, the cocoa powder, and the salt in a blender. Add the remaining milk and the maple syrup and blend for 30 seconds.

3. Add the dates and any soaking liquid and blend until mostly puréed (some small pieces of dates are fine).

4. Pour the mixture into a 2-cup measure. Add enough additional milk to equal 2 cups / 480 ml, if necessary.

5. Mix the chia seeds and the remaining 2 tablespoons of the coconut in a medium bowl.

6. Pour the liquid ingredients over the chia and coconut and whisk vigorously. Repeat twice at 5-minute intervals. Wait 10 minutes and whisk again.

7. Refrigerate the pudding for at least 6 hours or up to 2 days ahead. Whisk a few times, when you think of it, to prevent clumps of chia in the pudding.

SERVING

Whisk the pudding and serve in small bowls sprinkled with toasted coconut.

KEEPING

The pudding can be refrigerated in a covered container for up to two days. Whisk before serving.

VARIATION

Chocolate Espresso Chia and Coconut Pudding: Soak the dates in ⅓ cup / 80 ml strong espresso, mashing the dates into the espresso as they soften.

Chocolate Chunk Banana Bread Pudding

The humble origin of bread pudding dates back to thirteenth century England when a "poor man's pudding" was assembled from stale leftover bread, bits of fruit, and spices moistened with sweetened water. Contrast that lean and thrifty pudding with contemporary recipes often served in expensive restaurants, which are made with egg-rich breads, such as brioche or challah, baked in custards made with three or more eggs, heavy cream or whole milk, and sweetened with sugar. There's a lot to like about the technique and texture of these modern bread puddings, but clearly a recipe renovation is needed. In my version, cashew cream, coconut milk, and starch make the creamy custard, and a healthy dose of chocolate provides the wow factor. I use protein-rich, easy-to-digest sprouted bread, but any bread you like will do. Serve the pudding warm right out of the baking dish, or make it ahead and warm before serving. If you want to spice up brunch with Ms. or Mr. Sweetie, try the heart-shaped variation at the end.

MAKES 8 SERVINGS

6 slices sprouted wheat bread, or another bread

½ cup / 37 grams raw whole cashews, rinsed and soaked in boiling water to cover for 1 hour

½ can (13.5 to 14-ounce / 400 to 414-ml) unsweetened full-fat coconut milk, well-stirred (do not use light)

¼ cup plus 2 tablespoons / 76 grams organic granulated sugar

2 tablespoons / 30 ml pure maple syrup, Grade B or dark amber, or agave syrup

2 teaspoons / 10 ml pure vanilla extract

1 tablespoon / 7 grams tapioca starch or organic cornstarch

1 ripe medium-size banana

3 ½ ounces / 99 grams dark chocolate (any percentage), chopped into chunks

1. Cut the bread into roughly 1-inch / 2.5-cm chunks. Put the chunks into a large bowl and set aside until needed.

2. Drain the cashews and put them into a blender. Add the coconut milk, sugar, maple syrup, and vanilla. Blend, starting on low and increasing the speed to high for 1 minute or until the liquid is perfectly smooth. (If you have a high-speed blender, this will take about 1 minute. If using a standard blender, blend the ingredients in 2 or 3 batches until perfectly smooth.)

3. Add the tapioca or cornstarch to the blender and blend for 1 minute. Pour the liquid into a 2-cup measure and add enough water or non-dairy milk to equal 1⅓ cups / 320 ml.

4. Pour the liquid over the bread and set aside to soak about 15 minutes, stirring gently with a silicone spatula a couple of times, until the bread is soft and has absorbed most of the liquid.

5. While the bread soaks, position a rack in the middle of the oven and preheat to 375°F / 190°C. Oil the sides and bottom of an 8 x 8-inch / 20 x 20-cm baking pan.

6. Spoon the bread mixture into the prepared pan. Coarsely chop the banana and mix it into the soaked bread. Sprinkle the chocolate chunks over the top. Press some of the chocolate into the bread mixture.

7. Place the pan on the middle rack of the oven. Immediately reduce the heat to 350°F / 180°C. Bake for 15 minutes or until slightly puffed and firm to the touch. Let cool slightly before serving.

SERVING

Serve warm or refrigerate until cold. Reheat in the oven.

KEEPING

The bread pudding is best eaten the same day but may be refrigerated in a covered container overnight.

VARIATION

Bread Pudding Hearts: After the pudding has baked and cooled, refrigerate it until firm. About 30 minutes before you are ready to eat, remove the pudding from the refrigerator and cut small heart-shaped portions, or one large heart to share. Place on a baking sheet. Preheat the oven to 350°F / 180°C. Set the table while the pudding hearts heat in the oven back to melty, chocolaty goodness, about 15 to 20 minutes.

Chocolate Jello Shots

I'm glad I didn't know how to make these in my college days; I never cared for the red and green kind at bars and parties, but these would have been hard to resist. Made with Chocolate Vodka (page 257), or any good vodka, this bracing shot is definitely not for kids. Shoot two and you'll need a designated driver.

Note: The gel sets up very quickly, so if it is too firm for your taste, just warm it in a pan briefly with a little more water until liquefied and allow to set.

MAKES 6 SHOTS

1½ tablespoons / 4 grams agar flakes

¾ cup plus 2 tablespoons / 210 ml water, at room temperature

⅓ cup / 64 grams organic granulated sugar

¼ cup / 25 grams Dutch-process cocoa, sifted

Pinch fine sea salt

¼ cup / 60 ml Chocolate Vodka (page 257), or any premium vodka

1. Measure the agar flakes into a small saucepan. Pour the water into the pan. Do not stir or heat. Set aside for 10 minutes to allow the agar flakes to soften. This will help the agar dissolve thoroughly and easily.

2. Bring the agar mixture to a boil over medium heat and reduce the heat to low. Cover the saucepan and cook for 3 minutes, lifting the lid to whisk a few times. Check a spoonful of liquid for specks of agar. There should be none or very little. Cover and simmer longer if necessary, until the agar is completely dissolved.

3. Add the sugar, cocoa powder, and salt and whisk until dissolved. Remove from the heat and add the vodka.

4. Pour into six 2-ounce / 60-ml shot glasses and refrigerate until set, about 10 minutes. Serve cold.

KEEPING

Refrigerate the shots for up to three days.

Experience all the pleasures of an ice cream parlor or Italian *gelateria* in your own home with the recipes in this chapter. True, the eggs, cream, and other types of dairy found in traditional ice cream are gone, but these vegan versions are still undeniably rich and creamy. There's a boozy Chocolate Margarita Ice Cream, crowd-pleasing Peanut Butter and Jam Fudge Swirled Ice Cream, and a whimsical fat-free Watermelon Granita with Chocolate Seeds—wiht no artificial flavors, white sugar, lactose, or cholesterol! This is ice cream bliss, especially when you pair them with any of the toppings and creams in Chapter Eleven. You can choose from recipes based on commercial nondairy milks, avocado, canned coconut milk, and cashew cream, but you will need to seek out guar gum for all of them to ensure that the ice creams are made creamy and stay that way. (I use Bob's Red Mill; see Resources page 290.) Most of the recipes require an ice cream machine, but some go straight from blender to freezer.

Fran's Rulebook for Successful Frozen Desserts

1. **Read the recipe all the way through and plan your time, especially as ice cream and some of its components need to be made well ahead of time.**

2. **Prepare your *mise en place*: gather the equipment, freeze the ice cream maker canister, grind the sugar, chop or melt the chocolate, soak or roast and cool the nuts.**

3. **It is essential to wait until the base is ice cold—two to four hours or a day ahead—before churning. (A cold base churns faster, resulting in a creamier frozen dessert.)**

4. **Put a covered container big enough to hold the churned ice cream in the freezer to chill while the ice cream churns.**

5. **For more even freezing, when using a canister-type ice cream machine, use a silicone spatula to push the ice cream back into the machine as it freezes and moves to the top.**

6. **Immediately transfer the finished ice cream to the chilled storage container.**

TROUBLESHOOTING	
Ice cream is gritty	Allow the ice cream to melt. Blend, strain, and chill it thoroughly, then process again.
Ice cream is too soft	Freeze longer in the machine or freezer and serve in chilled dishes.

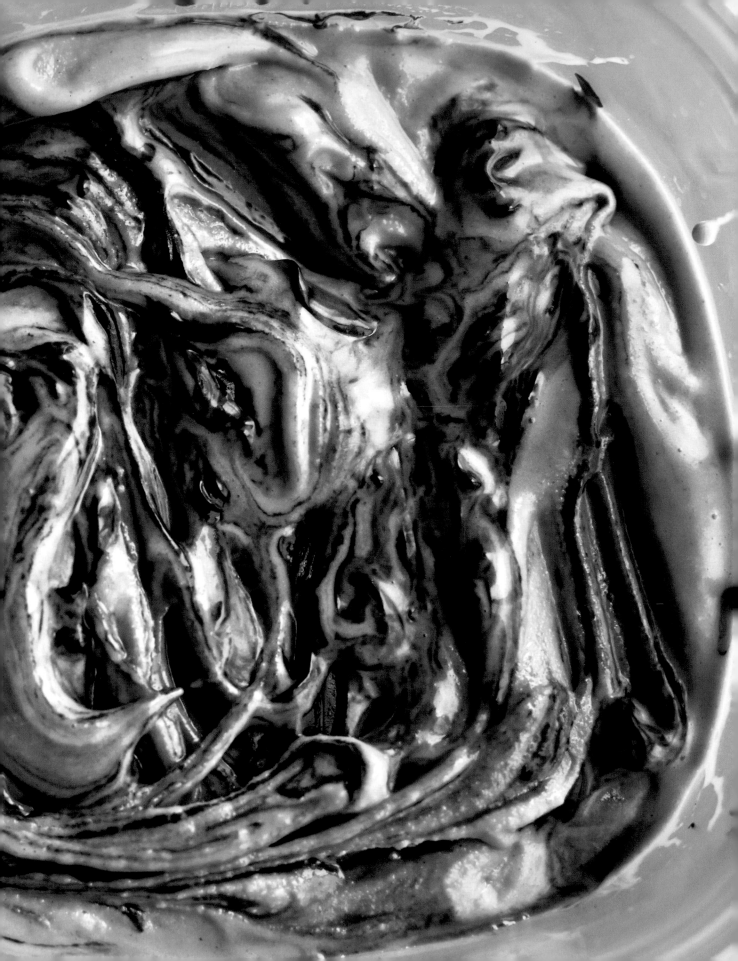

THE RECIPES

Chocolate Espresso Gelato

Peanut Butter and Jam Fudge-Swirled Ice Cream

Mint Chocolate Chip Ice Cream

Chocolate Mexican-Spiced Ice Cream

Chocolate Coconut Ice Cream

Chocolate Brownie Crumble Ice Cream

Chocolate Ginger Ice Cream

Chocolate Sorbet

Chocolate Margarita Ice Cream

Watermelon Granita with Chocolate Seeds

Chocolate Espresso Gelato

Gelato, Italy's version of ice cream, contains less sugar and significantly less fat than ice cream's typical 10 to 16%. So, it is easy to see why I "heard" the gelato recipes in my head asking me to take them over to the vegan side. For my first vegan gelato, I picked one of my favorite flavor combinations—dark chocolate and espresso—and used coconut milk for the fat. (You won't be able to detect any coconut taste.) A rich, just-sweet-enough gelato is the result.

MAKES ABOUT
3 ½ PINTS / 1.6 LITERS

1 can (13.5 to 14 ounces / 400 to 414 ml) full-fat organic coconut milk, (do not use light)

3 tablespoons / 14 grams instant espresso powder

1 cup / 207 grams organic granulated sugar

½ cup / 58 grams Dutch-process cocoa powder, sifted

3 ounces / 85 grams vegan espresso-flavored chocolate, finely chopped

2 ½ teaspoons / 5 grams arrowroot

¼ cup plus 2 tablespoons / 90 ml water, at room temperature

1 teaspoon / 5 ml pure vanilla extract

Chocolate-covered coffee beans, for serving (optional)

1. Add enough water to the coconut milk to equal 3 cups / 720 ml. Pour into a medium saucepan. Have a fine sieve set over a 4-cup heatproof measure or bowl nearby.

2. Mix the espresso powder into the coconut milk. Cook over medium-low heat to a gentle boil. Add the sugar and cook to a low boil over medium heat, whisking a few times until the sugar is dissolved.

3. Whisk half the cocoa powder into the liquid until dissolved, and then whisk in the other half until dissolved. Simmer on low heat for 3 minutes, adjusting the heat as needed so that small bubbles are visible around the sides of the saucepan and occasionally in the center. Add the chocolate and stir until it is melted.

4. Strain the mixture through the sieve into the heatproof measure or bowl. Rinse and dry the saucepan. Pour the base back into the saucepan and return the liquid to a simmer over low heat.

5. In a small bowl, dissolve the arrowroot in the water. (Remember the rule: arrowroot must never be dissolved in warm or hot liquid.)

6. Whisking constantly, add the dissolved arrowroot to the simmering mixture. The mixture will thicken. Cook only to a gentle boil and then immediately remove the saucepan from the heat. Add the vanilla.

7. Pour the mixture into a 4-cup / 1-liter container and cool to room temperature. Cover and refrigerate for at least 4 hours until thoroughly chilled before churning. Chilling the base thoroughly means faster churning, which results in a creamier frozen dessert.

8. When the mixture is cold, give it a good whisk. Pour into an ice cream maker and churn according to the manufacturer's directions. It will look like soft serve when it's ready.

9. Using a silicone spatula, immediately transfer the frozen gelato to the chilled storage container. Cover tightly, and freeze for 30 to 60 minutes until the gelato is firm enough to scoop.

KEEPING

Freeze the gelato in a covered container. For the best flavor and texture, eat the gelato within one week.

SERVING

Serve the gelato in chilled dishes. Garnish with a few chocolate-covered coffee beans if you like.

VARIATION

Affogato ("drowned" in Italian) is just a shot of espresso poured over a serving of gelato. For each serving of affogato, scoop a portion of gelato into a dish and freeze it for 15 to 20 minutes so it's quite firm when you pour the espresso over it. Serve immediately.

Peanut Butter and Jam Fudge-Swirled Ice Cream

Those of us who eat peanut butter straight from the jar and know that everything is better with chocolate will love this ice cream. Thick Fudge Sauce (page 277) is mixed into the freshly made ice cream instead of being churned into the base, allowing the fudge to remain distinct. Serve this ice cream with slices of banana, and it's a sure bet that Elvis will enter the building.

MAKES ABOUT
1 ½ PINTS / ¾ LITER

1 ¾ cups / 420 ml almond milk or
    soymilk
½ cup / 135 grams no sugar added
    peanut butter, smooth or crunchy
½ cup plus 2 tablespoons / 137 grams
    organic granulated sugar
¼ cup / 60 ml seedless strawberry
    or raspberry all-fruit spread or jam
1 ½ teaspoons / 7.5 ml pure vanilla
    extract
½ teaspoon guar gum
¼ cup plus 2 tablespoons / 90 ml
    Thick Fudge Sauce (page 277), plus
    more for serving (optional)
Roasted salted peanuts, chopped
    if you like, for serving

1. Process the almond milk, peanut butter, sugar, jam, and vanilla in a blender on high for 1 minute or until completely puréed.

2. Sprinkle the guar gum directly on the mixture. Blend on low for 30 seconds, then increase the speed to high and blend for 1 minute.

3. Pour the mixture into a quart container. Cover and refrigerate for 2 to 4 hours until thoroughly chilled before churning. Chilling the base thoroughly means faster churning, which results in a creamier frozen dessert.

4. When the mixture is cold, give it a good whisk. Pour it into an ice cream maker and process according to the manufacturer's directions. It will be thick and firm when it is ready.

5. Spoon half of the ice cream into the chilled container and swirl in 3 tablespoons of Thick Fudge Sauce. Repeat with the rest of the ice cream and another 3 tablespoons of the sauce. Cover tightly and freeze for 30 minutes to 2 hours until the ice cream is firm enough to scoop.

SERVING

Serve the ice cream in chilled bowls with a sprinkling of peanuts and, if you like, a drizzle of hot Thick Fudge Sauce (page 277).

KEEPING

Freeze the ice cream in a covered container. For the best flavor and texture, eat the ice cream within one week.

Mint Chocolate Chip Ice Cream

I like avocados for their taste, texture, and healthy nutritional profile. I eat them in salads, on crusty dense bread, mashed into a chunky guacamole, or simply halved and sprinkled with lime juice and flaked sea salt. Then, there is avocado-based ice cream! You may have already enjoyed some of the naturally vegan avocado ice creams that are standard fare in Mexico and other countries, and if you have, you know the good fat in this fruit churns into ultra creamy frozen desserts. You won't notice the slightly vegetal flavor of the fruit if you use just-ripe—not very ripe—fruit. But don't worry too much: It's the chocolate and mint that you'll taste the most. As a New Yorker with limited avocado choices, I use the creamy, neutral-flavored Hass from California.

MAKES ABOUT 1 ½ PINTS / ¾ LITER ICE CREAM

1 ½ cups plus 2 tablespoons / 390 ml almond milk

1 ¼ cups / 300 ml agave syrup or pure maple syrup, Grade B or dark amber

1 cup / 150 grams just-ripe Hass avocado, mashed (about ½ an average-size fruit)

¼ cup / 25 grams Dutch-process cocoa powder

1 teaspoon / 5 ml pure vanilla extract

½ teaspoon natural mint oil or ³⁄₈ teaspoon mint extract

½ teaspoon guar gum

3 ounces / 85 grams vegan mint chocolate, finely chopped

1 recipe Mint Chocolate Ice Cream Shell (page 279), for serving (optional)

1. Process the almond milk, agave, avocado, cocoa powder, vanilla, and mint oil in a blender on high for 1 minute or until completely puréed.

2. Sprinkle the guar gum directly on the mixture. Blend on low for 30 seconds, then increase the speed to high and blend for 1 minute. Taste the mixture. The mint should be strong but not overpowering. Add more mint oil cautiously, drop by drop, if needed.

3. Pour the purée into a 2-cup / 500-ml measure. Add enough almond milk to equal 2 cups / 480 ml.

4. Pour the ice cream base into a 2-cup / 500-ml container. Cover and refrigerate the base for 2 to 4 hours until thoroughly chilled before churning. Chilling the base thoroughly means faster churning, which results in a creamier frozen dessert.

5. When the mixture is cold, give it a good whisk. Pour into an ice cream maker and churn according to the manufacturer's directions. It will look like soft serve when it is ready. Add the chopped chocolate and process for another minute or two.

6. Using a silicone spatula, immediately transfer the frozen ice cream to the chilled container. Cover tightly and freeze for at least 3 hours until the ice cream is firm enough to scoop.

SERVING

Serve the ice cream in chilled bowls. Add a few tablespoons of Mint Chocolate Ice Cream Shell if you like.

KEEPING

The ice cream will stay creamy for at least five days in the freezer.

Chocolate Mexican-Spiced Ice Cream

I like chili-seasoned foods but prefer them on the mild side. If you're like me, you will be very happy with the flavor of this ice cream, which mixes smoky sweet ancho chili powder and pungent cinnamon into a luscious chocolate base. The chocolate flavor is up front, but as the ice cream melts in your mouth, the spice makes itself known. Three-eighths of a teaspoon of chili powder is just right for those of us with milder tastes, but heat seekers should feel free to spice it up even more. I prefer to make this ice cream with Dutch-process cocoa, but if you enjoy the fruity (or, as some say, sour) taste of natural cocoa, be sure to use a high-quality brand. Note that too much heat destroys the flavor of good cocoa, so simmer on low and don't overcook.

MAKES ABOUT 2 PINTS / 1 LITER

1¼ cups / 257 grams organic granulated sugar

1 cup / 104 grams Dutch-process or natural cocoa powder (non-alkalized)

¾ teaspoon / 2 grams ancho chili powder

½ teaspoon ground cinnamon

Pinch sea salt

1 cup / 240 ml boiling water, cooled 1 minute

2 tablespoons / 30 ml agave syrup

2 teaspoons / 10 ml pure vanilla extract

½ teaspoon almond extract

1 cup / 240 ml almond milk

¼ teaspoon guar gum

3 to 4 ounces / 85 to 113 grams dark chocolate (any percentage), finely chopped and mixed with a pinch of ground cinnamon and organic granulated sugar, for garnish (optional)

1. Sift the sugar, cocoa powder, chili, cinnamon, and salt into a medium saucepan.

2. Add the hot water and whisk over low heat until the dry ingredients are dissolved and a few wisps of steam are visible on the surface.

3. Increase the heat to medium-low and add the agave. Simmer for 2 minutes, whisking frequently. Make sure to stir the bottom and sides of the pan.

4. Remove the saucepan from the heat and add the vanilla and almond extracts. Cool 5 minutes.

5. Pour the almond milk into a blender and add the guar gum. Blend on low for 30 seconds, then increase the speed to high for another 30 seconds.

6. Add the contents from the saucepan to the blender and blend for 1 minute.

7. Pour the mixture through a strainer into a bowl.

Cover the bowl and refrigerate until very cold, 3 to 4 hours or overnight.

8. When the mixture is cold, give it a good whisk. Pour it into an ice cream maker and churn according to the manufacturer's directions. The ice cream is ready when it looks like soft serve.

9. Using a silicone spatula, immediately transfer the frozen ice cream to the chilled storage container. Cover tightly and freeze for 3 to 4 hours until firm enough to scoop.

SERVING

Serve in chilled cups sprinkled with finely chopped chocolate mixed with a pinch of cinnamon and sugar.

KEEPING

Freeze the ice cream in a covered container. For the best flavor and texture, eat the ice cream within one week.

Chocolate Coconut Ice Cream

This ice cream owes its exceptionally creamy, rich, melt-in-your-mouth texture and its coconut-forward flavor to a combination of canned full-fat coconut milk, coconut sugar, and candied coconut. Cocoa powder adds the chocolate note that follows. You might want to make a double recipe of the candied coconut and sprinkle some on each serving, or just to make sure you have enough left after nibbling to add to the ice cream!

MAKES ABOUT 1 ½ PINTS / ¾ LITER

CANDIED COCONUT (Makes 2/3 cup, packed)

½ cup / 120 ml agave syrup or pure maple syrup, Grade B or dark amber

½ cup / 44 grams toasted shredded coconut (see page 100)

ICE CREAM

1 can (13.5 to 14 ounce / 400 to 414 ml) unsweetened full-fat coconut milk (do not use light)

¾ cup plus 2 tablespoons / 185 grams organic granulated sugar, ground in a blender until powdered

½ cup plus 3 tablespoons / 108 grams coconut sugar, ground in a blender until powdered

2 tablespoons / 30 ml coconut milk or almond milk beverage

½ cup plus 1 tablespoon / 66 grams Dutch-process cocoa powder

1 ½ teaspoons / 7.5 ml pure vanilla extract

Pinch sea salt

½ teaspoon guar gum

MAKE THE CANDIED COCONUT

1. Pour the agave into a small skillet with high sides. Cook to a full boil over medium heat.

2. Remove from the heat and add the coconut, stirring to coat. Cool to room temperature. The candied coconut can be refrigerated in a covered container for up to 1 month.

MAKE THE ICE CREAM

1. Add enough water to the canned coconut milk to make 2 cups / 480 ml. Pour into the blender and add the granulated sugar, coconut sugar, and the nondairy milk. Blend on high for 1 minute until the sugar is thoroughly incorporated into the liquid. Add the cocoa powder, vanilla extract, and salt and process on high for 1 minute or until completely puréed.

2. Sprinkle the guar gum directly onto the mixture. Blend on low for 30 seconds, then increase the speed to high and blend for 1 minute.

3. Pour the ice cream base into a 4-cup / 1-liter container. Cover and refrigerate for 2 to 4 hours until thoroughly chilled before churning. Chilling the base thoroughly means faster churning, which results in a creamier frozen dessert.

4. When the mixture is cold, give it a good whisk. Pour it into an ice cream maker and churn according to the manufacturer's directions. It will look like soft serve when it is ready.

5. Using a silicone spatula, immediately transfer the frozen ice cream to the chilled container. Mix the Candied Coconut into the ice cream, cover tightly, and freeze for 2 to 4 hours until the ice cream is firm enough to scoop.

SERVING

Serve the ice cream in chilled bowls straight up or drizzled with slightly warmed Chocolate Dulce de Leche (page 234).

KEEPING

Freeze the ice cream in a covered container. For the best flavor and texture, eat the ice cream within one week.

Chocolate Brownie Crumble Ice Cream

Start with Sweet Thick Cashew Cream, then add almond milk, a little sweetener, a small amount of cocoa powder, and a teeny amount of guar gum to make this remarkably creamy chocolate ice cream. Mix in chewy chunks of Very Fudgy Chocolate Chip Brownies (page 128) or the Gluten-Free Brownie Bites (page 126) and you've got an extra-special treat. Brownies stay fudgy when frozen—making them a perfect add-in for any ice cream—but any leftover cake works well, too. I've been known to blow out birthday candles on the Blow Them Away Brownie Sundae variation at the end of this recipe.

MAKES ABOUT 1½ PINTS / ¾ LITER

1½ cups / 360 ml Sweet Thick Cashew Cream (page 284)

½ cup / 120 ml almond milk

¼ cup plus 1 tablespoon / 46 grams organic coconut sugar or ¼ cup / 50 grams organic granulated sugar

2 tablespoons / 30 ml agave syrup or maple syrup, Grade B or dark amber

2 tablespoons / 12 grams Dutch-process cocoa powder

⅛ teaspoon guar gum

Pinch fine sea salt

3 ounces / 85 grams very cold brownies or cake

1. Process the cashew cream, milk, sugar, agave or maple syrup, and cocoa powder in a blender on high for 1 minute until completely puréed.

2. Sprinkle the guar gum directly onto the mixture. Blend on low for 30 seconds, then increase the speed to high and blend for 1 minute. Add a pinch of salt.

3. Pour the ice cream base into a 4-cup / 1-liter container. Cover and refrigerate the base for 2 to 4 hours until thoroughly chilled before churning. Chilling the base thoroughly means faster churning, which results in a creamier frozen dessert.

4. When the mixture is cold, give it a good whisk. Pour it into an ice cream maker and churn according to the manufacturer's directions.

5. While the ice cream is churning, cut the cold brownies or cake into 1-inch / 2.5 cm pieces and refrigerate again until needed.

6. Add the brownies or cake when the ice cream looks like soft serve. Longer churning after the brownies

are added will bulldoze the bits into pieces that are too small.

7. Using a silicone spatula, immediately transfer the frozen ice cream to the chilled storage container. Cover tightly and freeze for 1 to 2 hours until the ice cream is firm enough to scoop.

SERVING

Serve the ice cream in chilled bowls.

KEEPING

Freeze the ice cream in a covered container. For the best flavor and texture, eat the ice cream within one week.

VARIATION

Blow Them Away Brownie Sundae: Place a brownie in a chilled dish. Top with 1 or 2 scoops of the Chocolate Brownie Crumble Ice Cream. Drizzle with Thick Fudge Sauce (page 277), add a dollop of Chocolate Coconut Whipped Cream (page 280), and finish with a dusting of organic vegan sprinkles (see Resources page 290).

Chocolate Ginger Ice Cream

Pungent, warming ginger is used in many cultures as a culinary spice as well as a medicine. My travel bag always holds ginger tea to soothe any digestive upset or ward off queasiness. Ginger is also considered one of the more potent anti-inflammatory spices. When it comes to food and flavor, the combination of ginger and chocolate is a personal favorite of mine, especially in this recipe, where the ginger adds a mild yet lingering hint of spice to the creamy chocolate ice cream. Since the flavor of fresh ginger is variable, I save the fresh root for making miso soup, salad dressing, and savory dishes, in which a few more coins of fresh ginger can be added along the way. Of course, ground spices are variable too, so you may need more or less than is called for in this recipe.

MAKES 1½ PINTS / ¾ LITER

1 can (13.5 to 14 ounces / 400 to 414 ml) unsweetened full-fat coconut milk, well-stirred (do not use light)

½ cup plus 1 tablespoon / 124 grams organic granulated sugar, ground in a blender until powdered

2 tablespoons / 18 grams organic whole cane sugar or coconut sugar, ground in a blender until powdered

¼ cup plus 1 tablespoon / 31 grams Dutch-process cocoa powder

2 to 3 teaspoons / 4 to 6 grams ground ginger

¼ teaspoon guar gum

Candied ginger, for serving (optional)

1. Add enough water to the coconut milk to make 2 cups / 480 ml and pour it into a blender. Add the granulated sugar and the whole cane sugar. Blend on high for 1 minute until the sugars are thoroughly incorporated into the liquid. Add the cocoa and 2 teaspoons of the ginger, and process on high for 1 minute or until completely puréed. Taste and add more ginger. The ginger flavor should be potent, as freezing will reduce the spiciness.

2. Sprinkle the guar gum directly onto the mixture. Blend on low for 30 seconds, then increase the speed to high and blend for 1 minute.

3. Strain the ice cream base through a fine sieve into a 2-cup / 500-ml container. Cover and refrigerate the base for 2 to 4 hours until thoroughly chilled before churning. Chilling the base thoroughly means faster churning, which results in a creamier frozen dessert.

4. When the mixture is cold, give it a good whisk. Pour it into an ice cream maker and churn according to the manufacturer's directions. It will look like soft serve when it is ready.

5. Using a silicone spatula, immediately transfer the frozen ice cream to the chilled storage container. Cover tightly, and freeze for 2 to 4 hours until the ice cream is firm enough to scoop.

SERVING

Serve the ice cream in chilled bowls sprinkled with the optional candied ginger.

KEEPING

Freeze the ice cream in a covered container. For the best flavor and texture, eat the ice cream within one week.

Chocolate Sorbet

Sorbets are soft, smooth frozen ices made without milk or other dairy products. My chef in culinary school taught me to add egg whites to yield an even smoother sorbet. This is not an option for vegan cooks. Moreover, egg whites also mute a sorbet's flavor. My extremely smooth, intensely flavored chocolate sorbet has no such problems. It uses no eggs, and will stay that way with no unpleasant iciness for up to a week (if it lasts that long).

Note: The sorbet will take longer to freeze than the richer frozen desserts made with nondairy milk and cream, and it will melt faster at room temperature. Place the serving dishes in the freezer until ready to serve.

MAKES 2 PINTS / 1 LITER

2 cups / 414 grams organic granulated sugar

4 cups / 960 ml water, at room temperature

½ cup / 120 ml pure maple syrup, Grade B or dark amber

1 cup / 104 grams Dutch-process cocoa powder, sifted

³/₈ teaspoon fine sea salt

8 ounces / 227 grams dark chocolate (70 to 72%), finely chopped

2 tablespoons / 9 grams instant coffee (optional)

1 tablespoon / 15 ml pure vanilla extract

1. Make the sugar syrup. Put the sugar into a large saucepan. Pour the water over the sugar and bring it to a boil over medium heat, whisking a few times after the water starts to boil. When a full boil is reached, add the maple syrup. Reduce the heat to medium, adjusting as necessary to keep the mixture at a low boil, and cook for 1 minute.

2. Whisk the cocoa into the sugar syrup in 2 additions until the cocoa is dissolved. Add the salt. Reduce the heat, adjusting as necessary to keep the mixture at a low boil for 8 minutes.

3. Remove the saucepan from the heat and immediately add half of the chocolate and the coffee if using. Whisk until the chocolate is melted, and then add the remaining chocolate. Add the vanilla. Keep the sorbet base in the saucepan for 5 minutes, whisking a few times.

4. Strain the base through a fine mesh strainer into a 3-cup bowl and cool to room temperature.

5. Cover and refrigerate the base for 2 to 4 hours until thoroughly chilled before churning. Chilling the base thoroughly means faster churning, which results in a creamier frozen dessert.

6. When the mixture is cold, give it a good whisk. Pour it into an ice cream maker and churn according to the manufacturer's directions. It will look like soft serve when it is ready.

7. Using a silicone spatula, immediately transfer the frozen sorbet to the chilled storage container. Cover tightly and freeze for 2 to 4 hours until the ice cream is firm enough to scoop.

SERVING

Serve in chilled bowls or glasses.

KEEPING

For the best flavor and texture, eat the sorbet within one week. The sorbet will be easy to scoop straight from the freezer.

Chocolate Margarita Ice Cream

Rim a cocktail glass with salt, fill it with ice cubes, and then pour in one ounce of premium agave-based tequila, a half-ounce of triple sec, and a half-ounce of freshly squeezed lime juice. Stir a few times until chilled. Sip slowly. That's my recipe for a perfect margarita. But when I began thinking about making a margarita-flavored chocolate ice cream, I had to play with perfection. Too much alcohol prevents ice cream from freezing, but too little "margarita mix" and the flavor won't come through. This is all to say that this ice cream required more tests than any of the recipes in this chapter. (I can assure you that even the rejected recipes were eaten or sipped!) When finally the recipe worked, using the Sweet Thick Cashew Cream as a base, it was clear to me and the testers that the hardest part about making this recipe is not drinking the base straight-up first.

Note: Because the freezing point of alcohol is much lower than water, boozy ice creams take longer to churn.

MAKES ABOUT A PINT / 500 ML

¼ cup / 25 grams Dutch-process cocoa powder

¼ cup / 60 ml pure maple syrup, Grade B or dark amber, or agave syrup

1 recipe Sweet Thick Cashew Cream (page 284)

2 tablespoons / 30 ml tequila

1½ teaspoons / 7.5 ml triple sec

¼ teaspoon fine sea salt

2 drops pure lime oil or the zest of one organic lime

¼ teaspoon guar gum

Flaked sea salt, for serving (optional)

Thinly sliced limes dipped in sugar, for serving (optional)

1. Add the cocoa powder and maple syrup or agave syrup to the blender. Blend on low to mix. The cocoa will not be completely dissolved. Do not wash the blender.

2. Add enough water to the Sweet Thick Cashew Cream to make 2 cups / 480 ml, then add 2 more tablespoons / 30 ml of water. Add to the blender. Blend, starting on low, then quickly increase the speed to high for 1 minute.

3. Add the tequila, triple sec, salt, and lime oil (or lime zest). Blend until incorporated.

4. Sprinkle the guar gum directly onto the mixture. Blend on low for 30 seconds, then quickly increase the speed to high and blend for 1 minute.

5. Pour the ice cream base into a 2-cup / ½-liter container. Cover and refrigerate for 2 to 4 hours until thoroughly chilled before churning. Chilling the base thoroughly means faster churning, which results in a creamier frozen dessert.

6. When the mixture is cold, give it a good whisk. Pour it into an ice cream maker and churn according to the manufacturer's directions. The ice cream will look like soft serve when it is ready.

7. Using a silicone spatula, immediately transfer the ice cream to the chilled storage container. Cover tightly and freeze for at least 3 hours or longer until the ice cream is firm enough to scoop.

SERVING

Serve the ice cream in chilled bowls with a sprinkle of flaked sea salt and garnish with thinly sliced limes dipped in sugar if you like.

KEEPING

Freeze the ice cream in a tightly covered container. For the best flavor and texture, eat the ice cream within one week.

Watermelon Granita with Chocolate Seeds

On a hot and humid New York City summer day, nothing beats a couple of slices of ice-cold watermelon to cool me off (as much as possible, anyway). Nothing, that is, until I made this rosy pink, icy cold, lime-scented watermelon granita for my frozen dessert class at the Natural Gourmet Institute for Health and Culinary Arts in New York City. Granitas are typically made by freezing fruity liquid in a shallow pan and scraping the mixture with a fork at regular intervals as it freezes. That's pretty simple, but I didn't want to be tied to setting a timer and scraping. I had heard about making granita in a food processor using frozen cubes of fruit purée, and I decided to test the process. It worked perfectly; the granita was fluffy and the watermelon taste shone through.

**MAKES ABOUT
1½ PINTS / ¾ LITER**

1½ pounds / 680 grams watermelon, cubed and seeded

¼ cup / 50 grams organic granulated sugar, ground in a blender until powdered

1 tablespoon / 15 ml fresh lime juice

1 to 2 ounces / 28 to 57 grams dark chocolate (any percentage), chopped into small chunks for the "seeds"

Flaked sea salt (optional)

1. Purée the watermelon cubes in a food processor or blender and pour into a bowl. (You should have 2 cups / 480 ml of juice.) Add the powdered sugar and lime juice to the purée and whisk briskly until the sugar is dissolved.

2. Pour the mixture into ice cube trays and freeze until hard. This can take up to 24 hours.

3. Make the granita: Put a 1-quart / 1-liter container with a lid into the freezer. Transfer the frozen cubes to a food processor. Limit the number of cubes to no more than a double layer at a time so that the granita does not get slushy. Pulse a dozen or so times in 2 to 3-second bursts until the cubes are finely chopped. The number of pulses will depend on your machine.

4. Scrape the granita into the chilled container, cover the container, and return it to the freezer; repeat with the remaining cubes if necessary.

SERVING

The granita is ready to eat right out of the food processor. Serve in chilled bowls and garnish with as many chocolate "seeds" as you like. I believe watermelon benefits from a sprinkling of flaked sea salt, and if you agree, sprinkle a bit over each bowl.

KEEPING

Freeze the granita in a covered container. For the best flavor and texture, eat the granita within one week. Fluff with a fork before serving.

CHAPTER NINE

Confections

You need not be a chocolatier to make irresistible confections like elegant Mendiants (disks of chocolate topped with any small bits of nuts, seeds, and dried fruit in your pantry) or my simplified Chocolate Peanut Butter Cups. My chewy No-Mallow Rice Crispy Treats don't require hunting down vegan marshmallow, and the Chocolate Hazelnut Butter ("Your-Name-Here-tella") contains lots more chocolate, nuts, and flavor than the popular European spread, but none of the dried skim milk powder. Every one of the recipes in this chapter can be made days in advance and stored in your refrigerator. The majority are also gluten-free, and one is raw.

Fran's Rulebook for Successful Chocolate Confections

1. Read the recipe all the way through and plan your time. (Since you will be chopping chocolate and melting it over a water bath, you may want to review "About Chocolate," pages 24 to 28.)

2. Prepare your *mise en place*: gather the equipment, prepare the pans, grind the sugar, chop or melt the chocolate, soak, roast, skin, or cool the nuts.

3. Keep the melted chocolate liquid over a water bath to prevent it from solidifying.

4. Keep the finished chocolate confections in an airtight container in layers separated by parchment paper, store them in the refrigerator or freezer, and serve cold.

TROUBLESHOOTING	
The mendiants got soft before I could serve them	Sorry. Make sure the mendiants are served cool but not cold, and don't put the tray next to the fireplace.
The dulce de leche was too thick/thin	Too thick? Stop cooking a little sooner next time. Thin with a little coconut milk. Too thin? Cook it longer.
The confection doesn't look perfect	There's always next time, but for now, you and your friends will be happy to eat the "mistakes."

THE RECIPES

Millionaire's Banoffee Tarts

Chocolate Peanut Butter Cups

No Mallow Rice Crispy Treats

Chocolate Olive Oil Glaze for Chocolate-Dipped Anything

Chewy Date Candies

Mendiants

Dukkah-Spiced Chocolate–Covered Matzoh

Chocolate Crostini

Chocolate Hazelnut Butter

Chocolate Dulce de Leche

Millionaire's Banoffee Tarts

Created with the assistance of Clare Gray, an RD and Natural Gourmet grad from London, this dessert combines the best parts of two wildly popular UK desserts: the Banoffee Tart and Millionaire's Pie. I saw banoffee-flavored tarts, truffles, and even ice cream all over London in the fall of 2011, but somehow neglected to learn more about it when I was there. So, I asked Clare when she interned with me and she explained that banoffee is traditionally made from short-bread, caramel, and bananas. I immediately understood the appeal and naturally wanted to incorporate at least one chocolate component. Clare suggested that the chocolate and caramel Millionaire's Tart and Banoffe would make a brilliant hybrid, and she was right. In short order, thanks to the caramel-like Chocolate Dulce de Leche, the Chocolate Cake to Live For, and the ripe bananas on my counter, we had an over-the-top treat. For even more good news, know that the tarts can be assembled a day ahead and sit out at room temperature for hours, making them the perfect party dessert.

   Notes: It is a real time saver to make the Chocolate Dulce de Leche in advance (it can be refrigerated for up to two weeks). The rest can be done the day before you serve the tarts. No ring molds? No problem: just layer in ramekins. It'll taste just as good. So will the chocolate crumbs from any moist cake—and leftover is fine, too. For a completely gluten-free dessert, use the gluten-free variation of the Chocolate Torte to Live For (page 69).

MAKES 4 LARGE SERVINGS

2 cups / 260 grams moist cake crumbs, from the Chocolate Torte to Live For (page 68) or the Bittersweet Chocolate Sheet Cake (page 116), divided

6 tablespoons / 72 grams dark chocolate (any percentage), coarsely chopped

2 large ripe bananas (but not overripe)

1 recipe (1 ¼ cups / 300 ml) Chocolate Dulce de Leche (page 234), at room temperature, or warmed in the jar in a water bath until pourable

6 to 8 ounces / 170 to 227 grams melted dark chocolate (any percentage), kept warm over a water bath (see page 28)

1. Line up four 4 x 1½-inch / 10 x 3.8 cm ring molds on a parchment-lined quarter sheet pan or another flat surface that can be moved to the refrigerator. Put ½ cup / 65 grams of the cake crumbs into each ring and press down to make a compact layer.

2. Sprinkle the cake crumbs with about 1½ tablespoons / 18 grams chopped chocolate.

3. Cut 1 banana at a time into rounds ¼ to ½ inch (6 to 12 mm) thick and place on the chocolate to cover, distributing evenly among the ring molds.

4. Pour or spoon 4 to 5 tablespoons / 60 to 75 ml of the Chocolate Dulce de Leche over the bananas to cover.

5. Pour 3 tablespoons / 45 ml melted chocolate over the Dulce, spreading to the edges of the ring. Refrigerate until the chocolate "disk" is set, about 20 to 30 minutes.

SERVING

Run a thin knife between the sides of the mold and the chocolate. Press down on the chocolate disk to release the ring and lift it off. Lift each tart onto a serving plate. A little messiness on the plate is encouraged. (If using ramekins, do not remove the tarts.)

   Allow 45 minutes (or up to 2 hours) for the tarts to come to room temperature so that the Dulce de Leche can soften. If you have some leftover Dulce, dot it onto the chocolate disks or onto the plate. Serve with a smile and a glass of water. This is rich!

KEEPING

The tarts can be made up to a day ahead and refrigerated, but remember to serve them at room temperature.

Chocolate Peanut Butter Cups

Molded chocolate candy cups filled with a confectioner's proprietary formula for sweetened peanut butter cream are one of the most enduringly popular American candies—none more so than Hershey's Reese's Peanut Butter Cups, invented in 1928 by H.B. Reese (a former employee of Hershey's). They were my favorite candy, until I overdosed on a multi-pound bag of the minis sent to me by my well-meaning mother during finals of my freshman year of college. Judging by the popularity of my Chocolate Peanut Butter Mousse in Chocolate Candy Cups in my last book, I am hardly alone in my inability to resist them. According to the feedback I received, the only problem with that recipe was that making the chocolate cups was too time consuming. So, this time I thought "outside the cup" and created a cream, which is piped or spooned over a chunk of chocolate in an actual cup and then topped with melted chocolate and peanuts. This makes the recipe infinitely easier and you get more of the chocolate peanut butter cream in each serving.

MAKES 4 LARGE OR 6 SMALL SERVINGS

1 cup / 146 grams cashews, rinsed, soaked at least 4 hours to overnight, and drained

²/₃ cup / 160 ml unsweetened canned full-fat coconut milk, well-stirred (do not use light)

1 cup / 207 grams organic granulated sugar

2 tablespoons / 12 grams Dutch-process cocoa powder

2 teaspoons / 10 ml pure vanilla extract

¹/₈ teaspoon fine sea salt

³/₄ cup / 202 grams smooth peanut butter

1¹/₂ to 2 ounces / 42 to 57 grams dark chocolate (any percentage), broken into pieces to fit into the bottom of the cups

2 ounces / 57 grams dark chocolate (any percentage), melted and kept warm in a water bath, for topping

Salted peanuts, chopped, for garnish

1. Put the cashews, coconut milk, and sugar into a blender. Blend starting on low for 1 minute. Increase the speed to high and blend until the liquid is perfectly smooth. Add the cocoa, vanilla, and salt and blend for 1 minute.

2. Pour into a deep bowl that is suitable for use with electric beaters. Beat the peanut butter into the cream in 3 additions, mixing on high after each addition until completely incorporated. The cream can be used immediately or refrigerated.

3. Place 1 or 2 pieces of chocolate in the bottom of each of 4 or 6 clear glasses. Spoon or pipe about ¹/₃ cup / 80 ml of the cream over the chocolate in each cup. Spoon about 2 teaspoons / 10 ml of melted chocolate over the cream. Serve immediately or refrigerate until the chocolate is set.

SERVING

Sprinkle the cups with chopped peanuts.

KEEPING

Refrigerate the cream in a covered container for up to three days. The cups can be made ahead and refrigerated for up to three days. Add the peanuts just before serving.

No Mallow Rice Crispy Treats

This recipe is my answer to those who love Rice Krispie Treats, but want a less sugary alternative. And you won't need to find the sometimes-elusive vegan marshmallows or mallow cream. Actually, it is my second answer, since the recipe is a chewier, more chocolaty update to the recipe in my last book.

Note: The agar powder and guar gum are necessary to the recipe; there are no substitutes.

MAKES ONE (8 X 8-INCH / 20 BY 20-CM) SQUARE PAN

4 cups / 113 grams crispy rice cereal (or a similar puffed rice cereal)

½ cup / 85 grams vegan chocolate chips

¾ cup / 180 ml brown rice syrup, warmed in the jar until liquid (see page 23)

¼ teaspoon agar powder

¼ teaspoon guar gum

2 tablespoons / 18 grams organic granulated sugar

2 tablespoons / 18 grams whole cane sugar, ground in a blender until powdered

½ cup / 140 grams cashew butter, jarred or homemade

2 teaspoons / 10 ml pure vanilla extract

1. Line an 8 x 8-inch / 20 x 20-cm square pan with parchment paper so that the paper extends up two sides.

2. Put the cereal and chocolate chips into a medium bowl, and set aside while you make the coating.

3. Pour the warm brown rice syrup into a small heavy-bottomed saucepan. Sprinkle the agar powder and guar gum over the syrup. Cook to a low boil, whisking constantly. Adjust the heat as needed so that the syrup is bubbling (but not boiling) vigorously.

4. Whisk the granulated and whole cane sugars into the rice syrup and cook for about 30 seconds until dissolved. Add the cashew butter, whisking to incorporate.

5. Remove from the heat and add the vanilla. Mix and pour over the cereal and chips. Be careful: Hot syrup mixtures can stick to your skin and burn. Mix with a silicone spatula until the cereal is coated. Some of the chocolate chips will melt. This is fine.

6. Spoon the mixture into the prepared pan. Place a piece of parchment paper or plastic wrap over the top and press hard into an even layer. Using a flat-bottomed cup to press is helpful.

7. Allow the bars to set up at room temperature for about 1 hour before cutting into squares. Use the longer pieces of parchment to lift the entire bar from the pan onto a cutting board or cut right in the pan.

KEEPING

Store at room temperature in an airtight container for up to four days.

Chocolate Olive Oil Glaze
for Chocolate-Dipped Anything

Shiny chocolate-dipped fruit, cookies, confections, and snacks like pretzels and potato chips look gorgeous, but most of the time, when dipped in melted chocolate alone, the final result is dull or speckled with white spots. Tempered chocolate, however, yields a glossy, speckle-free appearance. Directions for seed-tempering chocolate are found on page 28, but this recipe offers an alternative method: adding some mild tasting extra-virgin olive oil to melted chocolate. The result is not a true tempered chocolate, but this works very well as a chocolate dip and even a lusciously smooth cake glaze.

Note: Fruit must be thoroughly dry and cold before dipping (chocolate sets fastest on cold fruit). Rinse the fruit gently (do not wash berries more than 30 minutes before using), gently pat dry with paper towels and refrigerate until cold.

MAKES 1 CUP

6 ounces / 170 grams dark chocolate (70 to 72%), finely chopped

2 tablespoons / 30 ml mild tasting extra-virgin oil or neutral vegetable oil

2 pinches flaked sea salt (optional)

RECOMMENDED ITEMS FOR DIPPING:

Long-stem or standard strawberries

Blueberries, raspberries, blackberries

Cherries on the stem

Citrus segments (mandarin oranges or grapefruit, cleaned of all pith and "string")

Dried fruit

Pomegranate seeds

Sunflower seeds

Potato chips

Pretzels

Cookies

1. Line a sheet pan with a piece of plastic wrap, acetate, or parchment or a Silpat baking mat.

2. Melt half of the chocolate with the olive oil in a heatproof bowl set over a pan of simmering water (make sure the water does not touch the bottom of the bowl), stirring a few times until the chocolate is just melted. Add the rest of the chocolate and stir until melted.

3. Remove the bowl from the saucepan. Wipe the water from the bottom of the bowl. Crush the salt (if using) between your fingers and add it to the chocolate, stirring until the chocolate is completely melted and the glaze is smooth.

4. To dip larger items: hold by the end or stem. Dip each piece two-thirds of the way into the chocolate. Lift up and allow the excess chocolate to drip back into the bowl. Set each piece on the lined sheet pan and push forward just slightly, so the chocolate doesn't puddle too much. (Don't worry if it does.) Allow the chocolate to set at room temperature for about 15 minutes, then refrigerate on the tray until set. To dip smaller pieces, such as nuts or seeds, plunk a bunch at a time into a shallower bowl of chocolate and push them around with a fork until coated. Remove with a large fork or slotted spoon and allow the excess chocolate to drip back into the bowl. Place on the lined baking sheet to harden and then refrigerate.

5. Refrigerate until serving. The chocolate-dipped "anythings" will peel off the acetate, parchment, or Silpat when the chocolate has hardened.

SERVING
These treats are best on the day they are dipped.

VARIATIONS

Add a coating of chopped nuts, seeds, coconut or fine cake or cookie crumbs: After dipping the item, roll or sprinkle with any of the above toppings.

Make a free-form design by waving a forkful of melted chocolate over the item instead of dipping. If you want to create neat lines, pipe the melted chocolate through a small pastry bag, paper cornet, or squeeze bottle.

Chewy Date Candies

Take a handful of ingredients, a food processor, a quick pass with a rolling pin, and in 10 minutes you'll be snacking on a nutritious and satisfying chocolate-scented, sugar-free candy that can easily be made raw by using raw cacao powder and alcohol-free vanilla. The recipe calls for Medjool dates, but Deglet Noor or Halawi dates work as well. A little hot water may be needed if the dates are very dry, but rarely have I found this to be the case. What I have found to be the case in this recipe is the flavor-boosting power of soy sauce. I asked Elizabeth Andoh, a leading English-language expert on Japanese cuisine, if I was imagining this flavor boost, and she confirmed it exists. My preference is to add a dash of unpasteurized soy sauce (nama shoyu) to boost the chocolate flavor, but you can substitute any quality soy sauce or tamari, or just leave it out altogether and add a pinch of salt.

The candy stays chewy for weeks, right out of the freezer, or follow the directions in Variations (page 225) to make raw truffles, Tootsie Roll–shaped logs, or even a tart crust.

MAKES 24 (1½-INCH / 4-CM)
CANDY LOGS, 24 TRUFFLES,
OR ONE (6-INCH / 15-CM)
TART CRUST

6 ounces / 171 grams pitted Medjool dates (about 10)

⅓ cup / 32 grams Dutch-process cocoa powder

1 teaspoon / 5 ml pure vanilla extract

½ teaspoon nama shoyu (optional) or pinch of fine sea salt

⅔ cup / 68 grams finely ground walnuts

1. Rough chop the dates in a food processor with a few pulses on and off, and then process until the dates are very finely chopped. The dates may form a ball on the blade when finished.

2. Add the cocoa powder and process to incorporate.

3. Add the vanilla extract and the soy sauce or salt, if using. Add the walnuts and process for 2 minutes or until the walnuts are fully incorporated and the mixture is smooth and shiny.

4. Stop the machine and pinch a piece of the mixture between your fingers. It should be pliable and moist but not sticky. If it is sticky, add another tablespoon of cocoa powder. If it is too dry, add a few drops of very hot water.

5. Spoon the mixture onto a large piece of plastic wrap and cover with another piece of wrap. Press into a rough square. Roll to a ½-inch / 12-mm thickness and you have made the candy. (If the candy sticks to the wrap, refrigerate until it is cold and continue.)

6. Refrigerate or freeze the candy in a freezer bag until cold before cutting into squares. Chilling for at least 30 minutes improves the flavor.

SERVING
Cut the chilled candy into squares and grab one whenever you want!

KEEPING

All variations of the candy will stay chewy in an airtight container or freezer bag in the refrigerator for three weeks and in the freezer for one month.

VARIATIONS

Raw Truffles: Sprinkle ¼ cup / 30 grams cacao nibs, finely chopped nuts, or dark chocolate over the candy—or divide into thirds or quarters if you want to make an assortment. Press the fillings into the candy, then pinch or cut into 1-inch / 2.5-cm pieces. The best way to get the fillings mixed into the candy is to squeeze the pieces in the palm of your hand. Roll into balls in your hands or on a cutting board and then roll to coat in the cocoa powder. Store in an airtight container in the refrigerator or freezer, in layers separated by parchment paper.

Tootsie Roll–like Logs: Follow the directions for making truffles, but don't roll the balls in cocoa powder. Instead, roll into logs on a cutting board. It's easiest to cut even pieces when the logs are lined up so close together that they are touching. Use a sharp knife to cut 1½ inch x ¼-inch / 4 cm x 6-mm pieces and repeat until all the candy is used. Press the scraps together to make another log or two. If you are as fussy as I am, cut both ends of each piece for a nice flat edge. Store in an airtight container in the refrigerator or freezer.

Tart: Press the dough into a 6-inch / 15-cm diameter tart tin. Chill until firm. Store in an airtight container in the refrigerator or freezer. Fill with Chocolate Avocado "Buttercream" (page 272) for a very sweet treat or Magic Chocolate Mousse (page 182) to make a lovely little tart for two.

Mendiants

Mendiants are small chocolate disks topped with candied fruits and nuts. They look beautiful but can be time-consuming and tricky to make when using tempered chocolate and candying the nuts. I made a simpler version by using leftover ingredients. Melted chocolate left from a recipe test? Check. Walnuts or pine nuts? Yes. Four squares of candied ginger, a handful of dried cranberries . . . you get the idea. This is probably heresy but it works! I had only to rewarm the formerly melted chocolate. While the chocolate was melting, I lined a sheet pan with parchment and gathered the bits of fruit and nuts. Straight out of the refrigerator and onto a silver tray, the leftovers became elegant confections worthy of a grown-up party. I still think of them as fancy leftovers, though.

Notes: All amounts are approximate: use more or less depending on what you have. About a half tablespoon of melted chocolate makes a thin 2 to 2½-inch / 5 to 6-cm thin confection, but figure in a little bit of extra chocolate for chocolate that sticks to the spoon. If the leftover melted chocolate is streaked with white, warm it with a few small chunks of solid chocolate to "temper" it (page 28). Tempered chocolate sets fast, so you will have to add the toppings quickly. If the melted chocolate is not tempered, it will stay liquid for an hour, at least.

MAKES ABOUT 12 THIN MENDIANTS

3 ounces / 85 grams dark chocolate (70 to 72%), melted and kept warm in a water bath

6 walnuts, halved or quartered

10 blanched almonds, coarsely chopped (see Sidebar page 289)

½ ounce / 12 grams candied ginger, slivered or cubed

1¼ ounces / 35 grams any dried fruit, slivered or cubed if large

¼ ounce / 5 grams pine nuts (about 24)

1. Line a baking sheet with plastic wrap or parchment paper.

2. Drop a tablespoonful of the chocolate onto the sheet and use the back of a spoon to spread it into a thin round about 2 to 2½ inches / 5 to 6 cm in diameter. Keep the thickness of the round as even as possible. Make only 6 at a time to ensure that the chocolate doesn't set before the toppings are added.

3. For each mendiant, arrange a walnut half, a couple of pieces of almond, some of the ginger, a piece of another dried fruit, and 2 or 3 pine nuts on top of the chocolate, creating your own design. Repeat the process until you have used all of the melted chocolate, nuts, and fruits. Allow the mendiants to harden at room temperature. You can speed the process by placing the tray in the refrigerator.

SERVING

Mendiants (even made from leftovers) deserve to be served on an elegant tray. These are perfect party confections, or a lovely snack to enjoy at tea time. (Sip from a tea cup, not a mug!)

KEEPING

Store the mendiants in an airtight container in the refrigerator for up to four days.

Dukkah-Spiced Chocolate-Covered Matzoh

Recently, I went dukkah mad, and that madness led to the creation of this dish. Dukkah (also spelled duqqa or dukka) is an Egyptian spice blend made with nuts (usually hazelnuts, sometimes pistachios or almonds), cumin, sesame, coriander, fennel seeds, pepper berries, salt, some dried herbs, and chili pepper. The ingredients are lightly toasted and ground into a powder and make a divine dust for bread dipped in olive oil. During my dukkah delirium, I made batch after batch with different combinations of spices and nuts. I still had jars of them when my daughter asked me to make matzoh toffee for a Chanukah party. I spied the dukkah and thought, "Why not something different?" I slathered the matzoh with olive oil–enhanced Ganache Glaze, and finished with a shower of dukkah. The pieces were quickly devoured.

Note: This is my favorite version of dukkah, but if you have one you are happy with, of course, use it. Also: this stuff disappears fast! Instead of making more in the middle of the festivities, do what I did: Put out a tray of matzoh, a bowl of ganache, a few spreaders, a spoon, and a bowl of dukkah. It's a little messier, but good!

MAKES 4 PIECES OF MATZOH

DUKKAH TOPPING

1 ounce / 30 grams skinned hazelnuts or raw unpeeled almonds

1 ounce / 30 grams shelled pistachios, unsalted

1/4 cup / 35 grams natural sesame seeds

1 tablespoon / 5 grams coriander seeds

1 1/8 teaspoons / 4 grams anise seeds

1 teaspoon / 2 grams cumin seeds

3/4 teaspoon / 2 grams black peppercorns

1/2 teaspoon / 3 grams flaked sea salt

4 pieces matzoh (each about a 6 x 7-inch / 15 x 17-cm rectangle)

1 1/2 tablespoons / 22.5 ml extra-virgin olive oil, at room temperature

1 cup / 240 ml Bittersweet Chocolate Ganache Glaze (page 264) warmed in a water bath until spreadable

MAKE THE DUKKAH SPICE MIX

1. Toast the hazelnuts (or almonds) and pistachios in a dry skillet over low heat for about 2 minutes, shaking the pan so the nuts do not burn. Set aside in a bowl to cool.

2. Toast the sesame seeds, coriander seeds, anise seeds, cumin seeds, and peppercorns in the same skillet until fragrant, about 2 minutes, shaking the skillet frequently. Pour into a bowl and let cool completely.

3. Combine all the ingredients in an electric spice or nut grinder. Grind until the mixture looks like flaked sea salt, not too fine and not too coarse. (If you want to be authentic and use a mortar and pestle you will likely have to do this in 2 or 3 batches.)

4. Mix the salt into the dukkah and pour into a jar with a tight-fitting lid. Store in the refrigerator until needed.

MAKE THE CHOCOLATE-COATED MATZOH

1. Line up the matzoh on a parchment-lined sheet pan.

2. Stir the olive oil into the softened ganache. It is fine if the oil is not thoroughly incorporated.

3. Spread 4 tablespoons / 60 ml ganache on each piece of matzoh. Sprinkle with 2 tablespoons (about 26 grams), more or less to taste, of the dukkah. Refrigerate briefly to set the chocolate.

SERVING

Serve the prepared matzoh at once or refrigerate until the chocolate has hardened for a crunchier (and less messy) treat. Break or cut each coated matzoh into 12 pieces and arrange on a platter.

KEEPING

Keep any leftover pieces in a covered container at room temperature for two to three days.

Chocolate Crostini

Slice a good crusty baguette. Brush the bread with a little fruity extra-virgin olive oil, warm the ganache, and set aside while you enjoy your meal with friends and family. After dinner, pop back into the kitchen and finish the crostini. Or make a tray to serve at a cocktail party. I like to sprinkle the warm crostini with lemon salt or one of the smoked finishing salts found at The Meadow in New York City's West Village (see Resources page 290), but any finishing salt will do. The crunchy salt and drizzle of fruity olive oil on the chocolate-smeared bread is heavenly. Don't omit.

MAKES ABOUT 16 PIECES

1 good-quality (10-inch / 25-cm) whole grain or sourdough baguette

2 tablespoons / 30 ml fruity extra-virgin olive oil for the bread; plus about 1 tablespoon / 15 ml for drizzling

1⅓ cups / 320 ml Bittersweet Chocolate Ganache Glaze (page 264), warmed in a water bath until spreadable

Finishing salt or flaked sea salt for sprinkling

1. Slice the bread on a diagonal, about ½ inch / 12 mm thick. Arrange on a baking sheet and brush each slice lightly with the olive oil. Set aside until needed.

2. Fifteen minutes before you are ready to serve, preheat the oven to 375°F / 190°C. When the oven is at temperature, toast the bread for 5 to 8 minutes or until golden.

3. Remove the baking sheet from the oven and cool the bread until barely warm, about 5 minutes.

4. Spread each piece with about 2 tablespoons / 30 ml of the ganache, or enough to cover. Sprinkle lighly with salt and drizzle with a touch of olive oil. Serve immediately.

Chocolate Hazelnut Butter

I enjoy eating spoonfuls of "Fran-tella," my healthier and tastier version of the popular Italian chocolate and hazelnut spread, straight out of the jar. Making nut butters at home in a food processor is quick, easy, and cheaper than buying the jarred kind. Better yet, no added oil is needed when you allow the nuts to grind in a food processor for five to ten minutes. For the best flavor, roast the nuts first.

Notes: Roasting the hazelnuts is necessary to remove the skins and enhance the flavor. Even blanched hazelnuts benefit from five minutes in the oven (see Sidebar). Do not add salt or other flavorings until the nuts have transformed into a creamy, glossy paste. Start paying attention halfway through, as some nuts get oiler faster than others, and it's hard to know until they are grinding. Depending on the size and power of your processor, process one or two cups of nuts at a time. Chocolate extract may need to be mail-ordered, but it is worth seeking out; it adds an extra chocolate note. If you cannot find any, don't let that stop you from the recipe. The first tester was so pleased, she made jars of 'tella to give as holiday gifts.

MAKES ABOUT 1 ½ CUPS / 360 ML

1 cup / 140 grams whole hazelnuts, roasted and skinned (see Sidebar) to make ½ cup / 120 ml hazelnut butter

1 cup / 107 grams confectioners' sugar, sifted

½ cup / 58 grams Dutch-process cocoa powder, sifted

⅛ teaspoon fine sea salt

2 tablespoons / 30 ml boiling water

3 tablespoons / 45 ml almond milk, at room temperature, plus more as needed to adjust consistency

½ teaspoon pure chocolate extract (optional, but recommended)

1. Grind the hazelnuts in a food processor for 5 to 10 minutes until the nuts have transformed into a smooth, glossy nut butter. Scrape the sides of the processor once or twice if necessary. Stop processing before the nut butter gets oily.

2. Scrape the sides of the processor with a silicone spatula. Add the sugar, cocoa, and salt and pulse a few times until incorporated. The mixture will look like small crumbs.

3. Add the hot water and process for about 1 minute until incorporated, but not longer. The mixture will now look like large crumbles.

4. Scrape the mixture into a medium bowl. Mix 2 tablespoons of the almond milk and the chocolate extract into the mixture until incorporated. Repeat with the third tablespoon of almond milk. If the consistency looks good to you, spoon the spread into a jar. If it is still too thick, mix in more almond milk, one tablespoon at a time, with a silicone spatula, until the desired consistency is reached. (Do not add additional liquid to the processor, or the resulting hazelnut butter will be oily.)

SERVING

Slather the spread on anything you like, or eat it off a spoon, but do not say this is a healthy breakfast. Made thinner with extra nondairy milk, this butter is the icing on the Chocolate Hazelnut Six-Layer Cake (page 108).

KEEPING

Refrigerate the spread in a clean jar with a tight-fitting lid for up to five days.

Roasting and Skinning Hazelnuts

There are two methods for removing the skins from hazelnuts. Some people boil them with baking soda. The skins do pop off when they boil, but I still prefer to remove the skins by roasting them. Preheat the oven to 350°F / 180°C. Line a baking sheet with parchment. Spread the nuts in a single layer on the sheet and roast for 10 to 12 minutes, shaking the pan once or twice during the roasting. Pour the hot nuts into a clean towel, grab the corners to bundle it up, and rub the nuts vigorously against each other inside the towel until most of the skin comes off. Or pour them into a wire mesh strainer and rub them against the strainer (I do this over the sink). Some skin will remain, but that is fine. Roast blanched hazelnuts for only 5 minutes.

Chocolate Dulce de Leche

I stood firm in my conviction that chocolate would even improve *dulce de leche*—the superbly sweet, gooey, and creamy caramelized milk from Latin America, which is known in French as *confiture de lait* ("milk jam"). First, I had to find a way to replace the whole milk or sweetened condensed milk used in traditional recipes. Cashew cream was a fail, but canned full-fat coconut milk worked beautifully, after I added a tiny amount of the guar gum to stabilize the emulsion. Surprisingly, the coconut flavor—even with coconut sugar added—is just a whisper. I don't recommend doubling the recipe; it is difficult to get the reduction just right.

Use a bittersweet chocolate to temper the sweetness of this sauce. (Although if you have tasted conventional *dulce*, you'll notice that this one is far less cloying.) Be careful: Use a deep heavy saucepan and be very mindful that you are cooking a mixture that will bubble volcanically.

MAKES ABOUT 1¼ CUPS / 300 ML

1 can (13.5 to 14 ounces / 400 to 414 ml) unsweetened full-fat coconut milk (do not use light)

½ cup / 80 grams coconut sugar (substitute ¼ cup each organic whole cane sugar and organic granulated sugar)

1 tablespoon / 15 ml brown rice syrup or agave syrup

¼ teaspoon fine sea salt

⅛ teaspoon guar gum

2 ounces / 58 grams dark chocolate (68 to 72%), finely chopped

2 teaspoons / 10 ml pure vanilla extract

1. Combine the coconut milk, sugar, rice syrup, salt, and guar gum in a blender. Start blending on low and increase the speed to high. Blend for 1 minute until the sugar is dissolved.

2. Pour into a heavy-bottomed medium saucepan (about 8 to 10 inches across x 3 inches deep / 20 to 25 cm across x 7.5 cm deep) and cook over medium-high heat, whisking occasionally just until the mixture begins to bubble.

3. Raise the heat to high and stir constantly until the mixture starts to boil furiously. Stir frequently for 10 minutes, adjusting the heat up or down as necessary to maintain a steady boil.

4. Carefully pour the very hot liquid into a 2-cup / 500 ml heatproof spouted measuring cup. Wait for the bubbling to stop and note the amount. If the liquid measures 1¼ cups / 300 ml, or a little less, it can be finished. If not, cook longer until it has reduced further.

5. Once the mixture has reduced, wait about 1 minute until steam is no longer visible, and then add the chocolate and the vanilla extract. Stir until the chocolate is melted and the sauce is smooth. Pour the sauce into a clean jar. Use warm or at room temperature.

SERVING

Spread the Dulce de Leche on bread or use it as an alternative filling for the Chocolate Coconut Whipped Cream Layer Cake (page 100). Heat until liquid and use it as a dip for pretzels, pieces of cake, or cookies—use your imagination—or pour over Chocolate Coconut Ice Cream (page 204). This dulce is also the "caramel" component in the Millionaire's Banoffee Tarts on page 218.

KEEPING

The sauce can be refrigerated covered for up to two weeks in the jar. It will thicken considerably in the refrigerator. Warm refrigerated Dulce de Leche gently over low heat in a small saucepan to liquefy if desired.

CHAPTER TEN

Beverages

The superior sips in this chapter will quench your thirst from breakfast to cocktail hour and beyond. Start your day off right with a healthy Meal in a Glass Smoothie made with raw cacao and antioxidant-rich berries and superfoods. When five o'clock rolls around, be ready for a shot of cacao nib–infused Chocolate Vodka, or mix up a Chocolate White Russian (they may taste like milkshakes but they are potent). In between, cool off with a tall glass of brown-rice-and-almond–based Chocolate Horchata poured over ice. If warming up is in order, sip a mug of one of the hot cocoas or the Chocolat Chaud. And if you're part of the milk-and-cookies-before-bed crowd, create no-recipe vegan chocolate milk by mixing warm nondairy milk and All-Purpose Chocolate Syrup, and nibble a cookie from Chapter Five. Most of these beverages are ready to drink as soon as they are made, and many can be made ahead and refrigerated for convenience. Reheat or reblend as needed.

Fran's Rulebook for Successful Chocolate Beverages

1. **Read the recipe all the way through and plan your time.**

2. **Prepare your** *mise en place*: **Gather the little equipment you need (in this chapter it is often only a blender or saucepan) and prepare the few ingredients necessary, soaking rice or nuts, chopping chocolate, or washing fruits and veggies.**

3. **Measure carefully! These recipes may be short and sweet but the goodness is still in the details.**

THE RECIPES

Low-Fat and Luscious Hot Cocoa

Quick and Easy Homemade Hot Cocoa

Chocolat Chaud

Hot Chocolate Mexican-Style

Espresso Hot Chocolate

Cacao, Matcha, and Kale Smoothie

Chocolate Peanut Butter Cup Smoothie

Chocolate Date Thick Shake

Meal in a Glass

Raw Cacao Nib Smoothie

Chocolate Horchata

Chocolate Vodka

Chocolate White Russian

Low-Fat and Luscious Hot Cocoa

How can hot cocoa made with naturally low-fat nondairy milk taste so thick and creamy, or, as several testers wrote, "like a cup of warm, liquid chocolate pudding"? The secret is using a small but significant bit of starch dissolved in cool liquid (a.k.a. a starch slurry). The cocoa, which cooks in minutes, tastes best pot-to-mug but is easily made in larger quantities. Use a high-quality cocoa powder for the best taste. I highly recommend using Dutch-process cocoa powder, but if you grew up on Hershey's you might prefer natural cocoa powder (non-alkalized).

MAKES ONE SERVING

1 cup plus 2 tablespoons / 270 ml almond milk or another nondairy milk, divided

2½ tablespoons / 15 grams Dutch-process cocoa powder, sifted

1 tablespoon / 15 ml pure maple syrup, Grade B or dark amber, or agave syrup

2 tablespoons / 18 grams organic granulated sugar

Pinch fine sea salt

2 teaspoons / 5 grams tapioca starch, organic cornstarch, or arrowroot

½ teaspoon pure vanilla extract

¼ ounce / 7 grams grated dark chocolate

Vegan mini marshmallows (optional)

1. Combine 1 cup / 240 ml of the milk, the cocoa powder, the maple syrup, the granulated sugar, and the salt in a small saucepan and bring to a boil over medium-low heat, whisking a few times.

2. In a separate dish, dissolve the tapioca in the remaining 2 tablespoons / 30 ml of milk. Reduce the heat to low and, while whisking constantly, add to the hot milk mixture. After the liquid has reached a full boil, adjust the heat so that a low boil is maintained for 1 minute, whisking slowly but frequently. Add the vanilla extract and grated chocolate. Pour into a mug and garnish with the vegan marshmallows if you like.

Working with Starches

While tapioca starch, organic cornstarch, and arrowroot starches can be used with no change of measurement, their cooking times will be different. Tapioca needs to cook for one minute after the boil. Cornstarch requires one and one half minutes of slow boiling, while arrowroot-thickened mixtures must be removed from the heat as soon as the boil is reached, or they will thin out.

Quick and Easy Homemade Hot Cocoa

If you like basic hot cocoa, you'll be dog-earing this page, but you probably won't need to: The recipe is easy to remember and among the handful in the book with four or fewer ingredients. That does not mean it wasn't tested many times to get the taste just right. The only differences from your standard cocoa recipe are the uses of organic granulated sugar and nondairy milk. What cocoa you use is up to you. I make mine with Dutch-process cocoa, while my neighbor and colleague, Linda Long (author of *Great Chefs Cook Vegan*) prefers natural cocoa in her cup.

MAKES 1 SERVING

3 tablespoons / 39 grams organic granulated sugar

1 tablespoon plus 1 ½ teaspoons / 9 grams Dutch-process or natural (non-alkalized) cocoa powder, sifted if lumpy

Pinch fine sea salt

¾ cup / 180 ml any nondairy milk

Vegan marshmallows, for serving (optional)

1. Add the sugar, cocoa, and salt to a small saucepan. Whisk to combine.

2. Whisk the milk in gradually. Don't worry if the cocoa and sugar do not dissolve fully.

3. Whisking constantly, cook over medium-low heat until the first wisps of steam appear. Do not allow the mixture to boil. Reduce the heat to low and cook only until a few small bubbles appear around the sides. Pour into a mug and garnish with vegan marshmallows if you like.

Chocolat Chaud

My son Michael spent his junior year in college at the Sorbonne in Paris. When I visited, he had discovered *chocolat chaud* and excitedly explained, "Mom, it's like drinking a melted bar of chocolate." The kid with a fondness for Swiss Miss was forever changed, and I knew I had to take him back to the elegant Belle Époque La Maison Angelina on the rue de Rivoli for another "melted chocolate bar hot chocolate." Individual pitchers of thick, silken, and bittersweet *Chocolat Chaud Africain* are served from silver platters and accompanied by bowls of lightly whipped cream and glasses of water on the side. Of course, Angelina's recipe is a closely guarded secret, but my decadent homage will transport you to the Jardin des Tuileries all the same. You must use a premium high-percentage bittersweet chocolate, one that you love to eat, since that is what you will taste in the cup. The silver platter is optional.

MAKES 2 SMALL SERVINGS

2 ½ ounces / 71 grams dark chocolate (72 to 75%), finely chopped
Sugar to taste (optional)
½ cup / 120 ml nondairy milk or water

1. Melt the chocolate and nondairy milk together in a saucepan over low heat, whisking frequently. Pour the liquid through a strainer into a pitcher or into 2 small cups. Serve immediately with sugar and a glass of water on the side.

Chocolat à l'ancienne dit l'Africain

Antoine Rumpelmayer, who named the salon for his daughter-in-law, established La Maison Angelina in 1903. Angelina quickly became a favorite of the rich and famous, from royals to Coco Chanel and Marcel Proust. Expect to stand in line with tourists who come from around the world to order the famous *Chocolat à l'ancienne dit l'Africain*, which is named for the République Côte d'Ivoire in Africa, a former French protectorate and the origin of the Angelina cacao beans.

Hot Chocolate Mexican-Style

While I was on my way to Boston for the holidays, my nephew texted me to say he'd meet me at the Amtrak station so we could get to the Taza Chocolate Factory in nearby Somerville for the three o'clock tour. (Good nephew Josh knew his aunt was doing research for her vegan chocolate book and made reservations.) Cups of steaming hot chocolate, Mexican-style, were being passed when we arrived—vegans welcome! I had one made with almond milk. It was frothy and satisfying with just a hint of cinnamon and vanilla from Taza's high quality Mexican chocolate disks, which are made using traditional methods on antique or repurposed equipment. And all Taza ingredients are organic and direct trade (see Resources page 290). Get to Taza for a tour if you are in the area. Until then, try this version using their chocolate.

Note: In Mexico, hot chocolate is typically made with water, not milk, for a thinner, more intense chocolate beverage. For a thicker beverage, use almond or soy milk. You can mix the chocolate with a traditional *molinillo* (wooden Mexican whisk) or a standard kitchen whisk in the saucepan, but you may have a mess to clean up unless the saucepan is deep.

MAKES ONE SERVING

1 (1.3-ounce / 37-gram) disk of Mexican-style vegan chocolate, any flavor (Taza preferred)

½ cup / 120 ml nondairy milk or water

1 tablespoon / 15 ml rum, bourbon, or tequila (optional)

1. Use a Microplane grater to grate the disk of chocolate into a small bowl and set aside.

2. Heat the milk or water to just below boiling in a small saucepan with high sides.

3. Remove the saucepan from the heat and add the grated chocolate. Whisk continuously to prevent the chocolate from sticking to the bottom. Add any of the optional liquors and continue to whisk until the chocolate is completely melted.

4. Pour the chocolate mixture into a small pitcher and whisk vigorously for up to two minutes, until the chocolate is frothy.

5. Pour into a warm mug and serve immediately.

Espresso Hot Chocolate

I do not like flavored espresso. I like mine bordering on bitter without sugar. But one mid-morning, when I noticed a cup holding a few tablespoons of ganache next to my espresso machine, I thought, "Why not?" Now, every time I sip this bracing beverage from one of my brightly colored demitasse cups, I wonder, "Why didn't I think of this sooner?" Don't like your espresso on the bitter side like me? Go ahead and add some granulated sugar to your cup or a tablespoon of fluffy steamed almond milk.

MAKES 1 SERVING

1 tablespoon / 15 ml Bittersweet Chocolate Ganache Glaze page 264)

1 freshly made (1-ounce / 30-ml) shot espresso

Organic granulated sugar to taste (optional)

Frothed nondairy milk (optional)

1. If the ganache is solid after being refrigerated, warm it until pourable in a small bowl set into a saucepan containing a few inches of simmering water.

2. Stir the ganache into the espresso until thoroughly mixed. Add any or all of the optional ingredients and sip while hot.

Cacao, Matcha, and Kale Smoothie

Kale is the Michael Phelps of Team Cruciferous—a medalist in every Healthy Veggie Olympic contest. Blend that kale with cancer-fighting, energy-boosting, calorie-burning, and detoxifying matcha tea; flavanol-rich raw cacao; and the good fat in avocado, and your day is made. Or, you can choose to drink this smoothie just because it tastes really good. Matcha newbies, note that the taste is strong—a little goes a long way. Start with the smaller amount.

Note: If using a high-speed blender, the kale leaf can go in whole and the smoothie will be creamy in minutes. If using a standard blender, tear the kale into small pieces before adding it to the blender and process longer.

MAKES 2 SERVINGS

1¼ cups / 300 ml any nondairy milk

1 large kale leaf, stem removed

¼ medium avocado (about ¼ cup / 40 grams)

3 tablespoons / 15 grams raw cacao powder (or any cocoa powder)

2 tablespoons / 30 ml agave syrup or coconut sugar, or more to taste

1½ teaspoons / 3 grams matcha powder, more to taste

1 teaspoon / 5 ml pure vanilla extract

Pinch sea salt

1 cup / 140 grams ice cubes

1. Put all the ingredients in the blender in the order listed, except the ice, and blend until smooth and creamy. Start the blender on low and increase to high speed. Add the ice cubes a few at a time and blend until frothy. Pour into glasses and enjoy.

Chocolate Peanut Butter Cup Smoothie

I almost lived on peanut butter cup candies during finals as a freshman in college, and as a result I couldn't eat them again for years. But my preference for pairing peanut butter and chocolate eventually returned and remains to this day, only now I use better-quality peanut butter and chocolate. This quick, protein-packed, and healthy (but still rather decadent-tasting) smoothie, and the variation that follows, are in heavy rotation on my good mini-meal and snack list.

Note: If using a high-speed blender, the ice can go in all at once and the smoothie will be creamy in minutes. If using a standard blender, add the ice to the blender in batches and process longer.

MAKES 2 SERVINGS

1 cup / 240 ml any nondairy milk

1 medium frozen banana, cut into chunks

2 to 3 tablespoons / 34 to 51 grams peanut butter, chunky or smooth

2 to 3 tablespoons / 30 to 45 ml pure maple syrup, Grade B or dark amber, or agave syrup

1 ounce / 28 grams dark chocolate (use any percentage), melted

1 teaspoon / 5 ml pure vanilla extract

¼ teaspoon pure almond extract (optional)

1 cup / 140 grams ice cubes

1. Add the nondairy milk, banana, 2 tablespoons / 34 grams of the peanut butter, 2 tablespoons / 30 ml of the maple syrup, the melted chocolate, and the vanilla and almond extracts to a blender and blend on high until smooth. Add the ice cubes and blend until frothy. Taste and add additional peanut butter and sweetener if needed. Pour into glasses and enjoy.

VARIATION

Instead of maple syrup and melted chocolate, add a few tablespoons of the Chocolate Maple Syrup (page 275) or All-Purpose Chocolate Syrup (page 274) from the jar in your refrigerator, to taste.

Higher Protein Peanut Butter Cup Smoothie

Tofu adds a good portion of protein to this smoothie. I use organic sprouted firm tofu but any kind you like or have on hand will do.

MAKES 2 SERVINGS

1 cup / 240 ml any nondairy milk

4 ounces / 113 grams firm organic tofu

¼ cup / 67 grams peanut butter, crunchy or smooth

2 tablespoons / 34 grams organic granulated sugar, whole cane sugar, or coconut sugar

¼ cup / 25 grams Dutch-process cocoa powder

About 1 cup / 140 grams ice cubes

1. Put all the ingredients in a blender in the order listed, except the ice, and blend until smooth and creamy. Start the blender on low and increase to high speed. Blend until all the ingredients are completely puréed. Add the ice cubes a few at a time and blend until frothy. Pour into 1 or 2 glasses and enjoy.

Chocolate Date Thick Shake

Not far from the magnificent Joshua Tree National Park where I hiked with my children is Hadley Fruit Orchards. There, California dates reign supreme and the Hadley's Date Shake is said to be the best in the world. Expect long lines if you want one of those ultra-popular date shakes—especially the chocolate ones. I guess I can be grateful in one regard: Since ice cream is the base of Hadley's creamy shakes and I am a vegan, there would be no waiting in line for me. But I did get to watch as pitted Deglet Noor dates were blended into vanilla ice cream and milk and served up to throngs of people.

Years later, inspiration came from my desserts demonstration at the New York Veg Food Fest and my new high-speed Vitamix blender. As I figured out how to make a thick and creamy, no-apologies vegan version, I enjoyed every sip along the way. The dates serve as more than a sweetener in this recipe and their taste should be evident. If using a high-speed blender, the shake will be thick and creamy in minutes. If using a standard blender, process the nuts, dates, and ice in batches.

Note: It is essential to check every single pitted date for a stray pit or, as I found one morning, a moldy one. Dried dates are also sticky, so be sure to rinse them before soaking. If raw does not matter to you and you want to save time, the cashews and the dates can be soaked in boiling water for 2 to 3 hours. But no matter what method you choose, do not discard the soaking water! It is sweet, luscious liquid gold. I often peel soaked dates (I am not in the majority here), but this is a date shake and pieces of skin are just fine.

MAKES 1 LARGE SERVING

¾ cup / 110 grams whole raw cashews

½ cup packed / 115 grams any pitted dried dates

½ teaspoon pure vanilla extract or seeds from half a vanilla bean

3 to 4 tablespoons / 45 to 60 ml All-Purpose Chocolate Syrup (page 274) or Chocolate Maple Syrup (page 275)

1½ cups / 210 grams ice cubes

1. Rinse the cashews in a strainer, then put in a container and add enough water to cover the cashews by 2 to 3 inches. Refrigerate for 4 to 6 hours or overnight.

2. Rinse the dates in a strainer. Put the dates into a container. Add enough water to cover them by 2 inches. Soak the dates for 3 to 4 hours at room temperature or refrigerate them for up to 2 days (or cover the dates with boiling water and they will be ready to use in about 1 hour).

3. Drain and rinse the cashews. Put them in a blender and add ¾ cup / 180 ml water, which will barely cover the nuts. Start the blender on low and increase to high speed. Blend until the cashew cream is perfectly smooth. This will happen quickly in a high-speed blender but can be done in a standard blender in two batches and with longer blending.

4. Drain the dates in a strainer set over a measuring cup, saving the liquid. Add the dates, ¾ cup of the soaking liquid, and the vanilla to the cashew cream and blend until completely smooth.

5. Add 2 tablespoons / 30 ml of the chocolate sauce and the ice and blend until frothy. Taste and add more sauce or ice to taste.

6. Pour into a tall glass and serve immediately.

Meal in a Glass

The delightful food writer Kim O'Donnel talks about "eating down the fridge," which simply means making a meal or as many meals as you can by eating what you have on hand. That smart idea is the source of this recipe. My vegan assistant Megan and I got very hungry one afternoon right in the middle of a serious work crunch. I went into the kitchen, only a few steps away from the "office" in my small New York City apartment, to make us a fast-but-wholesome meal we could drink. Homemade nut milk, kale, frozen organic berries, cacao nibs, and nuts and seeds are always on hand in my place, and I'd just bought the highly touted superfoods lucuma and maca to try, so in they went, too. We liked what we later dubbed the "meal in the glass" and spent some time recreating it with measurements. You really need not measure though. Use a combination of healthy foods on hand, substituting cocoa powder for the cacao nibs if you wish. What is important to consider is what kind of blender you have. If you are using a high-speed blender, the beverage will be smooth and thick in a flash. Adding ingredients more slowly and blending longer is the key to making creamy mixtures in standard blenders. If using a standard blender, tear the kale into small pieces before adding it to the blender and process longer, stopping the machine a few times to clean the sides of the container. I prefer the high-speed kind and suggest that you start being very good ASAP and write a letter to Santa requesting a high-speed machine. It is worth it.

MAKES 2 SERVINGS

1 cup / 240 ml Basic Thick Cashew Cream (page 284)

½ cup / 120 ml water, at room temperature

1 large handful organic kale, stems removed

3 tablespoons / 24 grams cacao nibs

⅔ cup fresh or frozen organic blueberries

1 small frozen banana

Handful of walnuts

3 pitted Medjool dates (about 45 grams), or more for a sweeter smoothie

1 tablespoon / 9 grams lucuma powder

2 teaspoons / 6 grams maca powder

1 teaspoon / 5 ml alcohol-free vanilla extract

2 cups / 280 grams ice cubes

1. Put all the ingredients in a blender in the order listed, except the ice, and blend until smooth and creamy. Start the blender on low and increase to high speed. Add the ice cubes a few at a time and blend until frothy. Pour into 2 glasses and enjoy.

VARIATION

Creamy Meal in a Glass: Use any commercial nondairy milk to make the smoothie. It will not be "raw" but it will be delicious.

Raw Cacao Nib Smoothie

Cacao nibs are partially ground cacao beans that are the natural source of all chocolate products. If you've cracked open a cacao bean and eaten the nib inside you know it is bitter, with just a hint of chocolate flavor on the finish. I do like the flavor of the nib when it is infused into liquid, and I also like its crunch in place of nuts or seeds. In this recipe, you can add more or less cacao nib to taste. Look for raw nibs that are fermented and dried at temperatures below 118°F / 48°C for maximum nutrient retention. For a truly raw recipe, be sure to use raw agave syrup and alcohol-free vanilla extract for the cashew cream. This recipe specifies a high-speed blender, but a standard blender will do; just make sure to blend longer until the liquid is silky smooth. You can use nondairy milk, tamari instead of unpasteurized nama shoyu, any other sweetener, and pure vanilla to make this recipe. It will taste just as good, but will be what I call now "raw friendly" instead of really raw.

MAKES 1 LARGE SERVING

3/4 cup / 180 ml Basic Thick Cashew Cream (page 284)

1/4 cup plus 1 tablespoon / 75 ml water

3 pitted Medjool or 4 pitted Deglet Noor dates /
    46 grams, soaked and peeled

3 tablespoons / 24 grams raw cacao nibs

3 to 4 tablespoons / 45 to 60 ml raw agave syrup,
    to taste

1/2 teaspoon alcohol-free vanilla extract

1/4 teaspoon nama shoyu (optional)

1 cup / 140 grams ice cubes

1 to 2 tablespoons / 15 to 30 ml agave syrup or maple
    syrup (optional to add sweetness)

1. Put all the ingredients in a blender in the order listed, except the ice, and blend until smooth and creamy. Start the blender on low and increase to high speed. Add the ice cubes a few at a time and blend until frothy. Taste and add more sweetener if needed. Pour into a tall glass, and enjoy.

Chocolate Horchata

Horchata (pronounced or-CHA-tah) is a refreshing dairy-free rice- or nut-based drink from Mexico that's increasingly available in taquerías and burrito stands in the United States. (In Spain, horchata is based on the Chufa nut, which I've never seen here.) My recipe combines elements from *Horchata de Arroz* (rice) and *Horchata de Almendra* (almonds) but with healthy upgrades: Whole grain brown rice replaces white rice and organic granulated sugar and organic whole cane sugar replace refined white sugar. (You will need to soak the rice and almonds overnight, so plan ahead.) My Mexican and Salvadorian friends have told me about horchata flavored with mint, chocolate, or lime, and with enough ice to make the drink slushy. I like all these flavors too and find one cup of ice makes for the most refreshing version. Finally, for an adult version, tip some rum or tequila into the beverage for a frothy, potent, cooling cocktail.

If using a high-speed blender, the rice and nuts will be quickly pulverized and the horchata will be creamy and ready to drink in minutes, but the rice and nuts still need to be soaked and refrigerated for at least 24 hours, even if using a high-speed blender. If using a standard blender, it will be necessary to make the rice milk in 2 batches and to add the nuts half at a time as well. Be prepared to blend longer, stopping the blender a few times to clean the sides of the container. Have patience. The drink will be very good. Whether or not you use a high-speed blender, to strain or not to strain horchata is a personal choice. I like the slightly gritty texture, which is traditional in some communities, but strain through a nut milk bag or a fine mesh sieve if you prefer a smoother drink. The guar gum is optional but recommended to keep the beverage from separating if stored overnight.

MAKES 2 SERVINGS

¼ cup / 44 grams long grain brown rice

½ cup / 70 grams blanched whole almonds
   (see Sidebar page 289)

¼ cup / 50 grams organic granulated sugar

3 tablespoons / 27 grams organic whole cane sugar
   or coconut sugar

3 tablespoons / 18 grams Dutch-process cocoa
   or natural cocoa (15 grams)

1 teaspoon / 2 grams ground cinnamon, more or less
   to taste

1 teaspoon / 5 ml pure vanilla extract

½ teaspoon almond extract

⅛ teaspoon guar gum (optional but recommended)

1½ cups / 210 grams ice cubes, more for serving

1 to 2 teaspoons / 1 to 2 grams lime zest (optional)

1. Soak the rice and almonds: Rinse the rice in a sieve. Transfer into a container, pour in enough water to cover the rice by 2 inches, and refrigerate for 24 to 36 hours. Rinse the almonds. Transfer to a container, pour in enough water to cover the nuts by 2 inches, and refrigerate for 8 to 24 hours.

2. To make the drink, drain and rinse the rice first. Grind the rice with 1 cup of fresh water in a blender on high until the rice is pulverized and the resulting rice milk is smooth. This will take 5 minutes or longer in a standard blender.

3. Drain and rinse the almonds and add to the rice milk in the blender. Start the machine on low and quickly increase the speed to high. Blend until smooth, up to 5 minutes in a standard blender. Stop the machine a few times to clean the sides of the container, and have patience.

4. Add the granulated and coconut sugars, cocoa, cinnamon, and vanilla and almond extracts and blend on high until smooth. Scrape the sides of the blender with a spatula, pushing any unblended bits of rice or almond into the liquid. Add the guar gum if using and blend on high for 1 minute. Add the lime zest and 1 cup of ice cubes a few cubes at a time and blend on high until incorporated. Taste and add more sugar if desired. Pour over ice into tall glasses and serve immediately.

KEEPING

Horchata can be refrigerated in a covered jar for up to twenty-four hours: be sure to use the guar gum if keeping overnight. Shake very well or blend briefly before serving.

VARIATIONS

Spiced Chocolate Horchata: Add ¼ to ½ teaspoon ground chili powder.

Mint Chocolate Horchata: Add a handful of fresh mint leaves to the blender with the sugar.

Chocolate Vodka

As impossible as it might sound, there seems to be no universal drinking cheer in Russian. Chocolate Vodka certainly screams out for one, so I simply say, "To your health and enjoy responsibly!" All this takes to make are cacao nibs and some good vodka. Simply combine the two, shake the jar a couple of times a day for a week, strain out the nibs, and refrigerate or freeze. You'll have people screaming "*Da!*" before you know it. Drink an icy shot of the softly sweet and slightly bitter liqueur straight up or use it to make White or Black Russians (page 258).

MAKES 2 ¼ CUPS / 540 ML
INFUSED VODKA

2 ½ cups / 600 ml organic vodka

½ cup / 72 grams cacao nibs

1. Combine the vodka and cocoa nibs in a jar. Close the jar tightly and shake.

2. Let stand at room temperature for 1 week, shaking the jar once or twice each day.

3. Strain the vodka through a fine mesh sieve and discard the nibs. Strain the vodka a second time through an unbleached coffee filter into another clean jar and refrigerate or freeze.

SERVING

Drink a shot icy cold or use it as you would any vodka.

KEEPING

The infused vodka can be refrigerated or frozen for up to three months before the flavor starts going a little light.

Chocolate White Russian

The White Russian is the potent but easy to quaff cocktail that was a favorite of Jeff "The Dude" Lebowski (Jeff Bridges) in the Coen Brother's cult classic *The Big Lebowski*—only he called it "The Caucasian." I have enjoyed vegan versions of this cocktail made with nondairy creamer and have now upped the ante by starting with house-made cacao nib–infused Chocolate Vodka (page 257). My favorite creamer is So Delicious coconut milk creamer, but you can use any brand you like. (A cream-free Black Russian variation follows this recipe.) Whether to stir, float the cream on top, or to use equal parts vodka and coffee liqueur, I leave to you.

MAKES 1 DRINK

2 ounces / 60 ml Chocolate Vodka (page 257)

1 ounce / 30 ml coffee liqueur, such as Kahlua

½ ounce / 15 ml nondairy creamer

1. Pour the vodka and coffee liqueur into an old-fashioned glass filled with ice cubes and stir.

2. Pour the nondairy milk into the glass and leave it to float on top, or stir vigorously.

VARIATION

Black Russian: Pour the Chocolate Vodka into an old-fashioned glass filled with ice. Add 1½ ounces / 44 ml coffee liqueur and stir. Serve immediately.

CHAPTER ELEVEN

Master Recipes

Chocolate sauces for all reasons, impossible-to-resist frosting and buttercream to top your favorite chocolate cake, a splendid vegan honey, indispensable Basic Thick Cashew Cream: the recipes in this chapter are not only components for several different cakes, pies, and frozen desserts but they are also good on their own. To that end, it is wise to make more than you need for another recipe—you *will* be tempted to eat more than just the required taste tests along the way! With the exception of the Chocolate Avocado "Buttercream," which tastes best on the day it is made, all the recipes can be made ahead and refrigerated or frozen. The chocolate sauces can be thinned with water, nondairy milk, liquid sweeteners, or liquor to use as plating sauces for other desserts in the book.

Fran's Rulebook for Successful Master Recipes

1. **Read the recipes all the way through and plan your time.**

2. **Prepare your *mise en place*: gather the equipment, chop or melt the chocolate, melt the coconut oil, refrigerate the canned coconut milk (an extra can is advisable), soak the nuts.**

3. **Measure the ingredients carefully, using the correct utensil and method.**

4. **Pay attention to consistencies, and test as you go.**

THE RECIPES

Bittersweet Chocolate Ganache Glaze

Chocolate Coconut Ganache Glaze

Chocolate Confectioners' Sugar Glaze

Chocolate Orange Glaze

Creamy Chocolate Cupcake Frosting

Thick and Glossy Fudge Frosting

Chocolate Avocado "Buttercream"

All-Purpose Chocolate Syrup

Chocolate Maple Syrup

Raw Cacao Sauce

Thick Fudge Sauce

Chocolate Ice Cream Shell

Chocolate Coconut Whipped Cream

White Chocolate Cream Filling

Vanilla Custard Cream Filling

Chocolate Cranberry Cream Filling

Basic Thick Cashew Cream

Maple Cranberry Sauce

Vegan Orange Blossom Honey

Marzipan

Bittersweet Chocolate Ganache Glaze

It will take longer to read this recipe than to make it, but its success is all about the quality and taste of the chocolate and following the details in the recipe. As long as you stay within the percentages listed, any premium quality chocolate you enjoy eating is the one to use. The important part is to chop the chocolate very fine. Allowing the chocolate to melt into the milk for the full 4 minutes is *not* optional. And stir only until the chocolate and milk are emulsified—that is, glossy and smooth. Over-mixing may turn your silken ganache gritty. If the chocolate has not completely melted after the ganache is mixed, bring the water in the saucepan on the stove to a simmer and turn off the heat. Place the bowl of ganache on the saucepan for a few minutes, then stir very gently until the chocolate has melted and the ganache is smooth.

MAKES 2 CUPS / 480 ML

8 ounces / 227 grams dark chocolate (70 to 72%), finely chopped

1¼ cups / 300 ml organic almond milk or soymilk (more as needed to adjust consistency)

2 tablespoons / 18 grams organic granulated sugar

Pinch fine sea salt

1¼ teaspoons / 6.25 ml pure vanilla extract

2 teaspoons / 10 ml mild tasting extra-virgin olive oil (optional but recommended for sheen)

1. Add the chocolate to a heatproof bowl and set aside while you heat the milk.

2. Pour the milk into a small saucepan. Add the sugar and salt. Cook over medium heat, whisking a few times to a low boil.

3. Immediately remove the saucepan from the heat. Pour the hot milk over the chopped chocolate all at once. Rotate the bowl so the chocolate is completely submerged. Cover the bowl with a plate and let stand undisturbed for 4 minutes.

4. Add the vanilla and olive oil (if using) and whisk from the center out only until smooth and glossy. (If the chocolate is not completely melted, refer to the Sidebar on page 28 for instructions on using a water bath to melt the chocolate.)

5. Keep the bowl of ganache at room temperature while you test the final consistency. Dip a teaspoon into the ganache, set the coated spoon on a small plate, and refrigerate for 10 to 15 minutes. After chilling, the ganache on the spoon should be smooth and firm, but should still taste creamy. It is unlikely, but if the glaze is too firm, add a tablespoon of room temperature milk, and repeat the test. Add a second tablespoon if needed.

6. Pass the ganache through a strainer into a bowl. Whisking slowly will speed the process.

7. Allow the ganache to thicken at room temperature for 15 to 25 minutes, or until it will coat a spoon thickly with minimal dripping, but remain pourable. Stir a few times from the outside into the center before glazing.

KEEPING

The glaze can be refrigerated in a tightly closed container for up to five days and frozen for up to one month. The glaze hardens when it is cold and will need to be reheated. To reheat, spoon the glaze into a heatproof bowl that fits over a saucepan of barely simmering water. When about two-thirds of the glaze is melted, stir gently until it is smooth. Adjust the consistency as needed by stirring warm nondairy milk into the glaze a little at a time.

Chocolate Coconut Ganache Glaze

Canned coconut milk has far more fat (18 to 22% is typical) than nondairy milk, is quite thick, and has an apparent coconut flavor. The only ingredients on the label should be coconut milk, water, and guar gum, and organic is best. Some brands contain additives. Since canned full-fat coconut milk is so thick, it is essential that the chocolate be chopped so fine that it is almost powdered. This can be done in a food processor. Be sure to stir the coconut milk until it is thoroughly mixed before heating. The coconut sugar contributes a lovely fruity caramel flavor, but organic granulated sugar can be used with good results, too, to make an exceptionally creamy ganache glaze. Use as you would any chocolate glaze where a hint of coconut will enhance the dessert.

MAKES ABOUT 2 CUPS / 480 ML

8 ounces / 227 grams dark chocolate (68 to 72%), finely chopped

1½ cups plus 1 tablespoon / 375 ml canned unsweetened full-fat coconut milk, well-stirred, more as needed to adjust final consistency (do not use light)

¼ cup / 37 grams coconut sugar or organic granulated sugar (50 grams)

Pinch fine sea salt

1 teaspoon / 5 ml pure vanilla extract

1. Add the chocolate to a heatproof bowl and set aside while you heat the milk.

2. Pour the milk into a small saucepan. Add the sugar and salt. Cook over medium heat, whisking a few times to a low boil. Immediately remove the saucepan from the heat.

3. Pour the hot milk over the chopped chocolate all at once. Rotate the bowl so the chocolate is completely submerged. Cover the bowl with a plate and let stand undisturbed for 4 minutes.

4. Add the vanilla and whisk from the center out only until smooth and glossy. (If the chocolate is not completely melted, refer to the Sidebar on page 28 for instructions on using a water bath to melt the chocolate.)

5. Keep the bowl of ganache at room temperature while you test the consistency. Dip a teaspoon into the ganache, set the coated spoon on a small plate, and refrigerate for 10 to 15 minutes. After chilling, the ganache on the spoon should be smooth and firm, but should still taste creamy. It is unlikely, but if the glaze is too firm, add an additional tablespoon of room temperature milk, and repeat the test. Add a second tablespoon if needed.

6. Allow the ganache to thicken at room temperature for 20 to 30 minutes, until it coats a spoon thickly with minimal dripping, but still remains pourable. Stir a few times from the sides into the center.

KEEPING
Refrigerate up to a day ahead in a covered container or freeze for up to 1 month.

Chocolate Confectioners' Sugar Glaze

You won't need to chop or melt chocolate or add oil to make this luxurious chocolate glaze that is suitable for any cake. All it takes is bringing a kettle of water to just under the boil and sifting the sugar and cocoa. The glaze can also be refrigerated for a month in a covered container, so you may want to make a double batch.

MAKES ½ CUP / 120 ML,
ENOUGH FOR ONE 9-INCH /
23-CM CAKE

1 ⅓ cups / 140 grams confectioners' sugar

2 tablespoons plus 2 teaspoons / 16 grams Dutch-process cocoa powder

2 tablespoons plus 2 teaspoons / 40 ml boiling water

1 teaspoon / 5 ml pure vanilla extract

1. Sift the confectioners' sugar and cocoa into a small heatproof bowl.

2. Add the boiling water and whisk until the sugar and cocoa are dissolved and the glaze is smooth.

3. Add the vanilla and whisk until incorporated.

KEEPING

Refrigerate in a covered container up to one month. Allow time for the glaze to return to room temperature before using, stirring a few times. If the glaze becomes too thick to pour, stir in a teaspoon at a time of hot water until the desired consistency is reached.

Chocolate Orange Glaze

Drizzling this quick glaze over any simple cake will make a drab winter day—heck, any day—brighter. It's an added bonus that the juice makes this glaze lower in fat than those made with nondairy milks, and that it contains no added sugar. Choose an orange large enough and it alone might yield enough juice and zest for the recipe.

MAKES ⅔ CUP / 160 ML

Finely grated zest of 1 large organic orange

¼ cup / 60 ml freshly squeezed orange juice, strained

3½ ounces / 99 grams dark chocolate (70 to 72%), very finely chopped

2 teaspoons / 10 ml fruity extra-virgin olive oil

¼ teaspoon pure vanilla extract

⅛ teaspoon fine sea salt

1. Combine the zest, orange juice, and chocolate in a small saucepan. Cook over the lowest heat until the chocolate begins to melt.

2. Remove from the heat and stir until the chocolate is completely melted and the glaze is smooth.

3. Stir the olive oil, vanilla, and salt into the glaze. Pour into a bowl and allow the glaze to thicken at room temperature for 20 to 25 minutes or until the glaze has set enough to coat a spoon thickly. Stir a few times before using.

KEEPING

Refrigerate the glaze in a covered container for up to three days. Allow the glaze to return to room temperature before using, or warm it in a water bath.

Creamy Chocolate Cupcake Frosting

A shortening-free, super creamy frosting that can be piped through a pastry bag is a dream come true for me. Should you prefer to spread it on your cupcakes instead of filling a pastry bag, you may need to add an extra tablespoon or two of milk to thin it. The creamy consistency of this frosting makes it a delicious choice as a filling for the Intensely Chocolate Trifle, too (page 110).

MAKES ABOUT 1½ CUPS / 360 ML, ENOUGH FOR 12 TO 16 STANDARD-SIZE CUPCAKES

4 ¾ teaspoons / 4.75 grams agar flakes

¾ cup plus 2 tablespoons / 210 ml water, at room temperature, divided

½ cup / 120 ml canned full-fat coconut milk, well-stirred, plus more to adjust final consistency if needed (do not use light)

3 tablespoons / 45 ml pure maple syrup, Grade B or dark amber, or agave nectar

⅛ teaspoon fine sea salt

⅔ cup organic granulated sugar / 128 grams

⅓ cup / 32 grams Dutch-process cocoa powder

1 ounce / 28 grams dark chocolate (68 to 72%), chopped

4 ¾ teaspoons / 9.5 grams arrowroot

1 tablespoon / 15 ml pure vanilla extract

1. Measure the agar into a medium saucepan. Pour ¾ cup / 180 ml of the water over the agar, but do not stir or heat. Set aside for 10 minutes or longer to allow the agar to soften. This will help the agar dissolve thoroughly and easily.

2. Bring the liquid to a boil over medium heat, stirring a few times. Reduce the heat to low. Cover the saucepan and simmer for 5 to 6 minutes, stirring a few times to release any bits of agar that may be stuck on the bottom of the pan. Check a spoonful of liquid for undissolved agar. Cover and simmer longer if necessary, until the agar is completely dissolved.

3. Whisk the coconut milk, maple syrup, and salt into the dissolved agar and simmer for 2 minutes. Add the sugar and simmer for about a minute until dissolved. Add the cocoa slowly, whisking constantly until the cocoa is dissolved, and simmer for 2 to 3 minutes. Make sure you stir the bottom of the pot so the cocoa doesn't burn. Add the chocolate to the saucepan and stir until melted.

4. In a small cup, dissolve the arrowroot in the remaining 2 tablespoons / 30 ml of water. Whisking constantly, add the dissolved arrowroot to the simmering liquid. Cook only until a full boil is reached and not longer. (Arrowroot-thickened mixtures are in danger of thinning out if cooked too long.) The mixture will feel thick almost immediately. Remove the saucepan from the heat and add the vanilla extract. Pour into a 2-cup or larger measure. Stir gently but frequently until cooled to lukewarm.

5. Pour the cream into a shallow bowl and cool to room temperature. Then refrigerate until the cream is very firm. This will take 1 to 2 hours.

6. Before using, spoon the cream into a food processor. Pulse the cream a few times until creamy and easy to spread or pipe.

KEEPING

The frosting can be refrigerated in an airtight container for up to three days.

Thick and Glossy Fudge Frosting

While cocoa powder is bitter on its own, when used properly, it provides a strong chocolate flavor. Plus, in unsweetened cocoa powder seventy-five to eighty-five percent of the cocoa butter has been removed, making cocoa a valuable asset to a health-conscious chocolate chef. You'll want to swirl this glossy frosting thickly on any of the cupcakes in Chapter Three.

Note: Allowing the cocoa to bloom in hot liquid for about ten minutes unlocks its intense flavor.

MAKES ABOUT 3 ½ CUPS / 360 ML

- 1 ¼ cups / 129 grams Dutch-process cocoa powder
- 1 cup / 240 ml boiling water, plus more as needed to adjust final consistency
- ½ cup / 120 ml pure maple syrup, Grade B or dark amber, or agave syrup
- 3 tablespoons / 39 grams organic granulated sugar
- 3 tablespoons / 27 grams organic whole cane sugar, ground in a blender until powdered
- 3 tablespoons / 45 ml mild tasting extra-virgin olive oil or coconut oil, melted or solid
- ¼ teaspoon fine sea salt
- 2 teaspoons / 10 ml pure vanilla extract
- ¼ teaspoon chocolate extract (optional)

1. Sift the cocoa powder into a skillet or shallow 8 to 9-inch / 20 to 23-cm saucepan. Pour the boiling water and maple syrup over the cocoa and whisk to dissolve. Set aside for 10 minutes to allow the cocoa to bloom.

2. Add the granulated and whole cane sugars, oil, and salt to the skillet. Cook over low heat, whisking frequently, until wisps of steam are visible. Be sure to stir the bottom to keep the cocoa from burning. Cook for 2 minutes, adjusting the heat as needed to keep the chocolate steaming, and stirring frequently.

3. Raise the heat slightly, just enough so that the frosting bubbles slowly, and cook for 30 seconds, until the frosting is shiny and smooth and thick enough to spread. Immediately remove the pan from the heat, and add the vanilla and chocolate extracts, if using.

4. Check the final consistency of the frosting: Refrigerate a tablespoon of frosting in a small dish for 10 minutes. After chilling, the frosting should be thick and fudgy but still easy to spread. If it is too thick, add additional boiling water, a little at a time, and repeat the test. If no adjustment is needed, cool to room temperature in the skillet. It is ready to use as soon as it has cooled.

KEEPING

Refrigerate the frosting in a covered container for up to four days. Use at room temperature. If the frosting is too thick to spread easily, even at room temperature, whisk in additional hot water, a little at a time as needed.

Chocolate Avocado "Buttercream"

One of my favorite "fast food" snacks is a fully ripe buttery avocado sprinkled with flaky sea salt. But for desserts, the dark chocolate mutes the flavor of the ripe avocado, leaving just a hint of complementary fruitiness. Starting with a just-ripe, rather than a fully ripe, avocado avoids the subtle vegetal taste. I understand that the words "avocado" and "buttercream" may seem strange together—but be daring! As super tester James from Australia wrote, "It's fab! I tell you what, before I added the chocolate it looked like something out of *Ghostbusters*, but then I added the chocolate, and after a few seconds it looked like buttercream!"

Note: Organic confectioners' sugar is rarely as fine as conventional confectioners' sugar. It is essential that you sift the organic sugar twice. I have been known to sift three times. Also this is one recipe that tastes best on the day it is made.

MAKES 1 CUP / 240 ML

4 ounces / 120 grams (about ½ cup mashed) just-ripe avocado

1 tablespoon / 15 ml any nondairy milk

1 teaspoon / 5 ml pure vanilla extract

1½ to 1¾ cups / 164 to 191 grams organic confectioners' sugar, sifted twice

3 ounces / 85 grams dark chocolate (66 to 70%), melted

1. Mash the avocado with a fork in a medium bowl. Add the nondairy milk and vanilla extract and mix with electric beaters on high until smooth.

2. Add the confectioners' sugar, ¼ cup / 25 grams at a time, beating on low speed until just incorporated. Increase the speed to high and beat for 1 minute after each addition. Repeat until 1½ cups / 164 grams of the sugar is used. Taste the buttercream and decide if more sugar is needed.

3. When all the sugar has been added, stir the melted chocolate into the buttercream with a silicone spatula.

KEEPING

Refrigerate the buttercream in a tightly covered container for up to 1 day. Whip with a fork before using.

All-Purpose Chocolate Syrup (No Fat Added)

Real chocolate syrup, made without a drop of added fat, belongs in the refrigerators of chocolate lovers at all times—standing at the ready for all the puddings, ice creams, and pieces of cake waiting for a healthy drizzle of chocolate.

This recipe makes a glossy, deeply chocolate syrup that tends toward bittersweet. If you like your syrup sweeter, add more sugar. Regardless of how sweet you like it, the difference between powdery sauce and a smooth one with rich, full flavor is in the details, so while the recipe cooks in only 5 minutes, don't skip any steps. Blooming the cocoa first in very hot water deepens the chocolate flavor and helps prevent the powdery taste that is apparent in some cocoa-based desserts, particularly those made without fat. The small amount of maple syrup adds richness, not fat. Remember that cocoa, like chocolate, is easily scorched. Stir continuously, reaching the bottom and sides of the saucepan. I highly recommend using Dutch-process cocoa for the best flavor, but a premium natural cocoa can be used instead (see Resources page 290). If using natural cocoa, add another tablespoon each of sugar and maple syrup.

MAKES 1 CUP / 240 ML

¾ cup / 84 grams Dutch-process cocoa powder

¾ cup plus 6 tablespoons / 270 ml boiling water, divided

Pinch sea salt

½ cup plus 1 tablespoon / 124 grams organic granulated sugar

1 tablespoon / 15 ml pure maple syrup, Grade B or dark amber

¾ teaspoon / 3.75 ml pure vanilla extract

1. Sift the cocoa powder into a medium saucepan. Pour ¾ cup / 180 ml of the boiling water over the cocoa. Stir with a silicone spatula to moisten the cocoa. (The paste need not be smooth.) Remove from the heat and set aside for 5 minutes while the cocoa blooms.

2. Whisk the remaining 6 tablespoons / 90 ml of very hot water into the cocoa paste and add a pinch of salt. Cook over low heat, stirring with the silicone spatula for 2 minutes, making sure to reach the bottom and sides of the saucepan.

3. Add the sugar and maple syrup, and continue to cook over lowest heat for another minute. Taste the syrup carefully: it will be hot. If you want sweeter syrup, add another tablespoon each of sugar and water. When small bubbles start to form around the sides, it is time to turn off the heat. Stir the vanilla into the syrup.

4. Cool the syrup to room temperature in the saucepan, stirring once or twice while the syrup cools.

KEEPING

Store the syrup in a covered jar in the refrigerator for up to three weeks. Add a little very hot water to adjust the consistency, if needed.

Chocolate Maple Syrup

This recipe is my homage to Pete Kanik of Pete's Sweets. Pete produces excellent pure maple syrup in New York State and knows everything there is to know about what the colonists called "Indian Sugar." He and the New York State Maple Producers—second only to Vermont in their annual production—manufactured 564,000 gallons of maple syrup in 2011, their highest production rate in sixty-four years. And while you might have read that the brix (a measure of sweetness) in maple syrup has been declining—and that the unseasonably warm weather means a shortage of maple syrup to come—Pete says not to worry. I buy his maple syrup in gallon jugs, five at a time, to save money. I share the bounty with friends and neighbors, and always have plenty of excellent maple to use and enjoy.

Notes: Maple syrup is best stored in the freezer where it becomes viscous and is safe from fermentation. Do not use pancake syrup for this or any other recipe, even the organic kind. It is water, color, "natural flavor," and corn syrup—completely devoid of actual maple syrup.

MAKES ½ CUP / 120 ML

¼ cup plus 2 tablespoons / 90 ml pure maple syrup, Grade B or dark amber

¼ cup plus 1 tablespoon / 75 ml water, at room temperature

1 tablespoon / 10 grams maple sugar (substitute organic granulated sugar)

Pinch fine sea salt

¼ cup plus 1 tablespoon / 31 grams Dutch-process cocoa powder, sifted

½ teaspoon pure vanilla extract

1. Combine the maple syrup, water, sugar, and salt in a small deep saucepan. Cook over medium-low heat until bubbles appear around the sides of the saucepan. Increase the heat to high and bring to a boil. Boil for 1 minute.

2. Wait about a minute until the liquid is no longer steaming, and add the cocoa. Reduce the heat to low and whisk until dissolved, making sure you stir the bottom and sides of the pan. Remove the pan from the heat and add the vanilla. Cool to room temperature, stirring a few times.

3. Pour the syrup into a jar with a lid and cool to room temperature.

KEEPING

The syrup can be refrigerated in the jar for up to three weeks or frozen for up to two months.

VARIATIONS

Add 1 ounce / 28 grams dark chocolate (66 to 72%), coarsely chopped, to the syrup.

Replace the water with the same amount of strained orange juice. Add ⅛ teaspoon pure orange oil with the vanilla extract.

Raw Cacao Sauce

Blend all the ingredients until smooth and glossy—that's all it takes to make a dark and delicious raw chocolate sauce. Using nut oil instead of coconut oil can make for an interesting change of pace, but don't leave it out altogether: the oil ensures that the sauce is silken, not chalky. The unpasteurized soy sauce, nama shoyu, adds more to the flavor than you might expect from just ¼ teaspoon, but if you don't have the raw kind, use any soy sauce or tamari, or add a pinch of good quality sea salt.

MAKES ABOUT ¾ CUP / 180 ML

½ cup minus 1 tablespoon / 33 grams raw cacao powder

½ cup / 120 ml raw agave syrup

3 tablespoons / 45 ml warm water

1 tablespoon plus 1 teaspoon / 20 ml coconut oil, melted

1 teaspoon / 5 ml vanilla extract

¼ teaspoon nama shoyu, or any soy sauce or tamari

¼ teaspoon sea salt

1. Put all the ingredients into a blender. Blend, starting on low and moving to high speed, for at least 1 minute, until the sauce is smooth and glossy. The sauce can also be made in a food processor.

2. Pour the sauce into a jar and cover.

KEEPING

Refrigerate in the jar for up to two weeks. This sauce thickens as it chills in the refrigerator. Add water a little at a time to thin the sauce to your desired consistency.

Thick Fudge Sauce

Deep, dark, thick fudge sauce was a staple in my refrigerator during my pre-vegan days—and it still is, now that I've got this recipe to use! I dip bananas into it, spread it on bread, and eat it straight off a spoon. Heat the sauce until it is liquid (it will still be thick) and pour over ice cream, puddings, or whatever you fancy. This sauce tastes best warm.

MAKES ABOUT ¾ CUP / 180 ML

½ cup / 58 grams Dutch-process cocoa powder, sifted

Pinch fine sea salt

½ cup minus 1 tablespoon / 105 ml boiling water

5 tablespoons / 65 grams organic granulated sugar

2 to 3 tablespoons / 30 to 45 ml pure maple syrup, Grade B or dark amber

1 tablespoon / 15 ml mild tasting extra-virgin olive oil

1 teaspoon / 5 ml pure vanilla extract

1. Sift the cocoa into a heavy-bottomed skillet, preferably one with sloping sides. Whisk until the cocoa is free of lumps. Add the salt. Pour the water over the cocoa. Use a silicone spatula to mix to a paste.

2. Wait 5 minutes, then cook the mixture over medium-low heat for 1 minute, whisking frequently, until wisps of steam appear on the surface and a few small bubbles form around the sides. It is important to stir the bottom and sides so that the cocoa does not burn while it cooks and thickens; adjust the heat as necessary. The mixture may become lumpy as it cooks but will smooth out as you whisk.

3. Add the granulated sugar, maple syrup, and olive oil. Continue to cook, whisking constantly until the mixture boils. Immediately reduce the heat to low and whisk for 30 seconds.

4. Remove the saucepan from the heat. Add the vanilla and whisk slowly until the bubbling stops.

5. Cool the sauce to room temperature in the skillet, whisking a few times as it cools. Use immediately, or pour it into a container, let it come to room temperature, then cover and refrigerate.

SERVING

This sauce belongs on ice cream but go ahead and drizzle or pour this goodness over anything you like.

KEEPING

Refrigerate in a heatproof covered jar for up to two weeks. Warm by setting the jar in a small saucepan. Add water to reach halfway up the sides. Stick a spoon into the jar and heat the water to a simmer, stirring the sauce a few times.

Chocolate Ice Cream Shell

Smucker's Magic Shell—the chocolate sauce with the waxy taste and hydrogenated oil that hardens on ice cream—has the distinction of being the only junk food my mom didn't stock. But then again, she liked her ice cream straight up. I preferred the Carvel ice cream version in which cones were dipped in a similar waxy liquid chocolate that hardened immediately on the cold soft serve twist. After a futile search for the name of this favorite forgotten Carvel treat, I turned to my Facebook and Twitter friends. Based on the volume of immediate answers, it was clear I was not alone in my fond memories of the Carvel Brown Bonnet. Turns out, this magic ice cream topping, which is hard but slightly chewy, is super simple to make and requires only three ingredients (chocolate, vanilla, and olive or coconut oil). The best-tasting in my opinion—and in the opinions of many tasters—was a chocolate ice cream shell made with mild tasting olive oil. Just use good chocolate for the best tasting topping, but after that the flavor possibilities are endless. A mint-flavored variation follows the recipe.

MAKES 1 CUP / 240 ML

7 ounces / 198 grams dark chocolate (68 to 70%), finely chopped

2 tablespoons / 30 ml mild tasting extra-virgin olive oil or coconut oil, melted

½ teaspoon pure vanilla extract

1. Place the chocolate in a small heatproof bowl and set it in a saucepan of very hot water over the lowest heat. Allow the chocolate to melt undisturbed until about two-thirds is melted.

2. Remove the saucepan from the heat and stir with a silicone spatula until all the chocolate is melted. Stir the oil into the chocolate until incorporated. Add the vanilla.

3. Keep the shell in liquid form until ready to pour over the ice cream—do not refrigerate.

SERVING

Spoon a few tablespoons of the liquid shell over a dish of ice cream and wait a few seconds until it magically hardens. The liquid sauce will turn into a firm chocolate shell within a few seconds of touching ice cream and will turn matte when it hardens.

KEEPING

Store the Chocolate Ice Cream Shell in a jar in the refrigerator for up to two weeks. It will harden. To warm before using: place the jar in a small saucepan. Pour hot water to reach about halfway up the sides of the jar and warm over the lowest heat until liquefied.

VARIATION

Mint Shell: Add a few drops of pure mint oil or ¼ teaspoon mint extract.

Chocolate Coconut Whipped Cream

For such a simple concept, this recipe drove me mad. No matter how long I left the unopened can of full-fat coconut milk in the refrigerator, the coconut cream part of the milk frequently did not harden. I opened many cans of different brands only to find creamy (not hardened) fat, and unless that fat hardens whipped cream is not going to happen. Or so I thought. I finally realized that making this recipe work meant using a larger amount of confectioners' sugar and adding a small amount of guar gum to thicken and bind. Now, the texture of the cream was assured but my sanity was not: the cream was too sweet for me—that is until I reached for an unsweetened chocolate (99%). Of course, sweetness is a matter of taste, so feel free to use 75 to 85% chocolate instead. Skip the chocolate altogether for a vanilla version.

MAKES ABOUT 2 CUPS / 480 ML

1 can (13.5 to 14 ounces / 400 to 414 ml) unsweetened full-fat coconut milk (do not use light), refrigerated unopened, upright for at least 24 hours (2 days is better)

2 ounces / 57 grams unsweetened chocolate (99%), or substitute 75 to 85%, finely chopped

2 cups / 216 grams confectioners' sugar, sifted twice if organic, divided

¼ teaspoon guar gum, divided

1 teaspoon / 5 ml pure vanilla extract

1. Refrigerate the electric mixer bowl, or a metal bowl large enough to whip the cream, and the whisk beater.

2. Open the can of coconut milk directly from the refrigerator. With a spoon, scoop out only the solid part of the coconut milk (the cream) and place it in a the chilled bowl. Reserve 3 tablespoons of the thinner liquid coconut milk that remains in the can. (Refrigerate the rest for using as a liquid in desserts and smoothies.) Refrigerate the cream in the bowl while you melt the chocolate in the reserved milk.

3. Combine the reserved liquid coconut milk and chocolate in a small saucepan. Warm over the lowest heat until the chocolate is almost completely melted. Immediately remove the saucepan from the heat and stir until the chocolate is melted. Set the saucepan in a larger saucepan of very hot water to keep the melted chocolate from solidifying.

4. Remove the bowl of coconut cream from the refrigerator. Add 1 cup of the sifted confectioners' sugar and ⅛ teaspoon guar gum to the cream. Whip the cream on low speed for 1 minute using the chilled whisk attachment of your mixer. Increase the speed to high and beat for 1 minute. Turn off the mixer and clean the sides of bowl.

5. Add another ½ cup of the confectioners' sugar and the remaining ⅛ teaspoon of guar gum to the cream, and beat for 1 minute, starting on low and increasing the speed to high. Add the remaining ½ cup of confectioners' sugar and the vanilla and beat for another minute, starting on low and increasing the speed to high. The cream will be thickened.

6. When the melted chocolate is no longer warm, fold it gently into the whipped cream with a silicone spatula.

7. Refrigerate the cream in a covered container until set, about 4 hours or overnight. If the cream is too firm, stir vigorously or add a little of the extra liquid coconut milk.

KEEPING

The whipped cream can be made three days ahead and refrigerated in a covered container.

White Chocolate Cream Filling

This is an updated version of the cream that filled my infamous Organic Vegan Twinkies in 2007. The cream is so good though, that I had to find other reasons to use it. This cream still fills Twinkies, as well as the update to Éclairs (page 119). It is a component in Nesselrode Pie (page 160), makes a wonderful cake filling, and is lovely in parfaits layered with fruit, nuts, and chopped chocolate.

Note: You will need to find vegan white chocolate to make the cream. I buy white chocolate chips from kosher markets in my neighborhood, but the chocolate is available by mail order, too (see Resources page 290).

MAKES 1 1/2 CUPS / 360 ML

7 ounces / 198 grams organic firm tofu, drained

1 tablespoon / 15 ml mild tasting extra-virgin olive oil or coconut oil

3 tablespoons / 45 ml maple syrup, Grade B or dark amber, or agave syrup

3/8 teaspoon fine sea salt

1/4 cup / 50 grams organic granulated sugar, lightly ground in a blender

2 1/2 teaspoons / 12 ml pure vanilla extract

1/8 teaspoon pure almond extract (optional, but recommended)

5 ounces / 142 grams vegan white chocolate, melted and kept warm in a water bath (see Resources page 290)

1/4 cup plus 1 tablespoon / 75 ml almond milk or soy milk

1 teaspoon / 2.5 grams agar powder

1 tablespoon plus 2 teaspoons / 10 grams arrowroot

1. Crumble the tofu into a food processor. Add the oil, maple syrup or agave, and salt and process for 1 minute. Clean the sides of the bowl with a silicone spatula. Add the sugar and the vanilla and almond extracts and process for 1 minute.

2. Add the melted white chocolate. Pulse a few times to incorporate and process for 1 minute. Keep the tofu purée in the food processor while you cook the agar-arrowroot slurry.

3. Pour the almond milk into a small saucepan. Sprinkle the agar onto the milk and set aside for 1 minute. Add the arrowroot and whisk until the arrowroot is completely dissolved. Cook the slurry to a boil over medium-low heat, whisking almost constantly. The slurry will be so thick and gummy that the boil will look like sputtering lava. As soon as the sputtering and bubbling reaches the center, remove the saucepan from the heat.

4. Add the slurry to the food processor and pulse to incorporate. Process for 1 minute until the cream is smooth.

KEEPING

Refrigerate in a covered container up to a day ahead of using. The cream will thicken as it chills.

Vanilla Custard Cream Filling

A typical pastry cream, or stirred custard, is made on the stovetop using milk or cream, egg yolks, and starch. Butter may also be an ingredient. Flavorings include vanilla, chocolate, coffee, or liqueurs. A properly made pastry cream is silken and luxurious—and loaded with artery-clogging fat. This recipe, on the other hand, is made in a blender from a base of heart-healthy cashews. Use the custard in the Intensely Chocolate Trifle (page 110), or to fill the Éclairs (page 119). Spread a layer over a ganache-filled cookie crust, or spoon it over fresh fruit. Add a heavy grating of dark chocolate and a cookie and you will have a treat that is rich tasting without the bad fat.

MAKES ABOUT 1½ CUPS / 360 ML

5 ounces (about 1 cup) / 142 grams whole cashews, rinsed and soaked 4 hours to overnight

1 cup / 240 ml canned full-fat unsweetened coconut milk, well-stirred (do not use light)

6 tablespoons / 79 grams organic granulated sugar

1 tablespoon / 15 ml mild-tasting extra-virgin olive oil

Pinch fine sea salt

³/₈ teaspoon agar powder

⅛ teaspoon guar gum

1½ teaspoons / 7.5 ml pure vanilla extract

Seeds from 1 2-inch / 5-cm vanilla bean, or increase the vanilla extract to 1 tablespoon / 15 ml

IF USING A HIGH-SPEED BLENDER:

1. Drain the cashews in a strainer. It is important that the cashews are drained well before using. Blend the cashews, coconut milk, sugar, oil, and salt, starting on low and quickly increasing the speed to high for 2 minutes, until the purée is smooth, thick, and warm.

2. Add the agar powder and guar gum. Blend starting on low, and quickly increase the speed to high. Blend for about 2 minutes, or until the mixture boils; it will actually sputter. If you hear the motor laboring at any point, or if the cream stops moving, use the tamper to push the cream until it starts moving again.

3. Immediately pour the cream into a container. Stir in the vanilla extract and seeds, if using.

4. Cool to room temperature, cover, and refrigerate for 4 hours to overnight. The custard will become quite thick as it chills. Stir before using.

IF USING A STANDARD BLENDER:

1. Drain the cashews in a strainer. It is important that the cashews are drained well before using. Blend the cashews, coconut milk, sugar, oil, and salt, starting on low and quickly increasing the speed to high. You will need to do this in batches and blend longer, depending on the size of the machine. Add the guar gum and blend for 1 minute.

2. Pour the cream into a medium (8-inch / 20-cm) skillet. Add the agar powder and cook over medium-low heat, whisking continuously just until the custard boils. Remove from the heat and stir in the vanilla extract and seeds, if using.

3. Pour the cream into a container, cool to room temperature, cover, and refrigerate for 4 hours to overnight. The custard will thicken as it chills. Stir before using.

KEEPING

Refrigerate in a covered container up to a day ahead of using.

Chocolate Cranberry Cream Filling

Dried cranberries are easy to find year round, but for a summer version of the cream, use dried pitted cherries instead. I suggest you dollop this sweet-tart, pale-pink cream on puddings and gels, or use it as a component in a make-your-own parfait, or as a layer in the Intensely Chocolate Trifle (page 110). You could also use it to fill the Bûche de Noël (pages 116 to 118).

Note: Plan to make the cream at least four hours ahead, to allow it to thicken. It can be made up to a day in advance.

MAKES 1½ TO 1⅔ CUPS / 360 TO 400 ML

6 ounces / 170 grams (about ½ box) firm or extra-firm silken tofu, drained

½ cup / 111 grams organic granulated sugar, ground in a blender until fine

1 tablespoon / 15 ml coconut oil, melted

¼ teaspoon fine sea salt

⅛ teaspoon guar gum

3 tablespoons / 45 ml seedless raspberry jam

3 ounces / 85 grams dark chocolate (66 to 70%)

⅓ cup / 38 grams dried cranberries

1. Purée the tofu, sugar, oil, sea salt, and guar gum in a food processor for 1 minute until the mixture is creamy and no traces of tofu are visible.

2. Clean the sides of the processor and add the jam. Process until combined. Add the chocolate and pulse the machine on and off a few times. Process until incorporated.

3. Spoon the cream into a container, and cover and refrigerate for 4 hours or overnight to allow the flavor to develop. The cream will become firmer as it chills.

4. Bring the cream to room temperature. Stir hard with a silicone spatula and then stir in the cranberries. Refrigerate for at least 4 hours or overnight before using.

KEEPING

The cream can be made one day in advance and refrigerated in a covered container.

Basic Thick Cashew Cream

Cashew Cream is a valuable base ingredient that stands in for dairy cream in a variety of ways, and is used both uncooked and cooked. Refrigerate Cashew Cream for up to two days, or freeze it in ice cube trays so that the right amount is always available for quick defrosting (see Note on keeping). It's easy to thin the cream into cashew milk, as desired. A sweeter variation for making Cashew Cream follows.

Notes: To make the smoothest and best-tasting cashew cream, start with soaked whole raw cashews. If you want to speed the soaking process, use boiling water. The cashews will be soft enough to blend in one hour.

If using a high-speed blender, the Cashew Cream will be thick and smooth in minutes. If using a standard blender, blend the nuts in batches, processing longer. Stop the blender a few times to clean the sides of the container. The small amount of guar gum added is highly recommended to make the richest tasting cream, and one that does not separate.

MAKES ABOUT 1 3/4 CUPS / 420 ML

5 ounces (about 1 cup) / 142 grams whole raw cashews, rinsed and soaked 3 to 4 hours or overnight

2/3 cup / 160 ml water, at room temperature

1/4 cup / 60 ml agave syrup or pure maple syrup, Grade B or dark amber

1 teaspoon / 5 ml pure vanilla extract

1/4 teaspoon guar gum

1. Drain the cashews in a strainer. Put the rinsed nuts into a blender and add the water, agave or maple syrup, and vanilla. Blend, starting on low, and quickly increase the speed to high. Blend for about 1 minute until the cream is perfectly smooth.

2. Push any pieces of unblended cashews down into the cream and blend for 1 minute.

3. Add the guar gum directly onto the cream, making sure it doesn't land on the sides of the container. Blend on low for 30 seconds, then increase the speed to high and blend for 1 minute.

KEEPING

Pour the cream into a container, cover, and refrigerate for up to three days or freeze for up to two months. I freeze cashew cream in silicone ice cube trays, defrosting only the amount I need and giving the defrosted cream a good whisk before using. Store the frozen cubes in a zipper-lock bag until needed.

VARIATION

Sweet Thick Cashew Cream: Reduce the amount of agave or maple syrup to 3 tablespoons and add 3 tablespoons / 39 grams organic granulated sugar.

Maple Cranberry Sauce

This is the sauce to turn to when you want a pop of color and a tart counterpoint to a chocolate dessert. If you think like I do, you'll have bags of cranberries bought in winter in the freezer all year long. This sauce is chunky, but you can push it through a fine mesh sieve and make a gorgeous crimson coulis. (The variation follows.)

MAKES ABOUT 2 CUPS / 480 ML

3 cups (or one 12-ounce / 340-gram bag) fresh or frozen cranberries, picked over and rinsed (do not defrost if frozen)

1/2 cup / 120 ml pure maple syrup, Grade B or dark amber

4 to 5 tablespoons / 50 to 60 grams organic granulated sugar

1/3 cup / 80 ml orange juice

1 teaspoon / 1 gram finely minced zest of an organic or unsprayed orange

Pinch fine sea salt

1 teaspoon / 5 ml pure vanilla extract

1. Combine the cranberries, maple syrup, 4 tablespoons of the sugar, the orange juice, zest, and salt in a medium saucepan. Bring to a boil over medium heat. Reduce the heat to medium-low and cook at a low boil for about 10 minutes, stirring frequently, until the cranberries are soft and most of the liquid is absorbed. Remove from the heat and stir in the vanilla. Taste the sauce. If you prefer a less tart flavor, add the additional tablespoon of sugar and stir until dissolved.

2. Cool to room temperature in the saucepan. Spoon into a container, cover, and refrigerate until needed.

KEEPING

The sauce can be refrigerated up to four days ahead.

VARIATION

Cranberry Coulis: A coulis is a thick purée made from fresh fruit (often berries) or cooked fruit that is used as a sauce to accompany desserts such as puddings, ice cream, and cakes. Paint or smear some of this vibrantly colored sauce on a dessert plate and set a piece of cake atop for a glamorous presentation. Pour the cranberry sauce through a fine sieve into a bowl, pressing on solids. Discard the solids (or if you are like me and don't mind the crunch of seeds, save the solids to mix into hot cereal or yogurt). Makes 1 cup / 240 ml. Refrigerate the coulis in a covered container for up to one week.

Vegan Orange Blossom Honey

If you don't eat honey for ethical reasons or because you find it congesting, as I do, this orange-scented honey substitute is a superb alternative. I make a double recipe in a large saucepan so I always have a jar in my refrigerator for drizzling on nondairy yogurt, over puddings, on bread, and for dipping apples during the Rosh Hashanah holiday.

Note: It is very important to choose a saucepan with high sides when cooking sweet syrups, since they climb the sides quickly and furiously during cooking. A hot syrup boil-over will result in a messy cleanup or a serious burn, since the syrup sticks to skin. Be careful!

The cooked orange zest will have become deliciously candied. Keep it in a container at room temperature for a few days to munch.

MAKES ABOUT ⅔ CUP / 160 ML

⅓ cup / 80 ml brown rice syrup, warmed in the jar until liquid (see page 23)

¼ cup / 60 ml agave syrup

¼ cup / 60 ml pure maple syrup, Grade B or dark amber

1 teaspoon / 4 grams organic granulated sugar

Strips of zest from ½ of a medium organic orange

1. Combine the rice, agave, and maple syrups and the sugar in a medium saucepan with high sides and cook over medium heat to a boil. Add the orange zest.

2. Lower the heat and cook for 10 minutes, stirring a few times and adjusting the heat as necessary to maintain a low boil.

3. Remove the saucepan from the heat. Test the final consistency: Spoon a scant tablespoon into a small dish and refrigerate for 10 minutes. If the honey is thick enough, cool to room temperature in the saucepan. If not, cook it another few minutes.

4. Pour the syrup through a fine mesh strainer into a jar. Cover and refrigerate for up to 1 month.

KEEPING

Refrigerate in a tightly closed jar for up to one month.

Marzipan

Super tester James, a vegan baker in Australia, wrote, "WOW!! I made marzipan!" You can, too. You've probably seen intricately colored and decorated flowers, fruits, animals, and other items made from marzipan, a soft and pliable almond-based paste. When I needed a substitute for the meringue mushrooms I used to make for the Bûche de Nöel, I knew marzipan was the way to go. I am happy to report that making marzipan without refined white sugar, honey, or egg whites, which are some of the usual ingredients, and getting the proportions right, was far easier than I had expected. Make the mushrooms and other shapes, too, but save some of this almond-flavored paste to enrobe in chocolate and make lovely little candies, or press it into a Springerle cookie mold from House on the Hill (see Resources page 290) and cover a cupcake with the delicious stamped design.

Note: The marzipan may look oily after a few days in the refrigerator. Here's what to do. Wipe the oil off the marzipan with paper toweling and then dust with confectioners' sugar and/or cocoa.

MAKES ½ CUP / ABOUT 125 GRAMS

3 ounces / 86 grams blanched almonds (see Sidebar)

2 tablespoons / 12 grams organic confectioners' sugar, more for dusting

Pinch fine sea salt

2 tablespoons / 30 ml brown rice syrup, warmed in the jar until liquid (see page 23)

½ teaspoon pure vanilla extract

³⁄₈ teaspoon pure almond extract

1. Grind the almonds in a food processor until the nuts look like flour. Stop grinding before the nuts become oily. Add the sugar and salt and process until incorporated.

2. Add the rice syrup and vanilla and almond extracts. Process to a smooth paste, about 5 minutes. Squeeze a small piece between your fingers to make sure it holds together. If it does not, process longer or add a teaspoon more of rice syrup.

3. Scoop the marzipan onto a piece of plastic wrap. Cover with another piece and press until flattened to about 8 x 6 inches / 20 x 15 cm. If the marzipan is too soft to shape, refrigerate briefly.

KEEPING

Store the marzipan in a covered container in the refrigerator for up to three weeks. Refer to the Note in the introduction.

Blanching Almonds

To blanch almonds, pour them into a saucepan of boiling water. Let them sit a minute. Drain and dump them out into a bowl of ice water. Wait 2 to 3 minutes and pinch the skins off. Dry the blanched almonds before using, or roast them lightly in a 300°F / 140°C oven for 6 to 9 minutes, making sure they do not color.

Resources

VEGAN CHOCOLATE

Chocolate Alchemy
www.chocolatealchemy.com
3796 Stewart Road
Eugene, Oregon 97402
Organic, fair-trade deodorized cocoa butter

Chocosphere
www.chocosphere.com
PO Box 2237
Tualatin, Oregon 97062
877-992-4626
High-quality chocolates from around the world

Equal Exchange
www.equalexchange.coop
50 United Drive
West Bridgewater, Massachusetts 02379
774-776-7400
Organic and fair-trade chocolates

The Grenada Chocolate Company Ltd.
www.grenadachocolate.com
Hermitage, St. Patrick's
Grenada, West Indies
473-442-0050
Organic, fair trade small-batch chocolates made in Grenada, bean to bar. Because only dark chocolate is made, there is no worry about shared equipment.

Mama Ganache
www.mama-ganache.com
1445 Monterey Street
San Luis Obispo, California 93401
805-782-9868
Organic, fair-trade bulk chocolate, truffles, and confections

Mast Brothers Chocolate
www.mastbrothers.com
111 North 3rd Street
Brooklyn, New York 11249
718-388-2644
Single estate and single origin chocolates as well as a house blend. Not all bars are vegan.

Newman's Own Organics
www.newmansownorganics.com
Organic chocolates and other ingredients

Nibmor Raw Chocolate
www.nibmor.com
11 Middle Neck Road
Suite 208
Great Neck, New York 11021
718-374-5091
Organic, vegan chocolate with no gluten or dairy ingredients

Oppenheimer Chocolate U.S.A. Inc.
www.oppenheimerusa.com
544 Park Avenue
Brooklyn, New York 11205
718-852-5580
Kosher and vegan white chocolate chips

Organic Nectars
www.organicnectars.com
845-246-0506
Organic raw dark and white chocolates, agave nectar

Pacari Chocolate
www.pacarichocolate.com
2660 Blue Horizon Rd.
Sedona, AZ 86336
info@pacarichocolate.com
The first single-origin organic chocolate (including some raw bars) made entirely in Ecuador and produced according to fair standards

Sunspire
www.sunspire.com
The Hain Celestial Group, Inc.
4600 Sleepytime Drive
Boulder, Colorado 80301
800-434-4246
Dairy-free and gluten-free chocolate chips; some organic and fair trade

Taza Chocolate
www.tazachocolate.com
561 Windsor Street
Somerville, Massachusetts 02143
617-623-0804, ext.10
Organic, direct trade stone-ground chocolate

TCHO Chocolate
www.tcho.com
TCHO Ventures, Inc.
Pier 17
San Francisco, California 94111
415-981-0189
Dark chocolates; organic and fair practices

Theo Chocolate
www.theochocolate.com
3400 Phinney Avenue North
Seattle, Washington 98103
206-632-5100
The first organic, Fair for Life certified bean-to-bar chocolate factory in North America

BAKING INGREDIENTS

American Roland Food Corp.
www.rolandfood.com
71 West 23rd Street
New York, New York 10010
800-221-4030
Organic coconut milk, cocoa powder, roasted chestnuts, and more

Bob's Red Mill Natural Foods
www.bobsredmill.com
13521 SE Pheasant Ct
Milwaukie, Oregon 97222
800-349-2173
Baking supplies, guar gum, gluten-free flours, starches, coconut flour, nuts, oats, and much more

California Olive Ranch
www.californiaoliveranch.com
1367 East Lassen Avenue, Suite A-1
Chico, California 95973
530-846-8000
Extra-virgin olive oils made from their Northern California grown olives. The neutral tasting but rich Everyday Olive Oil is the oil I use to make virtually all of my desserts.

Chicago Vegan Foods
www.chicagoveganfoods.com
630-629-9667
Dandies vegan marshmallows

Crofters Food Ltd.
www.croftersorganic.com
7 Great North Road
Parry Sound, Ontario
Canada P2A 2X8
705-746-6301
Organic, non-GMO fruit spreads made with fair-trade sugar

Eden Foods, Inc.
www.edenfoods.com
701 Tecumseh Road
Clinton, Michigan 49236
888-424-3336
Organic nondairy milks, soy sauce, apple cider vinegar, agar flakes, matcha

Edward & Sons Trading Company, Inc.
www.edwardandsons.com
P.O. Box 1326
Carpinteria, California 93014
805-684-8500
Organic coconut products, including creamed coconut, coconut milk, coconut flour, and fine and thick shredded dried coconut. They also make great vegan sprinkles, ice cream cones, organic canned fruits and more.

Enjoy Life Foods
www.enjoylifefoods.com
3810 River Road
Schiller Park, Illinois 60176
847-260-0300
Vegan and gluten-free chocolate chips and chunks

Florida Crystals Corporation
www.floridacrystals.com
One North Clematis Street
Suite 200
West Palm Beach, Florida 33401
877-835-2828
Organic granulated cane and powdered sugar

Freddy Guys Hazelnuts
www.freddyguys.com
12145 Elkins Road
Monmouth, Oregon 97361
503-606-0458
Roasted hazelnuts from Oregon: simply the best

Frontier Natural Products Co-op
www.frontiercoop.com
PO Box 299
3021 78th Street
Norway, Iowa 52318
800-669-3275
Chemical-free and non-irradiated spices, organic extracts

Highland Sugarworks
www.highlandsugarworks.com
PO Box 58
Wilson Industrial Park
Websterville, Vermont 05678
802-479-1747
Organic maple syrup

Kalustyan's Spices and Sweets
www.kalustyans.com
Marhaba International, Inc.
123 Lexington Avenue
New York, New York 10016
212-685-3451
Premium quality ethnic spices, nuts, seeds, specialty ingredients, baking supplies

King Arthur Flour
www.kingarthurflour.com
135 US Route 5 South
Norwich, Vermont 05055
800-827-6836
Organic flours, baking ingredients, baking equipment

Lundberg Family Farms
www.lundberg.com
5311 Midway
P.O. Box 369
Richvale, California 95974
530-538-3500
Organic brown rice syrup

The Meadow - New York
www.atthemeadow.com
523 Hudson Street
New York, New York 10014
888-388-4633 / 212-645-4633

The Meadow - Portland
3731 N. Mississippi Avenue
Portland, Oregon 97227
888-388-4633 / 503-288-4633
*Fine chocolates and artisan
finishing salts*

**Mori-nu (Morinaga
Nutritional Foods, Inc.)**
www.morinu.com
3838 Del Amo Boulevard
Suite #201
Torrance, California 90503
310-787-0200
*Organic, non-GMO silken tofu
in 12.3-ounce aseptic boxes*

Nasoya
www.nasoya.com, www.vitasoy
-usa.com
Vitasoy USA
One New England Way
Ayer, Massachusetts 01432
800-848-2769
Organic tofu

Navitas Naturals
www.navitasnaturals.com
936 B Seventh Street Box #141
Novato, California 94945
888-645-4282
*Lucuma, maca, cacao nibs, raw
cacao powder, coconut products
and "superfoods"*

Pacific Natural Foods
www.pacificfoods.com
19480 SW 97th Avenue
Tualatin, Oregon 97062
503-692-9666
503-924-4570 consumer inquires only
Organic nondairy milks

Peeled Snacks
www.peeledsnacks.com
65 15th Street, Fl 1
Brooklyn, New York 11215
212-706-2001
*Organic unsweetened, sulfite-free
dried fruits*

Pete's Sweets
www.nysmaple.com/buy-local/
showproducer?producer=253
PO Box 647
Black River, New York 13612-0647
315-408-3761
My organic maple syrup supplier

Rapunzel (InterNatural Foods)
www.internaturalfoods.com/brands
/rapunzel-organic-fair-trade-foods.
html
1455 Broad Street, 4th Floor
Bloomfield, NJ 07003
973-338-1499
*Organic chocolate, cocoa powder,
and whole cane sugar (formerly Rapadura), organic fair-trade chocolate*

Singing Dog Vanilla
www.singingdogvanilla.com
PO Box 50042
Eugene, Oregon 97405
888-343-0002
*Organic fair-trade pure vanilla extract,
alcohol-free vanilla extract, vanilla
beans, non-irradiated cinnamon*

So Delicious Dairy Free
www.sodeliciousdairyfree.com
*Coconut milk beverages, coconut
milk yogurt*

Suzanne's Specialties, Inc.
www.suzannes-specialties.com
421 Jersey Avenue, Suite B
New Brunswick, New Jersey 08901
800-762-2135
Rice nectars, Ricemellow creme

Sweet and Sara
www.sweetandsara.com
43-31 33rd St, 4th Fl
Long Island City, New York 11101
718-707-2808
Vegan marshmallows

Tofutti
www.tofutti.com
50 Jackson Drive
Cranford, New Jersey 07016
908-272-2400
Nondairy cream cheese

Trader Joe's
www.traderjoes.com
*Grocery store with many
vegan products*

Vegan Essentials
www.veganessentials.com
1701 Pearl Street Unit 8
Waukesha, Wisconsin 53186
262-574-7761
*Online source for vegan
grocery items*

**Vermont Country
Naturals**
www.vermontspecialtyfoods.org
/member.php/lid/85
Joan Savoy
PO Box 238
Charlotte, Vermont 05445
800-528-7021
Organic maple syrup

Wholesome Sweeteners
www.wholesomesweeteners.com
8016 Highway 90-A
Sugar Land, Texas 77478
800-680-1896
*Organic granulated sugar,
organic dark whole cane sugar
(Sucanat), organic agave syrup,
organic coconut sugar*

VEGAN WINES

Querciabella
www.querciabella.com
Via di Barbiano 17
50022 Greve in Chianti FI
Italy
Tel + 39 055 8592 7777

Vegan Vine
www.theveganvine.com
One Hummingbird Lane
San Martin, CA 95046
(408) 686-1050

BAKING AND COOKING SUPPLIES AND EQUIPMENT

Amazon
www.amazon.com
Exponentially growing inventory of baking equipment and ingredients in grocery and gourmet food and home and kitchen categories. Everything from guar gum and agar powders to gold leaf and baking pans.

Beryl's Cake Decorating and Pastry Supplies
www.beryls.com
PO Box 1584
North Springfield, Virginia 22151
800-488-2749
Baking supplies, transfer sheets

Broadway Panhandler
www.broadwaypanhandler.com
65 East 8th Street
New York, NY 10003
866-266-5927
High-quality, professional bakeware and cookware

ChocoTransferSheets.com by Glarus Gourmet
www.chocotransfersheets.com

Glarus Gourmet, Inc.
4872 East 2nd Street
Benicia, California 94510
707-748-5658
Affordable transfer sheets

Cuisinart
www.cuisinart.com
800-726-0190
Electric stand and hand mixers, blenders, food processors, and other kitchen appliances

House on the Hill
www.houseonthehill.net
650 West Grand Avenue, Unit 110
Elmhurst, Illinois 60126
877-279-4455 (US only)
630-279-4455
Springerle cookie molds; great for molding marzipan

KitchenAid
www.kitchenaid.com
800-541-6390
Electric stand and hand mixers, blenders, food processors, and other kitchen appliances

New York Cake
www.nycake.com
56 West 22ND Street
New York, NY 10010
(212) 675-2253
This shop first opened its doors as the Chocolate Gallery more than 25 years ago. It is a one-stop shop for all baking needs, from cupcake papers to wedding cake toppers. Cake decorating and other baking classes are offered.

Pots and Pans.com
www.potsandpans.com
Pots and Pans Consumer
Relations/Meyer Corporation, US
One Meyer Plaza
Vallejo, California 94590

800-450-0156
Online cookware and bakeware outlet

Sur La Table
www.surlatable.com
Sur La Table
PO Box 840
Brownsburg, Indiana 46112
800-243-0852
High-quality bakeware, cookware, kitchen and baking supplies, and more

Vitamix
www.vitamix.com
8615 Usher Road
Cleveland, Ohio 44138
800-848-2649
High-speed blenders; exceptional customer service

Williams-Sonoma
www.williams-sonoma.com
877-812-6235
High-quality bakeware, cookware, kitchen and baking supplies, and more

Willpowder
www.willpowder.net
spice@willpowder.com
(866) 249-0400
Specialty pastry products like agar powder, guar gum, and xanthan. Bulk orders and small quantities available.

Zabar's
www.zabars.com
2245 Broadway
New York, New York 10024
212-787-2000 (store)
212-496-1234 (24-hour)
Famous for generations, selling high-quality kitchen and baking supplies, lots of food and more

BIBLIOGRAPHY AND READING LIST

Andoh, Elizabeth. *Kansha: Celebrating Japan's Vegan and Vegetarian Traditions.* New York: Ten Speed Press, 2010.

Asbell, Robin. *Sweet & Easy Vegan: Treats Made with Whole Grains and Natural Sweeteners.* San Francisco: Chronicle Books, 2012.

Beranbaum, Rose Levy. *Rose's Heavenly Cakes.* Hoboken: John Wiley & Sons, Inc., 2009.

——. *The Cake Bible.* New York: William Morrow Cookbooks, 1988.

——. *The Pie and Pastry Bible.* New York: Scribner, 1998.

Bloom, Carole. *Intensely Chocolate: 100 Scrumptious Recipes for True Chocolate Lovers.* Hoboken: John Wiley & Sons, Inc., 2010.

Carr, Kris and Chad Sarno. *Crazy Sexy Kitchen: 150 Plant-Empowered Recipes to Ignite a Mouthwatering Revolution.* Carlsbad, CA: Hay House, 2012.

Corriher, Shirley O. *CookWise: The Secrets of Cooking Revealed.* New York: William Morrow Cookbooks, 2011.

Costigan, Fran. *More Great Good Dairy-Free Desserts Naturally.* Summertown, TN: Book Publishing Company, 2006.

Daley, Regan. *In the Sweet Kitchen: The Definitive Baker's Companion.* New York: Artisan, 2001.

Ettinger, John. *Bob's Red Mill Baking Book.* Philadelphia: Running Press, 2006.

Falkner, Elizabeth. *Elizabeth Falkner's Demolition Desserts: Recipes from Citizen Cake.* New York: Ten Speed Press, 2007.

Figoni, Paula I. *How Baking Works: Exploring the Fundamentals of Baking Science,* 3rd ed. Hoboken: John Wiley & Sons, Inc., 2010.

Grogan, Bryanna Clark. *World Vegan Feast: 200 Fabulous Recipes from Over 50 Countries.* Woodstock, VA: Vegan Heritage Press, 2011.

Joachim, David. *The Food Substitutions Bible: More Than 6,500 Substitutions for Ingredients, Equipment and Techniques,* 2nd ed. Toronto: Robert Rose, 2010.

King Arthur Flour Baker's Companion: The All-Purpose Baking Cookbook, The. Woodstock: The Countryman Press, 2012.

Lebovitz, David. *The Great Book of Chocolate.* New York: Ten Speed Press, 2004.

Madison, Deborah. *Seasonal Fruit Desserts: From Orchard, Farm, and Market.* New York: Broadway Books, 2010.

Malgieri, Nick. *Chocolate: From Simple Cookies to Extravagant Showstoppers.* New York: Harper Collins, 1998.

——. *Great Italian Desserts.* New York: Little, Brown and Co., 1990.

McGee, Harold. *On Food and Cooking: The Science and Lore of the Kitchen.* New York: Scribner, 2004.

Medrich, Alice. *Bittersweet: Recipes and Tales from a Life in Chocolate.* New York: Artisan, 2003.

——. *Chocolat: Extraordinary Chocolate Desserts.* New York: Warner Books, 1990.

Page, Karen and Andrew Dornenburg. *The Flavor Bible: The Essential Guide to Culinary Creativity, Based on the Wisdom of America's Most Imaginative Cshefs.* New York: Little, Brown and Company, 2008.

Presilla, Maricel E. *The New Taste of Chocolate: A Cultural & Natural History of Cacao with Recipes.* New York: Ten Speed Press, 2000.

Rinsky, Glenn and Laura Halpin Rinsky. *The Pastry Chef's Companion: A Comprehensive Resource Guide for the Baking and Pastry Professional.* Hoboken: John Wiley & Sons, Inc., 2008.

Rombauer, Irma S., Marion Rombauer Becker, and Ethan Becker. *The All New All Purpose Joy of Cooking.* New York: Scribner, 1997.

Stewart, Martha. *Martha Stewart's Baking Handbook.* New York: Clarkson Potter, 2005.

Williams, Pam and Jim Eber. *Raising the Bar: The Future of Fine Chocolate.* San Francisco: Wilmor Publishing Corporation, 2012.

Wood, Rebecca. *The New Whole Foods Encyclopedia: A Comprehensive Resource for Healthy Eating.* New York: Penguin, 2010.

ORGANIZATIONS AND PUBLICATIONS

Center for Science in the Public Interest (CSPI)
www.cspinet.org
1220 L Street N.W. Suite 300
Washington, DC 20005
202-332-9110
Independent science-based public health group advocating nutrition and food safety

Ecole Chocolat
www.ecolechocolat.com
505 Montgomery, 11th Floor
San Francisco, California
213-291-8309
Online school for making chocolate; find lots of valuable information about chocolate on their website

Institute of Culinary Education, The
www.iceculinary.com
50 West 23rd Street
New York, New York 10010
212-847-0700
Offers a variety of professional and non-professional culinary arts programs

Natural Gourmet Institute for Health & Culinary Arts
www.naturalgourmetinstitute.com
48 West 21st Street, 2nd Floor
New York, New York 10010
212-645-5170
Offers a variety of health-supportive professional and non-professional culinary arts programs

North American Vegetarian Society (NAVS)
www.navs-online.org
PO Box 72
Dolgeville, New York 13329
518-568-7970
*A non-profit, tax-exempt educational organization offering information about veganism; publishes a magazine (*Vegetarian Voice*), and presents the popular annual Vegetarian Summerfest*

Organic Consumers Association (formerly the Pure Food Campaign)
www.organicconsumers.org
6771 South Silver Hill Drive
Finland, Minnesota 55603
218-226-4164
Research and action center for organic foods, food safety, and sustainability

Physicians Committee for Responsible Medicine (PCRM)
www.pcrm.org
5100 Wisconsin Avenue, N.W., Suite 400
Washington, DC 20016
202-686-2210
A non-profit promoting preventative medicine and good nutrition through a vegan diet, as well as alternatives to animal experimentation

Vegetarian Resource Group, The (VRG)
www.vrg.org
PO Box 1463
Baltimore, Maryland 21203
410-366-8343
Non-profit organization focused on vegetarian education; publishers of Vegetarian Journal, *vegetarian cookbooks, as well as a wealth of online guides, nutritional and ingredient information, recipes, and more*

Index

Note: Page references in *italics* indicate photographs.

A

Affogato (var.), 199
Agar, 15
Agave syrup, 23
Almond extract, 14
Almond milk, 18
Almond(s), 18
    Bittersweet Chocolate and Lemon Tartlets, *168, 169–70*
    blanching, 289
    Chocolate, and Orange Olive Oil Cake, 72–74, *73*
    Chocolate Chip Biscotti, 132–33, *133*
    Chocolate-Dipped Biscotti (var.), 133
    Chocolate Horchata, 254–55
    Coconut Macaroons (var.), 135
    Cookie Crust, 155
    Dukkah-Spiced Chocolate-Covered Matzoh, 228–29
    Marzipan, *288,* 289
    Mendiants, *226,* 227
    Mint Chocolate Horchata (var.), 255
    Opera Cake, 112–15, *114*
    Raw Nut Crust, 156
    Spiced Chocolate Horchata (var.), 255
Ancho chili powder, 20
    Aztec Truffles, *52,* 53–54
    Chocolate Mexican-Spiced Ice Cream, 203
    Spiced Chocolate Horchata (var.), 255
Anise, 20
    Chocolate Chip Almond Biscotti, 132–33, *133*
    Chocolate-Dipped Biscotti (var.), 133
    Dukkah-Spiced Chocolate-Covered Matzoh, 228–29
Apple cider vinegar, 16
Apricot preserves
    Sachertorte, 105–7, *106*
Arrowroot, 20, 240
Avocado(s)
    Cacao, Matcha, and Kale Smoothie, 247
    Chocolate "Buttercream," *272, 273*
    Mint Chocolate Chip Ice Cream, 202
Aztec Truffles, *52,* 53–54

B

Baking powder, 16
Baking soda, 17
Banana(s)
    Bread Pudding Hearts (var.), 191
    Cacao Nib Snack Cake, 82–83
    Chocolate Chunk Bread Pudding, 190–91, *191*
    Chocolate Peanut Butter Cup Smoothie, 248
    Cream Pie, Black Bottom, 171
    Creamy Meal in a Glass (var.), 252
    Meal in a Glass, 252
    Millionaire's Banoffee Tarts, 218–19, *219*
    Walnut Snack Cake (var.), 83
Banoffee Tarts, Millionaire's, 218–19, *219*
Bars
    Blondies, 130, *131*
    Gluten-Free Brownie Bites, 126–27
    Magic Cookie, 142–43
    preparing, tips for, 124
    Very Fudgy Chocolate Chip Brownies, 128–29, *129*
Beverages
    Black Russian (var.), 258
    Cacao, Matcha, and Kale Smoothie, 247
    Chocolat Chaud, 242, *243*
    Chocolate Date Thick Shake, 250, *251*
    Chocolate Horchata, 254–55
    Chocolate Peanut Butter Cup Smoothie, 248
    Chocolate Vodka, *256, 257*
    Chocolate White Russian, 258, *259*
    Creamy Meal in a Glass (var.), 252
    Espresso Hot Chocolate, 246
    High Protein Peanut Butter Cup Smoothie, 249
    Hot Chocolate Mexican-Style, *244, 245*
    Low-Fat and Luscious Hot Cocoa, 240
    Meal in a Glass, 252
    Mint Chocolate Horchata (var.), 255
    preparing, tips for, 237
    Quick and Easy Homemade Hot Cocoa, 241
    Raw Cacao Nib Smoothie, 253
    Spiced Chocolate Horchata (var.), 255
Biscotti
    Chocolate Chip Almond, 132–33, *133*
    Chocolate-Dipped (var.), 133
Black Bottom Banana Cream Pie, 171
Black Bottom Cupcakes, 86–88, *87–88*
Black Russian (var.), 258
Blondies, 130, *131*
Blueberries
    Creamy Meal in a Glass (var.), 252
    Meal in a Glass, 252
Bread
    Chocolate Crostini, 230, *231*
    Pudding, Chocolate Chunk Banana, 190–91, *191*
    Pudding Hearts (var.), 191
Brooklyn Blackout Cake, 94–96, *95*
Brownie(s)
    Bites, Gluten-Free, 126–27
    Chocolate, Crumble Ice Cream, 206, *207*
    Pudding Cakelettes, 79–81, *80*
    Sundae, Blow Them Away (var.), 206
    Very Fudgy Chocolate Chip, 128–29, *129*
Brown rice syrup, 23
Bûche de Noël, 116–18, *117*
Butter, Chocolate Hazelnut, 232

C

Cacao
    about, 30
    Matcha, and Kale Smoothie, 247
    Raw, Sauce, 276
    Raw, Superfood Truffles, *55*
Cacao Nib(s)
    about, 30
    Banana Snack Cake, 82–83
    Chocolate Vodka, *256, 257*
    Creamy Meal in a Glass (var.), 252
    Meal in a Glass, 252
    Raw, Smoothie, 253
Cakes
    Banana Cacao Nib Snack, 82–83
    Banana Walnut Snack (var.), 83
    Bittersweet Ganache–Glazed Chocolate Torte to
        Live For, 68–69
    Black Bottom Cupcakes, 86–88, *87–88*
    Brooklyn Blackout, 94–96, *95*
    Brownie Pudding Cakelettes, 79–81, *80*
    Bûche de Noël, 116–18, *117*
    Chocolate, Orange, and Almond Olive Oil, 72–74, *73*
    Chocolate Caramel Coconut Whipped Cream (var.), 101
    Chocolate Cherry Miroir, 102–4, *103*
    Chocolate Coconut Whipped Cream, 100–101
    Chocolate Date Muffins, 89
    Chocolate Fudge Cupcakes, 85
    Chocolate Hazelnut Six-Layer, 108–9
    Coffee, Chocolate Pecan Cranberry, 75–77, *76*
    Éclairs, 119–21, *120*
    Embellished Chocolate Cherry Miroir (var.), 104
    Embellished Torte to Live For (var.), 69
    frosting and decorating, 65
    Gluten-Free Chocolate Torte to Live For (var.), 69
    Gluten-Free Intensely Chocolate Trifle (var.), 111
    Intensely Chocolate Trifle, 110–11
    making cake crumbs from, 65
    measuring dry ingredients for, 63
    Mix-in-the-Pan Chocolate, 78
    The No-Oil-Added Chocolate Torte to Live For,
        70–71, *71*
    Opera, 112–15, *114*
    Orange-Scented Chocolate Cheesecake for your
        Thanksgiving Table (var.), 99
    preparing, tips for, 63–64, 91
    Sachertorte, 105–7, *106*
    showstoppers, preparing, 91
    troubleshooting, 64, 91
    Vanilla Chocolate Chip Cupcakes, 84
    White and Dark Chocolate Cheesecake, 97–99
Caramel
    Chocolate Coconut Whipped Cream Cake (var.),
        101
    Chocolate Dulce de Leche, 234, *235*
    Millionaire's Banoffee Tarts, 218–19, *219*
Cardamom, 20
Cashew(s), 19
    Bread Pudding Hearts (var.), 191
    Chocolate Chunk Banana Bread Pudding, 190–91, *191*

Chocolate Date Thick Shake, 250, *251*
Chocolate Peanut Butter Cups, 220
Cream, Basic Thick, 284, *285*
Cream, Sweet Thick (var.), 284
Cream Chocolate Pudding, Warm, 181
Cream Truffle Squares, Bittersweet, *42, 43*
Vanilla Custard Cream Filling, *282*
Chai-Spiced Truffles, 48–49
Cheesecakes
    Orange-Scented Chocolate, for your Thanksgiving
        (var.), 99
    White and Dark Chocolate, 97–99
Cherry
    Chocolate Miroir Cake, 102–4, *103*
    Chocolate Miroir Cake, Embellished (var.), 104
Chestnuts, 19
    Nesselrode Pie, 160–61
    Nesselrode Pudding (var.), 161
Chia (seeds), 16
    and Coconut Pudding, Chocolate Espresso (var.), 189
    Pudding, Chocolate, Date and Coconut, 189
Chocolate
    chopping, 27
    and cocoa percentages, 24–26
    cocoa powders, about, 29–30
    dark, labeling of, 24
    dark, pairing with wine, 57
    decorating with, 29
    extract, about, 14
    melting, 28
    storing, 27
    tempering, 28
    types of, 27
    vegan, buying, 26
Cinnamon, 20
Clabbered milk, about, 84
Cocoa butter, 14
Cocoa powder
    black, about, 30
    Dutch-process, about, 29, 30
    natural, about, 29, 30
    raw (cacao), about, 30
    substituting one type for another, 29
Coconut, 19
    Almond Macaroons (var.), 135
    and Chia Pudding, Chocolate Espresso (var.), 189
    Chocolate, and Date Chia Pudding, 189
    Chocolate Caramel Whipped Cream Cake (var.), 101
    Chocolate Chip Macaroons (var.), 135
    Chocolate-Covered Macaroons (var.), 135
    Chocolate Cream Pie, 166–67
    Chocolate Ganache Glaze, 266
    Chocolate Ice Cream, 204–5
    Chocolate Whipped Cream Cake, 100–101
    Macaroons, Chocolate-Dipped, 134–35
    Magic Cookie Bars, 142–43
    Milk Black Rice Pudding, 180
    Whipped Cream, Chocolate, 280
Coconut, creamed, 18

Coconut, cream of, 18
Coconut butter, 14, 18
Coconut cream, 18
Coconut flour, 15
Coconut milk, 18
Coconut oil, 14
Coconut sugar, 22
Coffee Cake, Chocolate Pecan Cranberry, 75–77, *76*
Coffee liqueur
    Black Russian (var.), 258
    Chocolate White Russian, 258, *259*
Confections
    Chewy Date Candies, 224–25
    Chocolate Crostini, 230, *231*
    Chocolate Dulce de Leche, 234, *235*
    Chocolate Hazelnut Butter, 232
    Chocolate Olive Oil Glaze for Chocolate-Dipped
        Anything, 222–23, *223*
    Chocolate Peanut Butter Cups, 220
    Dukkah-Spiced Chocolate-Covered Matzoh, 228–29
    Mendiants, *226*, 227
    Millionaire's Banoffee Tarts, 218–19, *219*
    No Mallow Rice Crispy Treats, 221
    preparing, tips for, 215
    Tootsie Roll-Like Logs (var.), 225
    troubleshooting, 215
Cookies. *See also* Bars
    Almond Coconut Macaroons (var.), 135
    Chocolate Chip Almond Biscotti, 132–33, *133*
    Chocolate Chip Coconut Macaroons (var.), 135
    Chocolate-Covered Graham Cracker S'mores (var.), 139
    Chocolate-Covered Macaroons (var.), 135
    Chocolate-Dipped Biscotti (var.), 133
    Chocolate-Dipped Coconut Macaroons, 134–35
    Double Chocolate Chunk, 146–47
    Gluten-Free Chocolate Chunk, 144–45, *145*
    Graham Crackers, 136–38
    judging doneness, 123
    Moon Pies, *140*, 141
    preparing, tips for, 124
    Round Graham Crackers (var.), *137*, 138
    S'mores, 139
    troubleshooting, 124
Cornstarch, 20, 240
Cranberry
    Chocolate Cream Filling, 283
    Chocolate Pecan Coffee Cake, 75–77, 76
    Coulis (var.), 286
    Sauce, Maple, 286
Cream cheese (vegan)
    Black Bottom Cupcakes, 86–88, *87–88*
    Orange-Scented Chocolate Cheesecake for your
        Thanksgiving (var.), 99
    White and Dark Chocolate Cheesecake, 97–99
Creamed coconut, 18
Cream Fillings
    Chocolate Cranberry, 283
    Vanilla Custard, 282
    White Chocolate, 281

Cream of coconut, 18
Creamy desserts. *See also* Pudding(s)
    Chocolate Jello Shots, *192*, 193
    Chocolate Panna Cotta, 176–77
    Magic Chocolate Mousse, 182–83
    Mocha Crème Brûlée, *186*, 187–88
    preparing, tips for, 173
    Stovetop Brûlée (var.), 188
    troubleshooting, 173
Crème Brûlée
    Mocha, *186*, 187–88
    Stovetop (var.), 188
Crème Fraîche Truffles, 60–61
Crostini, Chocolate, 230, *231*
Crusts
    Almond Cookie, 155
    Raw Nut, 156
Cumin, 20
Cupcakes
    Black Bottom, 86–88, *87–88*
    Chocolate Fudge, 85
    frosting and decorating, 65
    Vanilla Chocolate Chip, 84
Curry in a Hurry Truffles, 50–51

D
Date(s)
    Candies, Chewy, 224–25
    Chocolate, and Coconut Chia Pudding, 189
    Chocolate Espresso Chia and Coconut Pudding
        (var.), 189
    Chocolate Muffins, 89
    Chocolate Thick Shake, 250, *251*
    Creamy Meal in a Glass (var.), 252
    Meal in a Glass, 252
    Raw Cacao Nib Smoothie, 253
    Raw Cacao Superfood Truffles, 55
    Raw Chocolate Fudge and Mandarin Orange Tart,
        162–63
    Raw Truffles (var.), 225
    Tootsie Roll-Like Logs (var.), 225
Dukkah-Spiced Chocolate-Covered Matzoh, 228–29
Dulce de Leche, Chocolate, 234, *235*

E
Éclairs, 119–21, *120*
Embellished Chocolate Cherry Miroir (var.), 104
Embellished Torte to Live For (var.), 69
Equipment, 31–33
Espresso
    Affogato (var.), 199
    Chocolate Chia and Coconut Pudding (var.), 189
    Chocolate Gelato, 198–99
    Hot Chocolate, 246
    Mocha Crème Brûlée, *186*, 187–88
    Opera Cake, 112–15, *114*
    Stovetop Brûlée (var.), 188
    Truffles, 56–57
Extracts and essences (oils), 14

F Fats, 14
Flours
all-purpose, 14
coconut, 15
measuring, 63
non-wheat, 15
oat, 15, 81
tapioca, 20, 240
wheat, 14
whole wheat pastry, 14
Frostings
Chocolate Avocado "Buttercream," 272, *273*
Creamy Chocolate Cupcake, 270
quantities, for cakes, 65
Thick and Glossy Fudge, 271
Frozen desserts
Affogato (var.), 199
Blow Them Away Brownie Sundae (var.), 206
Chocolate Brownie Crumble Ice Cream, 206, *207*
Chocolate Coconut Ice Cream, 204–5
Chocolate Espresso Gelato, 198–99
Chocolate Ginger Ice Cream, 208
Chocolate Margarita Ice Cream, 210, *211*
Chocolate Mexican-Spiced Ice Cream, 203
Chocolate Sorbet, 209
Mint Chocolate Chip Ice Cream, 202
Peanut Butter and Jam Fudge-Swirled Ice Cream, 200, *201*
preparing, tips for, 195
troubleshooting, 195
Watermelon Granita with Chocolate Seeds, *212, 213*
Fruit. *See also specific fruits*
dried, buying and storing, 15
Mendiants, *226,* 227
zesting, 21, 74

G Ganache Glazes
Bittersweet Chocolate, 264, *265*
Chocolate Coconut, 266
Gelato
Affogato (var.), 199
Chocolate Espresso, 198–99
Ginger, 21
Chocolate Ice Cream, 208
Mendiants, *226,* 227
Truffles, Spicy, 46–47
Glazes
Bittersweet Chocolate Ganache, 264, *265*
Chocolate Coconut Ganache, 266
Chocolate Confectioners' Sugar, 267
Chocolate Olive Oil, for Chocolate-Dipped Anything, 222–23, *223*
Chocolate Orange, *268,* 269
quantities, for cakes, 65
Gluten-free baking mixes, 15
Gluten-Free Brownie Bites, 126–27
Gluten-Free Chocolate Chunk Cookies, 144–45, *145*
Gluten-Free Chocolate Torte to Live For (var.), 69

Gluten-Free Intensely Chocolate Trifle (var.), 111
Graham Cracker(s), 136–38
Magic Cookie Bars, 142–43
Moon Pies, *140,* 141
Round (var.), *137,* 138
S'mores, 139
S'mores, Chocolate Covered (var.), 139
Granita, Watermelon, with Chocolate Seeds, *212,* 213
Guar gum, 15
Gums, 15–16

H Hazelnut(s), 19
Butter, Chocolate, 232
Chocolate Six-Layer Cake, 108–9
Dukkah-Spiced Chocolate-Covered Matzoh, 228–29
roasting and skinning, 233
Honey
in vegan diet, 23
Vegan Orange Blossom, 287
Horchata
Chocolate, 254–55
Mint Chocolate (var.), 255
Spiced Chocolate (var.), 255
Hot Chocolate
Espresso, 246
Mexican-Style, *244,* 245
Hot Cocoa
Low-Fat and Luscious, 240
Quick and Easy Homemade, 241

I Ice Cream
Blow Them Away Brownie Sundae (var.), 206
Chocolate Brownie Crumble, 206, *207*
Chocolate Coconut, 204–5
Chocolate Ginger, 208
Chocolate Margarita, 210, *211*
Chocolate Mexican-Spiced, 203
Mint Chocolate Chip, 202
Peanut Butter and Jam Fudge-Swirled, 200, *201*
preparing, tips for, 195
troubleshooting, 195
Ingredients, 14–30
dry, measuring, 15, 63
ethical, note about, 16
organic, note about, 17

J Jello Shots, Chocolate, *192,* 193

K Kale
Cacao, and Matcha Smoothie, 247
Creamy Meal in a Glass (var.), 252
Meal in a Glass, 252
Kumquats
White Chocolate and Matcha Mousse Pudding, 184–85, *185*

L
Leavening agents, 16–17
Lemon
    and Bittersweet Chocolate Tartlets, *168*, 169–70
    Olive Oil Truffles, 44–45, *45*
Lucuma powder
    Creamy Meal in a Glass (var.), 252
    Meal in a Glass, 252
    Raw Cacao Superfood Truffles, 55

M
Maca powder
    Creamy Meal in a Glass (var.), 252
    Meal in a Glass, 252
    Raw Cacao Superfood Truffles, 55
Macaroons
    Almond Coconut (var.), 135
    Chocolate Chip Coconut (var.), 135
    Chocolate-Covered (var.), 135
    Coconut, Chocolate-Dipped, 134–35
Magic Cookie Bars, 142–43
Mangoes
    Coconut Milk Black Rice Pudding, 180
Maple sugar, 22
Maple (Syrup), 23
    Chocolate, 275
    Cranberry Sauce, 286
Margarita Chocolate Ice Cream, 210, *211*
Marshmallows
    Chocolate-Covered Graham Cracker S'mores (var.), 139
    S'mores, 139
Marzipan, *288*, 289
Master recipes
    All-Purpose Chocolate Syrup (No Fat Added), 274
    Basic Thick Cashew Cream, 284, *285*
    Bittersweet Chocolate Ganache Glaze, 264, *265*
    Chocolate Avocado "Buttercream," 272, *273*
    Chocolate Coconut Ganache Glaze, 266
    Chocolate Coconut Whipped Cream, 280
    Chocolate Confectioners' Sugar Glaze, 267
    Chocolate Cranberry Cream Filling, 283
    Chocolate Ice Cream Shell, *278*, 279
    Chocolate Maple Syrup, 275
    Chocolate Orange Glaze, *268*, 269
    Cranberry Coulis (var.), 286
    Creamy Chocolate Cupcake Frosting, 270
    Maple Cranberry Sauce, 286
    Marzipan, *288*, 289
    Mint Shell (var.), 279
    preparing, tips for, 261
    Raw Cacao Sauce, 276
    Sweet Thick Cashew Cream (var.), 284
    Thick and Glossy Fudge Frosting, 271
    Thick Fudge Sauce, 277
    Vanilla Custard Cream Filling, 282
    Vegan Orange Blossom Honey, 287
    White Chocolate Cream Filling, 281
Matcha, 17
    Cacao, and Kale Smoothie, 247
    and White Chocolate Mousse Pudding, 184–85, *185*

Matzoh, Dukkah-Spiced Chocolate-Covered, 228–29
Meal in a Glass, 252
Mendiants, *226*, 227
Milk (nondairy)
    clabbered, about, 84
    types of, 18
Mint
    Chocolate Chip Ice Cream, 202
    Chocolate Horchata (var.), 255
    Shell (var.), 279
Miso, 17
Mocha Crème Brûlée, *186*, 187–88
Molasses, 23
Moon Pies, *140*, 141
Mousse
    Magic Chocolate, 182–83
Muffins, Chocolate Date, 89

N
Nesselrode Pie, 160–61
Nesselrode Pudding (var.), 161
No Mallow Rice Crispy Treats, 221
Nut(s). *See also* Almond(s); Cashew(s); Hazelnut(s);
        Pecan(s); Walnut(s)
    Chocolate Peanut Butter Cups, 220
    Coconut Milk Black Rice Pudding, 180
    Crust, Raw, 156
    Dukkah-Spiced Chocolate-Covered Matzoh, 228–29
    Mendiants, *226*, 227
    Nesselrode Pie, 160–61
    Nesselrode Pudding (var.), 161
    roasting, 19
    types of, 18–19
    White Chocolate and Matcha Mousse Pudding,
        184–85, *185*

O
Oat flour, 15, 81
Olive oil, 14
Opera Cake, 112–15, *114*
Orange
    Blossom Honey, Vegan, 287
    Chocolate, and Almond Olive Oil Cake, 72–74, *73*
    Chocolate Glaze, *268*, 269
    Chocolate Sesame Truffles, 58, *59*
    Mandarin, and Chocolate Fudge Tart, Raw, 162–63
    -Scented Chocolate Cheesecake for your Thanks-
        giving (var.), 99

P
Panna Cotta, Chocolate, 176–77
Pastry Dough, Tender Olive Oil, 152–54, *153*
Peanut Butter
    Cup Chocolate Smoothie, 248
    Cups, Chocolate, 220
    Cup Smoothie, High Protein, 249
    and Jam Fudge-Swirled Ice Cream, 200, *201*
Peanuts, 19
    Chocolate Peanut Butter Cups, 220

Pecan(s), 19
    Chocolate Cranberry Coffee Cake, 75–77, 76
    Pie, Chocolate, 157–59, 158
    Raw Cacao Superfood Truffles, 55
    Slow-Roasted, 159
Pies
    Almond Cookie Crust, 155
    Black Bottom Banana Cream, 171
    Chocolate Coconut Cream, 166–67
    Chocolate Pecan, 157–59, 158
    Nesselrode, 160–61
    preparing, tips for, 149
    Raw Nut Crust, 156
    Tender Olive Oil Pastry Dough, 152–54, 153
    troubleshooting, 149
Pine nuts, 19
    Mendiants, 226, 227
Pistachios, 19
    Coconut Milk Black Rice Pudding, 180
    Dukkah-Spiced Chocolate-Covered Matzoh, 228–29
    White Chocolate and Matcha Mousse Pudding, 184–85, 185
Prune(s)
    Gluten-Free Brownie Bites, 126–27
    Purée, Homemade Sweetened, 127
Pudding(s)
    Bread, Chocolate Chunk Banana, 190–91, 191
    Bread, Hearts (var.), 191
    Chocolate, Almost-Instant, 178, 179
    Chocolate, Date, and Coconut Chia, 189
    Chocolate Cashew Cream, Warm, 181
    Chocolate Espresso Chia and Coconut (var.), 189
    Coconut Milk Black Rice, 180
    Nesselrode (var.), 161
    preparing, tips for, 173
    troubleshooting, 173
    White Chocolate and Matcha Mousse Pudding, 184–85, 185

R Raspberry Chocolate Silk Tart, 164–65, 165
Rice
    Black, Coconut Milk Pudding, 180
    Chocolate Horchata, 254–55
    Mint Chocolate Horchata (var.), 255
    Spiced Chocolate Horchata (var.), 255
Rice Crispy Treats, No Mallow, 221
Rice milk, 18

S Sachertorte, 105–7, 106
Salt, 20
Sauces
    Chocolate Dulce de Leche, 234, 235
    Chocolate Ice Cream Shell, 278, 279
    Cranberry Coulis (var.), 286
    Maple Cranberry, 286
    Mint Shell (var.), 279

    Raw Cacao, 276
    Thick Fudge, 277
Seasonings and spices, 20–21
Sesame seeds, 19
    Chocolate Orange Sesame Truffles, 58, 59
    Dukkah-Spiced Chocolate-Covered Matzoh, 228–29
Shake, Chocolate Date Thick, 250, 251
Shots, Chocolate Jello, 192, 193
Smoothies
    Cacao, Matcha, and Kale, 247
    Chocolate Peanut Butter Cup, 248
    High Protein Peanut Butter Cup, 249
    Raw Cacao Nib, 253
S'mores, 139
S'mores, Chocolate-Covered Graham Cracker (var.), 139
Sorbet, Chocolate, 209
Sorghum, 23
Soy, 21
Soymilk, 18
Starches, 20, 240
Sugars and sweeteners, 21–23
Syrups. See also Maple (Syrup)
    All-Purpose Chocolate (No Fat Added), 274
    Chocolate Maple, 275

T Tapioca flour or starch, 20, 240
Tarts
    Almond Cookie Crust, 155
    Bittersweet Chocolate and Lemon Tartlets, 168, 169–70
    Chocolate Fudge and Mandarin Orange, Raw, 162–63
    Millionaire's Banoffee, 218–19, 219
    preparing, tips for, 149
    preparing, with Chewy Date Candies (var.), 225
    Raspberry Chocolate Silk, 164–65, 165
    Raw Nut Crust, 156
    Tender Olive Oil Pastry Dough, 152–54, 153
    troubleshooting, 149
Tequila
    Chocolate Margarita Ice Cream, 210, 211
Tofu, 21
    Chocolate Cranberry Cream Filling, 283
    High Protein Peanut Butter Cup Smoothie, 249
    Orange-Scented Chocolate Cheesecake for your Thanksgiving Table (var.), 99
    White and Dark Chocolate Cheesecake, 97–99
    White Chocolate and Matcha Mousse Pudding, 184–85, 185
    White Chocolate Cream Filling, 281
Tootsie Roll-Like Logs (var.), 225
Tortes
    Bittersweet Ganache–Glazed Chocolate, to Live For, 68–69
    Embellished, to Live For (var.), 69
    Gluten-Free Chocolate, to Live For (var.), 69
    The No-Oil-Added Chocolate, to Live For, 70–71, 71

Trifles
  Gluten-Free Intensely Chocolate, (var.), 111
  Intensely Chocolate, 110–11
Triple sec
  Chocolate Margarita Ice Cream, 210, *211*
Truffle(s)
  Aztec, *52, 53*–54
  Bittersweet Chocolate, 40–41, *41*
  Chai-Spiced, 48–49
  Chocolate Orange Sesame, 58, *59*
  coatings for, 36
  Crème Fraîche, 60–61
  Curry in a Hurry, 50–51
  Espresso, 56–57
  Lemon Olive Oil, 44–45, *45*
  melted chocolate and cocoa coatings for, 37
  preparing, tips for, 35–36
  Raw Cacao Superfood, 55
  Raw (var.), 225
  serving and storing, 36
  Spicy Ginger, 46–47
  Squares, Bittersweet Cashew Cream, *42, 43*
  troubleshooting, 37

V
Vanilla beans, seeded, reusing, 49
Vanilla Chocolate Chip Cupcakes, 84
Vanilla Custard Cream Filling, 282
Vanilla extract, 14
Vodka
  Black Russian (var.), 258
  Chocolate, *256, 257*
  Chocolate Jello Shots, *192, 193*
  Chocolate White Russian, 258, *259*

W
Walnut(s), 19
  Banana Snack Cake (var.), 83
  Chewy Date Candies, 224–25
  Creamy Meal in a Glass (var.), 252
  Magic Cookie Bars, 142–43
  Meal in a Glass, 252
  Mendiants, *226, 227*
  Raw Nut Crust, 156
  Raw Truffles (var.), 225
  Tootsie Roll-Like Logs (var.), 225
  Very Fudgy Chocolate Chip Brownies, 128–29, *129*
Watermelon Granita with Chocolate Seeds, *212, 213*
Whipped Cream, Chocolate Coconut, 280
White and Dark Chocolate Cheesecake, 97–99
White Chocolate
  about, 27
  Cream Filling, 281
  and Matcha Mousse Pudding, 184–85, *185*
  Orange-Scented Chocolate Cheesecake for your
    Thanksgiving (var.), 99
  White and Dark Chocolate Cheesecake, 97–99
White Russian, Chocolate, 258, *259*
Wine, pairing with chocolate, 57

Z
Zest, citrus, notes about, 21, 74

More Advance Praise for *Vegan Chocolate*:

"When those of us of the grains, beans, and veggies persuasion want to indulge in a sweet treat, it has to be something spectacular—and preferably chocolate! There's no better guide to the world of delectable chocolate desserts than Fran Costigan; that they happen to be egg- and dairy-free is icing on the vegan cake."

—Nava Atlas, author of *Wild About Greens* and *Vegan Holiday Kitchen*

"Fran's infectious passion for chocolate radiates from these voluptuous yet amazingly approachable recipes. From breakfast smoothies to show-stopping desserts and even nightcaps, Fran finds a way to sneak a little chocolate bliss into every corner of your day. Warning: these hedonistic recipes aren't for the faint of heart! (I admit it. I actually licked page 92.)"

—Dynise Balcavage, author of *Pies and Tarts with Heart* and *The Urban Vegan*

"Fran is a pioneer of the vegan baking world. . . . As a fellow chocoholic, I am thrilled that Fran is sharing her extensive collection of decadent chocolaty creations with the world. Any vegan will feel like a kid in a candy store flipping through the mouthwatering pages of this book. Bravo Fran!"

—Chloe Coscarelli, cookbook author and winner of Food Network's *Cupcakes Wars*

"Fran Costigan absolutely delights with her book *Vegan Chocolate*. This expansive cookbook—filled with drop dead gorgeous photos and decadent recipes—will inspire chocolate lovers everywhere to get into the kitchen and create something extra-special."

—Allyson Kramer, author of *Great Gluten-Free Vegan Eats*

"A treasure. . . Chef Fran Costigan raises the vegan chocolate bar to such great heights that every-one will be shown a luscious path to confectionary nirvana. Chef Fran's talent and wizardry are gifts to be shared. We cherish and savor all her decadent creations."

—Bart Potenza and Joy Pierson, owners of Candle Cafe, Candle 79, and Candle Cafe West

"Fran Costigan's stunning new book is a game changer. . . . Nothing is missing from these sumptuous chocolate desserts except the dairy, eggs, refined sugar, and cholesterol.

—Tal Ronnen, *New York Times* bestselling author of *The Conscious Kitchen*

"Take a chunk of dark chocolate, a spoonful of sugar, and put it in the pan with Fran, and what you get is a collection of divinely inspired, sophisticated desserts that make me ponder only one thing: which one to make first? . . . . Vegan dessert books may abound, but only Fran Costigan reveals the true meaning of chocolate: it may seem rich, indulgent, and even sinful, but as I dip my finger into a bowl of Chocolate Panna Cotta, I realize it is ever so necessary."

—Miyoko Schinner, author of *Artisan Vegan Cheese*